Ranganathan Series in Library Science, 8

REFERENCE SERVICE

Some other books by the author

Anuvarga-suchi-kalpa
Classification and communication
Classified catalogue code
Depth classification
Five laws of library science
Grantha-adhyayanartha-hai
Granthalaya-prakriya
Heading and canons
Library development plan
Library legislation
Literature for neoliterates
Organisation of libraries
Philosophy of library classification
Public library provision and documentation problems
Rural adult education
Social bibliography
Social education literature
Union catalogue of learned periodical publications in South Asia

Ranganathan Series in Library Science

1 *Library movement in India, a symposium*, ed by P N Kaula
2 *Classified catalogue code with additional rules for dictionary catalogue code*, by S R Ranganathan, ed 4
3 *Library administration*, by S R Ranganathan, ed 2
4 *Colon classification*, ed 6
5 *Social science research and libraries*, ed by S R Ranganathan and Girja Kumar
6 *Library Manual*, by S R Ranganathan, ed 2
7 *Education for leisure*, by S R Ranganathan, ed 4
8 *Reference service*, by S R Ranganathan
9 *Elements of library classification*, by S R Ranganathan, ed 3

Reference Service

Second Edition

S R Ranganathan

SARADA RANGANATHAN ENDOWMENT
FOR LIBRARY SCIENCE
Bangalore 560 078

Shiyali Ramamrita Ranganathan (1892)

First Edition	1940
Second Edition	1961
Second Edition Reprint	1989
Second Edition Reprint	1992
Reprint	1996
Reprint	1999
Reprint	**2006**

2:7
N61

ISBN: 81-7000-466-7

Rs.750/-

Published By:
Ess Ess Publications
4837/24, Ansari Road,
Darya Ganj,
New Delhi-110 002
Ph.No. 23260807, 51563444, Fax: 51563334
E-mail: info@essessreference.com
url: www.essessreference.com

For:
Sarada Ranganathan Endowment for Library Science
702, 'Upstairs',
42nd Cross, III Block,
Rajajinagar,
Bangalore-560 010.
Ph.No. 23305109
E-mail: srels@vsnl.com

Printed in India at: Printline, New Delhi

To

SHRI T SUNDARACHARIAR

A Walking Concordance

CONTENTS

CONTENTS

Part J
Long Range Reference Service

Part K
Illustrative Actualities

The Five Laws of Library Science

1. Books are for use
2. Every reader his book
3. Every book its reader
4. Save the time of the reader
5. A library is a growing organism

ग्रन्थालय-शास्त्र-पञ्च-सूत्राणि

ग्रन्थालयी सदासेवि पञ्चसूत्री परायण : ।
ग्रन्था अध्येतुमेते च सर्वेभ्यः स्वं स्वमाप्नुः ॥
अध्येतुः समयं शेषेदालयो नित्यमेव च ।
वर्धिष्णुः एव चिन्मूर्तिः पञ्चसूत्री सदाजयेत् ॥

FOREWORD TO EDITION 1

I most willingly accede to Rao Sahib S R Ranganathan's request that I should write a Foreword to his book; and indeed I deem it an honour to be allowed to do so. Mr Ranganathan's contributions to library science are so well known, both in India and elsewhere, that a new volume from his pen is assured of as warm a welcome as any of its predecessors. I have found this present volume stimulating and wholly delightful. It covers an immense range. It is not only scientific in the strictest sense of the word, but also abounds in the most practical wisdom. And when I add that it is full of a broad humanity, I am not referring merely to the wit and humour which adorn its pages, but to the author's love of good books and good literature which shines out in every chapter, and to his ardent desire to make both more readily accessible to the world at large.

I have had the privilege of meeting Mr Ranganathan in the great library over which he presides, and in which, with the assistance of Mr C Sundaram, his [Chief Reference Librarian], he guides and inspires all those who seek after knowledge; and it is therefore an added pleasure for me to write these lines. The proverb says that good wine needs no bush, and a book by Mr Ranganathan needs no commendation from me; but I wish for it a successful career and very many readers, and I am quite sure that it will make new friends wherever it goes. There is in it an exquisite quotation of some words spoken by Sita to Rama: "I do not instruct; I only remind you out of my love and regard for you". Mr Ranganathan tells us that these words describe what should be the correct attitude of the reference librarian; I can think of no words more exactly appropriate to describe the attitude of the author himself in this book.

MAURICE GWYER
(*Chief Justice of India*)

New Delhi,
13 *December* 1940

Part A

Introduction

CHAPTER 0

CONSPECTUS

1 This book is divided into ten parts. These are numbered by the letters A to K, with the omission of the letter I.

2 Each part is divided into chapters. These are numbered by Indo-Arabic numerals. The total number of chapters is 66.

3 Each chapter is divided into sections and subsections. These are numbered decimally in Indo-Arabic numerals. In other words, the numbers of the sections should be read and treated as if they were pure decimal fractions. A decimal point should be taken as understood at the beginning of the number of each section. Then, the sequence of the numbers of the sections will become intelligible.

4 The digits in the numbers of most of the sections are mnemonic.

5 There is a bibliography at the end of the text. Each item in it is given a serial number. It consists of a capital letter followed by an Indo-Arabic numeral. At the appropriate place in the text, this serial number is inserted within square brackets.

6 The index follows the bibliography. Each index number is made of the letter denoting the part followed by the number of the section in which the reference occurs.

7 The text is illustrated by 167 case studies. These are scattered throughout the book in their appropriate places. The location of each case study is indicated in the index under the heading "Case study".

A The succeeding chapters of part A—that is, this part itself—are largely of a reminiscential nature. If desired, they may be skipped over by students in the first reading.

B Part B is on the "Emergence of Reference Service". Its chapter 1 begins with the definition of 'reference service' and traces its origin to the Laws of Library Science. The remaining chapters trace the evolution of library, its function, and its techniques. They culminate on the emergence of reference service and its nature.

C Part C is on the "Initiation of Reader". Its first three chapters are on the initiation of an adult reader without previous experience of a library. These deal with the what, the why, and the how of initiation into the structure, organisation, and functioning of a library with open access. There are also chapters on the initiation of the youth into the use of a college library and of the children into the use of a school library.

D PART D is on "General Help to General Reader". It has a chapter on the psychology of a reader, explained from the angle of reference service. Five of its chapters deal with the various qualities of books, making reference service necessary. Its last chapter is on the possible wrong behaviour and the psychology of a reference librarian.

E PART E is on the "Mystic Picture of Reference Service". Its chapters indicate the light shed obliquely on reference service by the *Vedas*, the *Ramayana*, the *Mother* of Sri Aurobindo, and the terminology in the Sanskrit language.

F PART F is on "Ready Reference Service". It has chapters on the what, the why, and the how of ready reference service.

G PART G is entitled "Find Me Out". One of its chapters indicates how answers were found out in the Madras University Library for 54 of the reference questions received during one month. Another chapter gives 108 'Facts to Find' questions for practice by students.

H PART H is on "Reference Book". Its chapter 1 traces the evolution of the reference book. Its other chapters describe with illustrations the wide variety in their subject-coverage, scope, up-to-dateness, and arrangement. The last chapter gives a skeleton to help the student in making a systematic study of the structure and contents of a reference book. This part is not a bibliography of reference books.

J PART J is on "Long Range Reference Service". Its chapters deal with the what, the why, and the how of long range reference service. The last chapter gives a skeleton to help the student in making a systematic study of the structure and contents of a bibliography.

K PART K is entitled "Illustrative Actualities". Its chapters describe in detail the routeing of six long range reference problems, as it was done in the Madras University Library. Its chapter 8 describes the deferred joy of a reference librarian, coming to him at a time when his ego can no longer feed itself on what he hears about his own work.

CHAPTER 1

REFERENCE SERVICE EXPERIENCE AS A STUDENT

11 At School

As a pupil at school, I never had access to a library. For, there was no library in the school. There was only a cupboard of specimen copies of text-books in an everlocked room. It was seldom thrown open to us. Nor was there any other library in our town—Shiyali. Therefore, there was no question of reference service. There was hardly a library in those days—the first decade of the present century—in any school or in any town. Indeed, pupils of my generation had never heard the term 'library' uttered by anybody. Still less then was the term 'reference service' known.

12 No Reference Book

The only books known at the school stage to most persons of my generation were the prescribed text-books. At home we had copies of the epics; but they were mostly manuscripts. Some homes had just a few printed books; but they were all text-books of the earlier generation. The teacher occasionally used a dictionary; but we were seldom allowed to look it up. In geography, we had to learn by rote statements such as "Birmingham is noted for hardware", "Reading is noted for biscuits", and "Sheffield is noted for cutlery". These statements were all picked up from the prescribed text-book. But we had never heard of a directory or year-book. Nor had we heard of an encyclopaedia. We knew only of a single simple prescribed school atlas. This completed our list of printed reference books.

13 Living Reference Book

But, I was fortunate to have daily use of two living reference books. One was Tiruvenkatachariar, my Sanskrit teacher during all the six years of my school. The other was Anantaramayyar, a teacher in the infant school and a co-tenant in my house. Both had an intimate knowledge of our indigenous encyclopaedias called the *Puranas*, the epics, and some other literary pieces. Both had an intimate knowledge of the religious practices, of the biographies of the saints and mystics, and of the local histories of the chief temple-towns, belonging to their respective creeds. They enjoyed answering questions. They filled my mind with much information in the humanities, and in some social sciences, but nothing in the natural sciences or the arts and crafts. I am now able to recognise their help to me through all the six years at school, as reference service of inestimable value. Of course, they gave all the information from within themselves. They could not help me to help myself with externalised memory or reference books. Later in life, I had the chance to look up and confirm most of the information in books.

14 At College

I moved into college on 18 March 1909. The college was in Madras. It was in the front rank among the colleges of the University. It had a 'General Library' for loan and a 'Consulting Library' for study within its room. In respect of the former, any interested student can put in an application slip at 10 a m on an appointed day of the week. Luck favouring, he may get the book at 4 p m. There was no help in the choice of book either in the class room or in the library. The professor seldom mentioned any title other than that of a prescribed text-book. In the library, we never came into contact with any human being, except the attender mutely handing over the book at 4 p m on the appointed day of the week.

15 No Reference Service

We had a slightly better experience in the Consulting Library. It was generally used as a waiting room between classes. E M Macphail, a Professor of History, once happened to enter the Consulting Library. He threw us into a roar of laughter by his remark, "I thought I was entering a fish market". Our roar of laughter completely drowned, for the moment, the normal noise of the Consulting Library. The attendant in charge of the library was Daniel. He had one essential quality of a reference librarian—geniality. But he could read only the backs of books. At the end of a term, I had the benefit of a sort of reference service from him. He introduced me to Milne's *Weekly problem papers* and his *Companion to weekly problem papers*. He said, "Prof Chinnatambi Pillai has been copying out something from these two books"! This is the only kind of reference service experienced by me till my leaving the college!!

16 No Reference Book

While in the college, we were never introduced to any encyclopaedia, biographical dictionary, directory, year-book, or bibliography. We had no occasion to know if the College Library had any reference book at all. The only volumes of the *University calendar*, doled out to us in the Consulting Library, were those containing the examination question papers. Each of us had to buy a copy of the *College calendar*. But we did not find much use for it. We did not know that it was a reference book. In fact, we had not heard the term 'reference book' uttered by anybody at any time in our college days. We were asked to buy a copy of some *English dictionary*. But we were not helped to make a full or an intelligent use of it. The only bibliography, known to us, was the *Catalogue of the College Library*. It was a tattered copy at the library barrier. It was an alphabetical catalogue cut into a number of subject sequences. We were not given any instruction in its use. It was all a matter of hit or miss. Even this experience was only in the case of the few longing to take out a book home.

17 Unexpressed Wish

I used to take out books from the General Library now and then. It was, as a rule, a random choice. Sometimes, the book drawn would be trashy. Sometimes, it would be beyond my capacity. I had to wait till the appointed day and hour to return such books to the library, though unsuited to be read. Occasionally, the book happened to be an enjoyable one. In those days, I had a vague feeling. I could not then express it properly. I can now express it in the words, "I wish I could get some reference service from a reference librarian, in the choice of suitable books for reading and in finding the information needed to satisfy my curiosity about many things."

18 First Use of Reference Book

I went to Teachers' College in July 1916. There was much free time. There was a library in the college. Some of the books occupied my free time. One of the professors used to help me in the choice of books. His evaluation of the books on education was very helpful. This was a new experience. But few students took advantage of this. This enabled me to make a full use of the Professor's reference service. Once, he put into my hands the volumes of Dutta's *Survey of real income in India*. It had many statistical tables. The Professor said, "Glance through the tables. Prepare some charts and histograms for the college exhibition". This work made me understand the structure and the contents of a statistical reference book. It also trained me in drawing information from it to suit a particular purpose. This experience thrilled me. I was glad to finish off my formal student stage with this intensive experience with at least one reference book. Of course, I did not then know the term 'reference book'. But that made no difference in the joy of the experience of the first acquaintance with a reference book:

CHAPTER 2

REFERENCE SERVICE EXPERIENCE AS A TEACHER

21 Individual Instruction

On 9 July 1917, I changed from the student's bench to the teacher's chair. I had my first experience as teacher in the Government College, Mangalore. The Principal, N R Krishnamma, was pleasant and youthful. He gave full freedom to do my teaching in my own way. The classes were small. And yet the scatter of the ability of the students was immense. I found mass-teaching ineffective even with a class of a dozen students, if done from day to day and from hour to hour. But, the concept of individual instruction had not been passed on to us while at the Teachers' College. Indeed, I learned later that the concept had not entered modern India, though it was being preached and practised by John Dewey since the turn of the century. However, in her usual way, necessity appeared as the mother of invention. I decided to help each student individually and to allow him to grow at his own speed along his own lines. Very soon, I found myself letting the students work their own way with the aid of books and in doing experiments in the laboratory, myself going round and helping each to get over his individual difficulties.

22 Need for Variety in the Standard of the Books

Very soon, this led me to sense that the prescribed text-book did not suit every student in equal measure. Some found it too easy. They finished it quickly and found nothing more to do. Some others found it too difficult. They felt repelled from the subject and found study irksome and unprofitable. They looked depressed. Still others found the prescribed text-book to be to their standard. They studied with zest. This experience made me realise the need for text-books of different standards and with different approaches to the subject. I also realised the need for different text-books of the same standard. But the students could not afford to buy many text-books.

23 Formation of Class Library

I asked the Principal for funds to buy a variety of text-books in a variety of standards and to buy several copies of some of them. He readily gave the necessary funds. The books arrived in a few days. I then explained to the Principal the advantage of leaving the books in my charge, instead of getting them locked up in the general library in charge of the semi-literate care-taker called librarian. He readily agreed. He did not allow any red tape or tradition to clog the way. The result was the formation of a class library. All live books; no dead stuff. All new books; no old stuff. Unhampered access to students. Ample guidance on the spot in the selection of books. Of course, I need not have taken on myself the full load of looking after the library if the college had a competent professional librarian. Then, mere collaboration with the librarian would have been sufficient.

24 Budding of Reference Service

The class library gave ample opportunity to find out for each student his exact book—of the right standard and the right approach suited to him. It gave me opportunity to feel the joy of marching with each student at his own pace. Each student was found to be fully occupied in learning. The forwards did not feel bored. The backwards did not feel depressed. It was joy for the teacher; and it was equally joy for every one of the taught. The teacher-in-me had evidently compelled me into this kind of personal service to the students in the choice of the right book for the right student, in the right way and at the right time. The librarian-in-me had not then sprouted out. I now realise that what I was then led to do was reference service—the true work of a librarian.

25 Full Use of Departmental Library

On 9 July 1921, I was posted to the Presidency College, Madras. My Department had already a splendid collection of books. But the college as a whole had only one clerk and two attendants to look after its library system. The departmental library was in the custody of the teachers. This made it possible for me to continue the method of individual instruction and of helping each student personally in the choice of books best suited to his capacity and standard of attainment. This was found to be truly helpful. For, though the classes were small, the ability-scatter was great. Work with the students in the library was even more helpful with the advanced senior students of the Presidency College than with the junior students in the Mangalore College. For, the individual variation in interest and capacity was greater in the former than in the latter. The benefit of personal help in the choice of books was unmistakeable in the Presidency College. This was a happy period in my career as a teacher. I hardly realised at that time my being thus unconsciously prepared for my future career as librarian. Yes; my preview of the joy of doing reference service began quite unawares even while practising as a teacher.

26 Vicarious Satisfaction

During all the six and a half years as a teacher, the pleasant experience of seeing the students getting satisfaction from the library service, inaccessible to myself in my student days, gave me vicarious satisfaction. I now realise that I had really integrated in those years the function of a teacher with that of a reference librarian. Indeed, I had been spending much of my time in the area of overlap between the regions of a teacher and of a reference librarian.

CHAPTER 3

REFERENCE SERVICE EXPERIENCE AS AN ADULT USER OF LIBRARY

31 Public Library

In the year 1916, I had occasionally stepped into the Connemara Public Library in Madras. It was the only public library, even be it so only in name. In reality, it was an annexe to the Museum. It did not lend out books. However, it had an impressive building. Its reading room used to be nearly empty, except for the sight-seers coming to the museum peeping in to see and sit for a while in the majestic long corridor in the centre, functioning as the reading room. Its great length, its enormous height, the penetrating smell of naphthalene, the massiveness of its chairs and tables laid bare by the absence of occupants, the mellow light trickling through the coloured glass on the sides of the roof, and the serene watchful look of the sentinels perched up high on the platform inside the enclosure at the centre—all these combined inspired awe. It was an ordeal to wade through the alphabetical entries of the huge repulsive tomes of paste-down catalogue to locate, all by oneself, some title of interest. For there was hardly anybody in the library, who could be approached for help. Indeed, except for the sublibrarian—an administrator with no concern about readers—there was nobody in the library with a knowledge of books and some ability to help readers in the choice of books or in the obtaining of information.

32 University Library

The young Madras University Library was then a tenant in the building of the Connemara Public Library. Its part of the long corridor was even more deserted. After my return to Madras in 1921, I began to visit the University Library almost every Saturday and Sunday. It had just begun to build up a small but intrinsically heavy collection of treatises in the subjects taught to the honours level in the colleges. In my own subject, I had no difficulty in choosing my books. This was as a result of the familiarity gained in helping the students in the Library of my Department in the college. The library staff itself had none to help readers either in choosing books for study or in finding out information from the books.

33 Trace of Reference Service

Trivikrama Row and N S Sivarama Ayyar were looking after the collection. They were good and kind to the few readers visiting the library. Of course, the few readers were mostly teachers in the colleges of the University. The two gentlemen in the library had ample native intelligence. But, they had not gone beyond the school-final class. Therefore, they could not know the inside of the severely advanced books being collected in the library. They had three assistants. These had not completed even the school course. They could only read the backs of books. As a teacher of the Presidency College and as a frequent visitor to the library, I was allowed the indulgence of looking through the accession registers. There was a separate accession register for each of the faculties recommending books. There were only a few pages of entries in each. This made it easy to choose books from the accession register. While scanning the entries in the register, Sivarama Ayyar would occasionally disclose the name of the professor who recommended a particular book or that of a professor who frequently borrowed a particular book. Sometimes, these remarks helped in the evaluation of some of the books. In other words, these remarks carried with them a trace of reference service! That was all the unmeant, unrecognised, reference service experienced in that library.

34 Hoarded Collection

Nobody knew in those days that a library should have a learned staff, designated reference librarians, to receive readers with geniality and confidence, to help readers in looking up references and finding information, and to give them pin-pointed personal help in the choice of the books needed for their respective purposes. It was only in 1937 that R Littlehailes, the then Vice-Chancellor, had the designation 'Reference Librarian' accepted by the University. Nobody realised in those days that the poor attendance in the library was largely traceable to the absence of reference librarians to render personal reference service to readers. Nor did anybody feel concerned about the poor attendance. Nobody realised in those days the absurdity of the plenty in the library being hoarded and locked up, while the potential consumer either did not come to the library or even after coming to the library had to go away without drawing the best possible help out of its collection, because of the absence of provision of reference librarians as 'salesmen' for getting the intellectual commodities assembled in the library put across persistently and even aggressively to the probable consumers.

35 Reluctance to Become Librarian

Experience as a user of the library had prejudiced me against work in a library. It appeared to be low level, dull, mechanical, janitorial work, without need for much of learning or intelligence and without any grip or human touch or human value. This made me indifferent to the advice of N Raghunatha Ayyangar, my good friend and co-teacher in the college, to apply for the post of University Librarian just then created. But his persistence made me sign an application with great reluctance. I took no further interest in the matter. However, the University happened to select me for the post. On 4 January 1924, I had to change over from the college to the library. I did so with a heavy heart. I little knew at that moment that the focal point of the work attached to the office of librarian was essentially the same as the one to which I had been accustomed as a teacher, viz, to help each person individually to get his information and to choose the books best suited to him.

CHAPTER 4

OBSERVATION OF REFERENCE SERVICE

41 Preparation for Observation

On 30 September 1924, I landed in London. The purpose was to study Library Science and to observe library service. On the recommendation of Sir Frederick Kenyon, the Principal Librarian of the British Museum Library, I joined the School of Librarianship in the University College, London. The first two months were spent in studying the books and the periodicals in the library of the School. It contained useful books on several branches of Library Science, but hardly anything of value on reference service. Nor were there many articles on the subject in the periodicals on Library Science. But there were a few notes on 'Information Desk'. In the course given at the School also, very little was done on reference service. But something was said about information desk, and directories, and year-books. Even the course on Bibliography, given by Esdaile, was turned more on Physical Bibliography, Descriptive Bibliography, and Historical Bibliography than on Subject Bibliography the tool for reference service.

42 First Contact with Reference Books

In December 1924, W C Berwick Sayers allowed me to pick up practical experience in library work in his Public Library at Croydon. I worked there as an apprentice for about a month. I found two collections, called respectively 'lending library' and 'reference library'. The latter term denoted that the books in it could not be borrowed but should be studied within the room only. It contained copies of many of the serious books found in the lending library. But I found something new in its collection—new to me from India. These were the reference books—directories of diverse industries and trades, telephone directories and street directories of several cities, who's who of many countries, dictionaries of biography, year-books of various institutions, several general encyclopaedias, many other cyclopaedias restricted to different subject-fields, such as physics, technology, philosophy, psychology, education, social sciences, law, and even on particular authors such as

Browning and Dickens, and a considerable collection of bibliographies on several subjects. I studied their structure and scope with avidity.

43 Information Desk

Thereafter, I visited nearly 120 libraries. In every library, there was a reference library. Every reference library contained an Information Desk, answering the description given in the lectures in the School. There was always somebody on duty at the desk. He had within his arm's reach a battery of business directories, money market reports, railway time-tables, and similar materials of current ready reference value. He was continuously approached by reader after reader for some information or other. He tossed out a reference book to one. He himself found out the information for another. He gave the information from memory to still another. My memory went back in time. I asked myself, "Is it not this kind of organisation that I had been all along feeling the need for?" My mind went back to India. I asked myself, "When will our people have access to a similar information service?"

44 Research Consultant

But, I was disappointed in one respect. Help to readers in the choice of books and in the extension of their knowledge was not very visible in many libraries. However, I soon had a re-assurance on this form of service to readers. E C Richardson delivered a lecture in the Use of Libraries Series organised at the University College. He mentioned the term 'Research Consultant'. It captivated me. He described that term as denoting a scholar of erudition, whose extensive and intensive knowledge of his own subject of specialisation was harnessed by the Library of Congress. He was not made a regular member of its staff. He was used as a 'retainer' is used in the legal profession. Whenever a reader was in need of help in the consultant's subject of specialisation, the services of the latter were requisitioned. The help may be needed for the preparation of a bibliography to suit the specific needs of the reader; or, it may be needed for chalking out a special course of reading; or, it may be for pursuing a specific problem not covered clearly or comprehensively by widely known books or periodical articles. My memory went back in time. I asked myself, "Is it not this kind of reference service in a library that I had been longing for as a student, as a teacher, and as an adult user of libraries?" I was emboldened to believe, "I had not been, after all, wishing for the moon. This kind of reference service is possible; and it should be practicable in a library."

45 Reference Service in Incipient State

Richardson's lecture made me look for the practice of reference service in the libraries visited thereafter. But, few went beyond Information Desk Service. I discussed with the librarians the absence of reference service of a deeper quality in their respective libraries. Some traced it to shortage of staff. Some others said that reference service required a special training which was not available. Still others said that it required personnel with qualifications superior to those found necessary for other forms of library work, but that the salary scale prevalent in libraries could not either attract or retain persons with such superior qualifications. A few gave the naive reply that the readers did not generally expect such reference service and that they were satisfied with information desk service. Some missed the essence of reference service. They overlooked the service having to be personal to an individual reader facing a particular requirement at the moment. They equated reference service with the supply of reading lists prepared in a general way with no particular person in view. Such lists were no doubt prepared and distributed widely by many libraries in association with library extension talks. This form of service appeared to my mind to come midway between public relation work and reference service. It was more like the work of sale-promoters; while reference service was like actual salesmanship itself with the consumer right at the shop and the consequent obligation to find for him the right commodity in co-operation with him, and not merely give him a list of commodities. Reference service can emerge only in the reader-books-librarian juxtaposition characterised by a compelling purpose. I was led to the conclusion that reference service was then only in an incipient stage in public libraries.

46 Illusion

In university libraries, the position appeared to be even worse. Reference service was not even in an incipient stage. It was not practised at all. And yet the readers in a university library usually go deep into their subjects. They need a good deal of hunt through several books and back volumes and current issues of diverse periodicals. This hunt has to be made systematically. It requires special training reinforced by practice. A reference librarian will have both of these in a greater measure than a student can be expected to have. Even if an experienced teacher had both of these, he cannot find the time for an exhaustive hunt. Thus, reference service is a necessity in a university library. But why was it not given? The answer given was, "The teacher helps the student in that way." Was it so? What did the teacher do? Did he help each student individually in the measure of his "individuating peculiarities"? This was test number one. Did he give help in the student-books-teacher juxtaposition? This was test number two. If both the tests were satisfied, the university library may abstain from giving reference service. If the teacher merely gave a list of books to be read by the members of his class, it was nothing short of an illusion to call it reference service. And my impression was that most university libraries were under that illusion. There was perhaps a reason for such an illusion to be used as an excuse for not making provision for reference service. The university libraries were not then managed by professional librarians. They were largely managed by honorary librarians drawn from among professors or controlled by professors or by Library Committees made of professors.

CHAPTER 5

PRACTICE OF REFERENCE SERVICE

51 Planning for Reference Service

On 21 July 1925, I resumed work in the Madras University Library, after return from study tour in Europe. I came back convinced that library service was even a greater challenge to me than teaching service. I was also equally convinced of the great potency of library service in working for the social betterment of the community. It would fulfil many of my nebulous unexpressed cravings developing steadily from student stage onwards. There was no more reluctance to embrace library service as the career for life. The challenge of library service was worthy of grappling with as life's work. It had every promise of occupying the whole life and of leading to the fulfilment of the journey through life in the present body. While on board the ship, the devotion of the Captain of Dumana to his duty, his untiring hour-to-hour attention to every detail in the ship, and above all his never-failing cheerfulness impressed me greatly. Being the only Indian passenger on the ship, he sought my company quite often. His complete identification of himself with his work, coupled with a similar thing observed by me in my childhood in Tiruvenkatattayyangar, our village temple priest, and in my college days in Edward B Ross, my professor in the Madras Christian College, confirmed my faith in the path of Karma Yoga. In my voyage, I was intensively planning my future library work—first in the Madras University Library and then in the country at large. Some part of the planning, such as the one concerning classification was based on actual work and trial with the ship's library. But a good part of the planning had to be in thought only. Reference service belonged to the latter part. I sensed that the successive steps should be to

1 Classify the books in the library;
2 Re-arrange the books in classified sequence;
3 Introduce open access;
4 Learn the art of reference service by doing it myself;
5 Demonstrate the educational and social values of reference

service by taking up the work as an additional load, without asking for additional staff, for a few years; and finally

6 Secure the necessary additional staff after the value of reference service is appreciated by the public as a result of the demonstration.

52 Preparation for Reference Service

The first four steps for the introduction of reference service, depended entirely on myself. No doubt, they meant hard work, great responsibility, and some amount of risk. But it was mostly creative work. It therefore charmed me to take the extra load of work, responsibility, and risk. The work was lived with joy all the waking hours in the day and on all the days of the year. Sundaram and Sivaraman were already working in the library as temporary staff for seeing the second supplement to the library catalogue through the press. They were the only graduates in the staff. They were willing workers. They were loyal. They too shared with me the delight of meeting the challenge of the reorganisation of the library in general and of the eventual introduction of reference service. For, they readily appreciated my description of the social benefit of reference service and of the few details about it already formed in my mind. These two colleagues were a great prop to me. This was a providential advantage. Another providential factor: Without thinking and as if by reflex action, I took the first five steps to lie entirely within the discretion and the powers of the librarian himself. I did not take up the proposal to the authorities for sanction—neither to the Library Committee nor to the Syndicate of the University. I did not even report to them about these five steps at any stage. An aside at this stage: In later years, I have been finding many librarians creating trouble for themselves, losing the chance to reorganise and revitalise their libraries, and also creating a pestering precedent to other librarians by surrendering their own rights and powers in the internal working of the library and asking for "sanction"—it may be out of ignorance or as a cheap way of advancing themselves in the eyes of the members of the authorities. My appeal goes to the library profession to give up this practice.

521 Phasing of the Five Steps

The whole process was brought within the range of practicability and comfort by phasing the five steps in a helpful way. The phasing consisted of two factors. One main class was taken up at each phase. Within each main class chosen, the phases were,

1 Classification of the books;

2 Rearrangement of the books classified, in a new sequence;

3 Giving open access to the new sequence; and

4 Doing reference service for the subjects brought into the new sequence

The subjects were taken in the following sequence for the reasons given against each.

1 English literature. This was a compulsory subject for all the students. Even otherwise, it was the most sought subject. My own extensive and intensive study of English literature in my undergraduate years had given me a fair insight into the highways and by-ways in the subject. Some of my old colleagues in the teaching profession were willing to help me in the work. Lastly the design of the Colon Classification for Literature was simple and the schedules were self-formed.

2 Education. This was my favourite subject. There were friends like M S Sabesan ready to work with me in designing the facets and the schedules for this subject. The ramifications in the subject, as reflected in embodiment as books, were relatively simple. My intimate relation with the teachers of the city and my previous position in the organisation of the Madras Teachers Guild enabled me to bring in readers for the books on Education. They willingly participated in the evaluation of the new steps taken.

3 Psychology. This had much affiliation with Education. Here also, the ramifications of the subject, as reflected in their embodiment as books, were relatively simple. I had studied the subject with some interest as a student in Teachers' College. The design of the facets and the schedules for the subject was relatively easy.

The other subjects were taken up later. During the first three years, the classification had all to be done by me. This was of much help in designing the classification. It must be stated here that the design of the schedules of the Colon Classification was done concurrently with the work of classifying the books in the library. The reference service also had to be done almost all by myself. This again was an advantage. It enabled me to test the efficiency of the schedules of classification and make the necessary amendments from time to time. While doing reference service, many of its techniques emerged and got formulated in mind in easy instalments. As and when a sufficient number of them had taken shape, they were brought up for discussion in the monthly meetings of the Staff Council [R 37]. Little by little, Sundaram began to share the work with me. He was an intelligent man. He was also a shrewd observer. We could put our heads together and evolve the techniques of reference service with confidence.

53 Demonstration of Reference Service

There was no special publicity turned on reference service. The service publicised itself. It was something novel for the few persons happening to call at the library. Apart from its novelty, they found it useful to themselves. Each found his books readily with the help obtained from open access, classified arrangement, and reference service. Every book also found its readers with the very same aids. Above all, the time of the reader was saved considerably. There was no boredom of sitting idle till the attendant would bring the books. The reader was continuously kept pleasantly occupied in browsing the books. He had somebody in the library to discuss his book needs with him. Thus, his subjective time went without any waste whatever. Naturally, every visitor to the library talked about this new arrangement in the library with his friends not accustomed to go to the library. This roused curiosity. The curiosity attained sufficient intensity in some to make them go to the library and gain personal experience of the new service. On reaching home, each of these became a voluntary "publicity agent" for the library. Thus, the chain action gradually spread itself over an ever-increasing number of students, graduates, and teachers in the city. In about two years, the chain action spread out into the other towns of the state too. Occasionally, a plaintive protest against the new system of open access and reference service used to reach my ears. It was weak in its strength. It was also private in its origin. It used to come from some teachers. They had been my colleagues before my migration to the library field. A special pleading used to be somewhat as follows.

"The new thing you are doing is certainly useful to me. But it is not an unmixed good."

"How?"

"You allow the full advantage of this system to the students also."

"What's wrong with it?"

"Some of the students come to the class as well informed as myself! I find it difficult to tell them anything new. What am I to teach?. . ." But this was only from some gramophone type of teachers. The others welcomed the students coming well posted with published information and knowledge. This enabled the development of the subject in the class room into its further reaches—jointly by the teacher and the taught. Class-room discipline became easy. There was the happy sign of attention and interest in the face of most of the students. This was the version of some teachers.

531 Evaluation of the Demonstration

In about three years, the demonstration had done its work effectively. As already indicated above, the educational value of the trinity of classified arrangement, open access, and reference service came to be realised by many. It was classification that made open access useful. It was open access that made reference service possible. It was reference service that brought practically universal support to classification and open access. The social value was not so obvious. It was of a deferred, indirect, and hidden kind. However, some deep thinkers used to discuss it with me with penetration, appreciation, and satisfaction. Among them were Sir P S Sivaswamy Ayyar, F H Gravely, M S Sabhesan, Edward B Ross, S Kuppuswamy Sastri, M A Candeth, A Chakravarty, and the parents of some of the students of the university. Their evaluation of reference service added to the enthusiasm of my co-workers in the library.

54 Averted Obstruction to Reference Service

But there were troubles ahead. They took shape on the request for sanction of additional staff, to meet the year-to-year increase in the volume of work. No doubt, the increase in work was largely due to the inherent attraction of open access, reference service, and a large annual accession of the latest worthwhile books. It was also due to deliberate public relation work to persuade more persons to accept the service of the library. The main streams of obstruction were two.

541 Futurist Obstruction

The first obstruction came from a foreigner, belonging to the then ruling nation. He had the typical mind of the foreign bureaucracy. He sensed the ultimate social good and enlightenment bound to flow from widespread library service to students and graduates. On my side, care had been taken to make out a case for additional staff on the basis of increase of readers and of work in general. No mention had been made of the need for additional competent persons to strengthen reference service. But, he had learnt of the introduction of reference service. He had known of its spear-head value in the extension and intensification of library service. He therefore started his vehement opposition to the request for staff. He explicitly traced the increase in work to reference service. He pleaded in the Library Committee that reference service was spoon-feeding, that it would sap away the originality and the spirit of self-help in the students, that it was unnecessary for the teachers, that it was presumptuous for librarians to claim to be omniscient, and that reference service was not a legitimate function of the library. Fortunately, I was myself the *ex-officio* Secretary of the Committee. That was an advantage. The immediate physical presence of the whole personality and the chance for quick give and take carried conviction to the other members of the Committee more easily than hundreds of type-written words could have done. All the other members of the Committee—Indian as well as foreign—voted him down. The request for additional staff received approval with only one dissentient voice.

542 Obstruction as Cult

The second stream of obstruction arose out of local political factors. The opponents had had no experience of library service at any time—not even after the university library had begun to function and to give reference service. For them, the library was only an administrative department, lending itself as an additional means to grind their political and personal axes. It was not necessary for them to base their support or opposition to any proposal on its intrinsic merits or its social value. "Whose proposal is it?" The answer to this question would decide their attitude. If the proposal came from certain quarters, it was their cult to oppose it. Those opposing the proposal for the library were not, then, in a majority. The majority consisted partly of those politically opposed to the obstructionists. These supported the proposal because the other side opposed it, not necessarily on the basis of its merits or of its social value. For, mutual opposition was a cult of the political parties. The other part of the majority consisted of professors and other scholarly persons. Some of them were regular visitors to the university library. They had seen the new life humming there. The grounds, on which sanction for additional staff was sought, appeared sound to them. Therefore, they too supported the proposal. As a result, sanction was accorded. Additional staff came into the library. Reference service was intensified. The spiral of growth began to rise smoothly in the library.

55 Reference Service on Full Steam

Through the grace of God, all such obstructions soon became mere deposits in the memory. My busy life with readers did not allow such deposits to come to the surface of the memory in those days. By 1930, reference service had put on full steam in the Madras University Library. Five smart young graduates formed the squad of reference librarians. They had specialised in different subjects in their degree course. The universe of knowledge was roughly shared among the five. They started reference service with a short in-training course given by me. They learnt the art of reference in great detail during the process of actually giving the service in full faith and with the zeal of a pioneer. Their place of work was the stack-room and the adjacent catalogue room. They had no files to distract their thought from giving personal service. Their hours were staggered as determined by the statistically ascertained fluctuation in the density of readers. They staggered their annual holidays as determined by the statistically ascertained monthly fluctuation in the density of visitors to the library. Reference service was maintained all the thirteen hours on all the 365 days of the year. At peak hours, the members of the Technical Section normally engaged in classification and cataloguing work and those of the Maintenance Section reinforced the Reference Section. I myself was always a standby to be called in during crowded hours and to pursue problems too refractory for normal investigation. The readers enjoyed reference service. They felt benefited. We enjoyed it too. It was an additional gratification to hear of the appreciative way in which people talked about this service in the clubs and on the marina in the evenings, in the homes and the hostels in the night, in the common rooms of the colleges and the Bar room of the High Court during the day, in the buses, in the trams, and even in railway trains. The joy was even greater when visitors from other parts of India and from other countries referred to our reference service as something unique in its conception, in its intensiveness, and in its very existence on such a planned, large, and continuous scale.

56 Further Development into Documentation

All this happened twenty years ago. Along with the World War II, a smothering cloud descended on this organisation. It was a heart-break to see the dwindling of the number of readers and the withdrawal of reference librarians from reference service. The situation deteriorated considerably after 1942. Fortunately, I had to leave the library in 1944. This minimised the pain. Within three years all the disappointment disappeared. For shortly after the close of the war, joy centred on full-fledged reference service came back in re-doubled measure. For, many opportunities came to witness very intensive reference service being given in several industrial libraries in several countries. Emphasis shifted from whole books embodying macro thought to articles in periodicals embodying nascent micro thought. To highlight this shift, reference service of that intensive kind to specialists is now being denoted by the new term 'Documentation'. Documentalists are being recognised as forming a profession [R 20] with a necessary part to play in the future well-being of humanity.

57 Future of Reference Service in India

India should fall into line with this world trend. I trust that it will not be very long before each one of our forty university libraries will practise reference service. I trust that the public libraries beginning to function will straight away begin to practise reference service. Lastly, I trust that the libraries of our business enterprises and of the departments of the governments of our land will begin to practise documentation service. India can then continue to contribute much to the world-pool of thought on reference service and documentation.

CHAPTER 6

GENESIS OF THE BOOK

61 First Version of the Ideas

The observation of the working of libraries in Europe during 1924-25 led to some intensive thinking. An urge came to reduce the diverse library practices to a few fundamental laws. In about three years, the Five Laws of Library Science took shape. Then came the making of all possible inferences from the Five Laws. At first, the observed library practices were verified to be a part of these inferences. The practice of 'Information Desk' found a place in this part of the inferences. It was found to be essentially an implication of Law 4 "Save the time of the reader" [R 28]. Another part of the inferences from the Five Laws were found to be new. Reference service—particularly the one of the long range variety—found a place among them. It emerged in the first instance as an implication of Law 1 "Books are for use" [R 24]. Then, it emerged again as an implication of Law 2 "Every reader his book" [R 25]. Here its facet facing the readers emerged. It next emerged as an implication of Law 3 "Every book its reader" [R 26]. Here its facet facing the books emerged. It again emerged as an implication of Law 4 "Save the time of the reader" [R 27]. Here its facet facing time emerged. The results of this *a priori* study of reference service were verified while doing floor duty in the Library. The results were then embodied in edition 1 of the *Five laws of library science* (1931). This formed the first published version of my thought on reference service.

62 Pressure from the Library School

A School of Library Science was founded in 1929. From 1929 to 1931, it was conducted by me in the Madras University Library under the auspices of the Madras Library Association founded in 1928. From 1932 to 1943, I conducted the School under the auspices of the university itself. From 1929 to 1938, it gave only a Certificate Course of ten weeks. During this period, I used to give only about three talks on reference service. The students found the version in the *Five laws of library science* to be sufficient for their recapitulatory study. From 1938, the School gave a post-graduate Diploma Course of one full academic year. I then began to give talks and direct practical work on reference service for about ten weeks. This had necessarily to be more elaborate than the brief version in the *Five laws*. The students needed an elaborate book for recapitulatory and follow-up study. This pressure from the Library School prompted me to write out a book on the subject.

63 Pressure from Inside

Apart from this pressure from outside, an inner pressure had been slowly developing all along. It was urging the embodiment of my thoughts on reference service in the form of a regular book. This inner pressure originated from a desire to lay bare as fully as possible all the implications of the Five Laws in the field of reference service. This was an intellectual urge. But this book could not be given priority over the other books on classification, cataloguing, and administration. Therefore, the idea was driven down to the subconscious level year after year. In the meantime, the inner pressure was gradually gaining in strength with the accumulation of interesting case-studies picked up from the actual reference service in the library. Sundaram and myself used to discuss frequently the difficult reference problems pursued, the different routes followed in their pursuit, the difficult books negotiated, the difficult readers served, and the general principles getting distilled out of these experiences. By 1939, these experiences had accumulated to a considerable volume. A ripeness came over us. Books on other essential branches of library science had been already written and published. The inner pressure had its way. The writing of the first edition was started.

64 Pressure from the Library

In the meantime, the work in the library had increased considerably. The daily attendance of readers had increased steadily. The pressure on reference service increased in consequence. But due to various causes, beyond the control of the library, only three of the five places in the Reference Section had been filled permanently. The other two places used to fall vacant every six months on an average. With the increased volume of work, it was difficult to train each new recruit solely through oral instruction from day to day. This increased the pressure on the three permanent members of the section and on myself. The feeling came that this pressure could be reduced if there were a detailed book on reference service with plenty of illustrative case-studies, which can be put into the hands of the new recruits.

65 Edition 1

The first edition of this book was the result of all the three pressures mentioned above. It was an ambitious venture. It consisted of five parts as described below.

Parts 1 to 3: Reference service;

Part 4: Bibliography; and

Part 5: Bibliography of reference books and bibliographies.

It was brought out in two volumes in the years 1940 and 1941 respectively. Part 5 occupied the whole of volume 2. The other four parts were put into volume 1. By 1939, I had formed a desire to associate my colleagues with me in the writing of books. Sundaram was the seniormost of them. He had a flair to express himself. He had also gained a considerable experience in reference service. In fact, he was the best known member of the staff on account of his able and untiring work as the chief reference librarian. He was therefore invited to become the co-author for volume 1. But by the time parts 1 to 2 were completed, he dropped out. Parts 3 and 4 had therefore to be written all by myself. Sivaraman was the next in seniority. He had gained considerable experience in classification and cataloguing. He was invited to become the co-author for volume 2. The intention had been to find facilities to send him abroad to visit the important national libraries of the West and collect correct descriptions of reference books and bibliographies by actually examining the books. But war conditions prevented this procedure. Therefore volume 2 had to be based only on the few reference books and bibliographies available in the Madras University Library and on secondary sources for the rest.

66 Present Version

The present version is differently organised. I command no facilities to prepare an enlarged and up-to-date new edition of the *Bibliography of reference books and bibliographies* [R 2]. It is therefore dropped out. Further, the five parts of edition 1 lack the homogeneity necessary to go into a single book. This is true even of the first four parts. Therefore, volume 1 of edition 1 has been replaced by the following group of three independent but related books:

1 Reference service;
2 Documentation and its facets; and
3 Enumerative bibliography.

661 Book on Reference Service

The book on Reference Service is the focal point in the proposed set of three books. It covers the same ground as parts 1 to 3 of edition 1. It has been rearranged. It has also been re-written. It has 18 new chapters. These are,

1 All the chapters of Part A;
2 Chapter 1 of part B;
3 Chapter 5 of part C;
4 Chapters 1, 2, 3, and 5 of part E;
5 Chapter 8 of part H;
6 Chapters 6 and 7 of part J; and
7 Chapter 8 of part K.

A reference librarian should be thoroughly familiar with the idiosyncracies of reference books. He is their essential consumer. At the same time, he cannot be its producer either as author or as publisher. For the latter reason, the proposed group of books does not include a full-fledged book on Reference Book. For the former reason, an account of reference books viewed from the angle of the reference librarian is retained as part H of the present book.

662 Book on Bibliography

On the other hand, every reference librarian has to be at once a consumer and a producer of bibliographies. A detailed knowledge of the production as much as of the use of bibliographies is a necessary part of the equipment of a reference librarian. And yet the area of the production of bibliographies is separable from the area of reference service proper. This fact has been taken advantage of in transferring part 4 of edition 1 to a separate book. For, the volume of information to be given on reference service and bibliography taken together is found to be too great for inclusion in a single book. This proposed book will be called *Enumerative bibliography*.

663 Book on Documentation

Bibliography-building has been traditionally laying its emphasis on whole books embodying macro thought—that is, on macro documents. Further, tradition includes within the area of bibliography not only subject lists but also various other kinds of lists of books prepared by different agencies, such as the publisher, the bookseller, the cataloguer of a library, the producer of state and national bibliographies, linguist bibliographer, and so on. On the other hand, in recent years, as a result of social pressure and the urge to increase productivity, much thought is being devoted exclusively to subject bibliography. The production of subject bibliography has begun to lay emphasis on articles in current periodicals—that is on nascent micro documents—on the side of its contents and on the needs of specialist research workers on the side of its consumers. To mark this new field now being vigorously cultivated, the term 'Documentation' has come into use. Documentation has now gained greatly in importance in the local, national, as well as international level. This accounts for the second book in the proposed group of books being on *Documentation and its facets*.

CHAPTER 7

SUGGESTIONS TO BEGINNERS AND TEACHERS

71 Five-Fold Method

Reference service cannot be learnt merely by listening to lectures or by reading books on it. Both these methods are, of course, necessary; but they are not by themselves sufficient. The students and the teachers alike should adopt the five-fold method [R 21] of:

1 Apprentice or clinical method;
2 Lecture method;
3 Practical or workshop method;
4 Preparatory work with reference materials; and
5 Discussion method.

These five methods will have to be carefully telescoped in respect of time.

72 Apprentice Method

The beginner should be made to work as an apprentice with a regular reference librarian in a library. He should watch the work of the reference librarian in his eliciting from the reader an exact enunciation of the information or the piece of knowledge sought at the moment. The successive steps in the facet analysis used in the process should be followed (*see* sec. 52, 54, and 55 of part J of this book). Then the beginner should follow the reference librarian in his search for the right documents, the diverse routes followed, and the checking up with the reader at the different stages of the pursuit. All through the apprentice course, the beginner should record his experience in his case-study-book. This should be like the clinical lessons in a medical course.

73 Lecture Method

After the gain of some experience through apprenticeship, the student should be given formal lectures on the theory of reference service—its what, why, and how. I have found it to be entertaining as well as effective to start from the Five Laws of Library Science and to arrive at the answers to the above questions as necessary implications of the Five Laws. The logical process of inference should be interspersed with case studies taken from the experience of the teacher as well as of the students. The process is indicated in parts B, C, F, J, and K of this book.

74 Practical Method

A certain number of hours of apprenticeship and of formal lectures should fit the student to do some practical work in reference service. This should be done under the guidance and supervision of the teacher. In reference service, there should be a more intimate supervision over the practical work of students than in a natural science such as physics or an applied science such as surveying. In the the latter cases, the probable risk is only to the instruments used. There is no human 'object' involved. But in reference service, no disservice should be done to the reader. Nor should any prejudice be produced in his mind about the library. The reader is often a busy person. His faith in the efficiency of the library should not be prejudicially affected by any inordinate delay in completing the service or by the giving of unsatisfactory service. Therefore, the teacher or demonstrator, as the case may be, should closely watch, help, and give a final check up to the practical work of a student. All through the practical course, the student should enter systematic notes in his case-study-book.

75 Preparatory Work

Knowledge about reference books and bibliographies should grow continuously all through the life of a reference librarian (*see* chapters 4 and 6 of parts F and J of this book). In fact, it should begin at the student stage itself. The basic knowledge of the oft-used reference books and bibliographies should be acquired at the student stage itself. But, it will be boring to a beginner to devote several hours to a systematic study of the structure and contents of a reference book or a bibliography all by itself and all by himself. Yet it should be possible for him to do such a study purposively and with some zeal and enjoyment after gaining some experience in apprenticeship and practical work. For, by that stage the inescapable necessity to know the reference books and bibliographies would have been realised by the student. An outline scheme for a systematic study of the structure and contents of reference books and bibliographies is indicated in chapter 8 of part H and chapter 7 of part J of this book. Each student should complete a systematic study of a prescribed assortment of reference books and bibliographies during term time as part of his course. His note-book of preparatory study should be scrutinised by the teacher week by week. He should be helped by the teacher, week by week, in improving his preparatory study. A student tends to fag out quickly in this work. Therefore, the teacher should furnish the necessary stimulus and act as a helpful prop. The student's note-book of preparatory study should be certified by the teacher to have been satisfactorily done to a proper standard, before the student is declared fit to practise as a librarian.

76 Discussion Method

Discussion method is a recognised method in education. It is also called tutorial method. Unlike in the lecture method, in the discussion method the student is kept in an active and participating state instead of the passive one of listening. The discussion hours should be used to ram in several of the points in the technique of reference service, on the basis of the experience gained by the students during apprenticeship, practical work with readers, and preparatory work with reference books and bibliographies. Ample use should be made, during discussion hours, of the case-study-books of the students as well as of the teacher. The discussion hours should be judiciously interspersed amidst the hours of the other methods of teaching and learning.

77 Warning for the Period of Transition

Teaching of library science is now in a period of transition in India and in some other countries. It is particularly so in respect of reference service in most countries. Let us take India as an example. For ten years from 1929, there was only one Library School in the country. That was the school started by me in Madras. Admission to the school was then restricted to librarians of experience and to a few other persons considerably above the average in their general education and ability. The students felt themselves to be pioneers in the field. The teachers too had all the fervour of pioneers. In spite of most of their thought and time having to be turned on to the building up of the library and its service from scratch, they voluntarily taught library science outside their normal office hours. This is a measure of their fervour and urge to teach. Hundreds of years ago, Vatsyayana [V9] had described the psychology of a pioneer in full fervour and with great ability. To adapt one of his verses to our context,

> A pioneer feels the thrill of delight. His whole personality gets merged in his work; it involuntarily expresses itself in the work. Rules and methods and incentives are not for him. He transcends them all; and yet his work is better than that of the long-settled person guided by rules and precedents.

शास्त्राणां विषयस्तावत् यावत् मन्दरसाः नराः ।
[रसास्वादे प्रवृत्ते तु नैव शास्त्रं न च क्रमः ॥

So it was in the Madras School some twenty years ago. Now, several schools have come into being. Raw youth are admitted into them. Very often, unemployed young persons crowd into the library schools. The teachers are no longer under the spell of pioneership. The library staff have their hands full on account of the large sums of money paid as grant by the University Grants Commission and on account of serious research work beginning to hum in all the departments. Teaching has degenerated to the dictation of a few notes. Diplomas are given and taken. The result is proving to be deplorable. The employers have begun to ridicule the work of the library schools. Fortunately, there is now a trend to appoint full-timed teachers. For some years, these will be young persons. These teachers should, deliberately and without shirking, adopt all the five-fold methods of teaching reference service. The students too should adopt all the five-fold methods of learning reference service.

Part B

Emergence of Reference Service

CHAPTER 1

REFERENCE SERVICE AND THE LAWS OF LIBRARY SCIENCE

10 Definition of Reference Service

Reference service is the process of establishing contact between a reader and his documents in a personal way. 'His documents' means every one of the precise documents needed by him at the moment. It also means all the documents likely to be of use to him at the moment. It further means establishing the contact without any loss of time for him. It is not possible to do all this for a reader without an intimate understanding of his precise interest at the moment. To get this understanding, there must be an intimate communion between the librarian and the reader. From the first moment of the reader asking for help to the last moment of his getting all his documents, the librarian will have to be personally administering to the needs of the reader. Therefore, reference service is essentially personal service.

101 Illustration by Contrast

This may be made concrete as follows. At the time of a university convocation, each new graduate is served with a copy of the *Bhagavad-gita*. There is nothing personal in this service. For, all the copies are alike. Any graduate can be served with any copy of the book. Or again, on the occasion of a marriage festival, each guest is served with a cocoanut. Here all the cocoanuts are virtually alike. They are, in a sense, copies of one another. Therefore, there is nothing personal in serving them. But, the books in a library are not all alike. They are not copies of one another. Each book is an individual. So also, each reader is an individual. Therefore, each book has to be matched with each reader according to their respective 'individuating particularities'. This matching needs personal attention on the part of the librarian. In other words, this calls for personal service. Therefore, reference service is personal service. Its definition may be made clearer as follows. Reference service is personal service to each reader in helping him to find the documents answering his interest at the moment, pin-pointedly, exhaustively, and expeditiously.

102 Definition of Reference Librarian

A librarian is a reference librarian at the moment of doing reference service to a reader. The happiest moment in the life of a librarian is the moment of his doing reference service. The greatest joy of a reference librarian is attained at the moment of the blossoming of joy on the face of a reader as a result of the satisfaction got by the reference service received by him.

11 First Law and Reference Service

The First Law of Library Science is "Books are for use". The use of a book meant by the First Law is the use of its thought-content—that is, the expressed thought embodied in the book. According to the First Law, librarianship is connecting the right reader and the right book. This connection should be brought about almost aggressively, though pleasantly and persuasively. Any library, organised to work whole-heartedly with the First Law as its primary normative principle, demands reference service to be done profusely by its reference librarians. The First Law is indeed a hard task-master. One admits its dictum at one's peril. For, it says, "If the books are really collected and kept for use, the task of the librarian is not exhausted by merely advertising the library and its books. Nor can he force readers to accept the books of his own choice. On the other hand, he must know the books that readers will use with willingness and benefit to themselves. To find them out, he must co-operate with the readers. To co-operate is to help the readers to carry out their respective plans and wishes—to help them to help themselves." This is the kind of personal service expected by the First Law from the reference librarian. From the side of readers too, the request for individual personal service should come without any hesitation whatever. That is the wish of the First Law [R24].

12 Second Law and Reference Service

The Second Law of Library Science is "Every reader his book." This Law spells out in detail the insistence of the Laws of Library Science, as viewed from the angle of readers. According to this Law, the reference librarian should find out pin-pointedly the books needed by every reader for his use. Here, 'books' means, not merely conventional books but also parts of books and articles in periodicals, answering the needs of a reader pin-pointedly. The term includes also, other materials carrying information or knowledge, such as pictures, drawings, diagrams, gramophone records, and other kindred portable materials.

121 Definition of Document

For convenience of reference, the generic term 'document' has been brought into use, of late, to denote any or all such portable information-carrying or knowledge-carrying materials. The conventional books of appreciable size are called 'macro documents'. All other books of too tiny a size and all the other kinds of materials are called 'micro documents'. Naturally, the contents of a macro document will cover an appreciable area of knowledge. Therefore, the thought, normally taking a book for its embodiment, is called 'macro thought'. So also, the thought embodied in a small part of a book, a pamphlet, an article in a periodical, a picture, a drawing, a diagram, a gramophone record, or any similar materials, is called 'micro thought'.

122 Document-Journey

We may now re-state the Second Law in the form "Every reader his document". In finding his document for every reader in a pin-pointed way, the reference librarian should participate with the reader in his document-journey. His role is not that of a teacher or instructor. Far from it. It will not even be that of an adviser. It is all too presumptuous on the part of the reference librarian to call himself in either of these ways. It also takes away from the dignity of the reader. A reader may even be offended by such a term. For this reason, I do not support the term "readers' advisory service" used by our British colleagues in the place of 'reference service'. The reference librarian is only a companion to the reader in his document-journey. Perhaps, he is a companion more familiar, by practice, with the highways and the by-ways in the world of documents. In particular, he will know each of the reference books carrying information in a readily assimilable form; he will also know the structure and the mode of distribution of information in each of them; with this knowledge, he can help each reader to get his information. Similarly, he will be familiar with the important lists of books, including the library catalogue. These are called bibliographies. He will know the highways and by-ways in the bibliographies on diverse subjects. He will also know about the standards of the books. With this knowledge, he can help each reader with the books or the documents exactly answering his special needs and standards. This is the kind of personal service expected by the Second Law from the reference librarian. From the side of the readers too, the request for such pin-pointed personal service should come without any hesitation whatever. That is the wish of the Second Law [R25].

13 Third Law and Reference Service

The Third Law of Library Science is "Every book its reader". Here too, we must replace the term 'book' by the term 'document'. Micro document as well as macro document is meant in this context. This Law spells out in detail the insistence of the Laws of Library Science, as viewed from the angle of the documents. The demand of the Third Law will often transcend the capacity of aids like reference books, bibliographies, and catalogues. Books are mute. They are inert. They cannot make a journey into the world of readers to find out their respective readers. This entire journey will have to be done on their behalf by the reference librarian all by himself. In fact, the Third Law expects the reference librarian to act as the canvassing agent for every book and every document in the library. It asks him to be the interpreter of every book, to its potential readers. Thereby, he should convert them into its actual readers. He should move freely in the world of readers, even as a marketing agent for a commodity does in the world of consumers. He must know the qualities of the books and the documents well, even as the marketing agent has to know the qualities of his commodities well. He must be on the look out for every possible opportunity to find suitable readers for the books and the documents in the library. In fact, he must catch the reader in the right mood or prepare him into the right mood to use his books and documents, be they informational, recreational, or knowledge-giving, or inspirational. In the hands of the reference librarian, the library should be like a kaleidoscope. He should keep turning its facets, in order to win over suitable readers to each one of its facets. This is the wish of the Third Law. [R26].

14 Fourth Law and Reference Service

The Fourth Law of Library Science is "Save the time of the reader". This Law expects from the reference librarian something more than the first three Laws. It introduces the new factor 'time' into the service. It goes further in its demands on the reference librarian than the first three Laws. To satisfy it, the reference librarian should have great familiarity with the world of books and documents in general. He should also be fully familiar with the inside of all the reference books and with the battery of bibliographies available including the catalogue of the library itself. He should acquire speed in their use. He should also have an alert mind. He should be an adept in library classification. He should have special competence in facet analysis on the basis of the five fundamental categories of time, space, energy, matter, and personality. He should develop capacity to facet-analyse the question of the reader. In the course of this facet analysis, he should be able to fill up all the unexpressed elements in the question posed by the reader. He should then be able to put the grid obtained by that facet analysis on the world of the documents and on the catalogue and the bibliographies, and pick out the right documents without any loss of time.

141 Support of the Business World

The Fourth Law gets full support for such a reference service from the business world. For, the business world—the industrial and the commercial enterprises—values time. For it, time is money; and money is time. According to the Fourth Law, the money spent on reference service and reference librarians comes back to the community—be it the nation as a whole or a particular enterprise—in ever increasing measure, in the form of the saving of the precious time of the best brains—be they in the top-management or in the research team or in the field team. The business sense has been awakened in most nations since the World War II. It is alarmed at the wastage of the research-potential caused by the inadequacy of reference service. It has started investigating the size of this wastage by the methods of Operation Research. Half the time of the research worker has been found to be spent away in the general browsing of the published documents, in order to find out the particular few documents, relevant to the work on hand and therefore worth study. This is avoidable wastage of research time. According to the Fourth Law, one of the necessary elements in the machinery to be set up for the elimination of this wastage is reference service. The reference librarian should scan the bibliographical documents and the original documents themselves and place before the research worker just the documents rich in the matter relevant to the research-work on hand and worth study. That is the kind of sharing the literature-search with the research worker and of expeditious service expected by the Fouth Law from the reference librarian. From the side of the research worker too, the willingness to demand such personal service and to share the literature-search with the reference librarian should come without any hesitation whatever. That is the wish of the Fourth Law [R27].

15 Fifth Law and Reference Service

The Fifth Law of Library Science is "A library is a growing organism". In particular, the documents in a library continuously grow in quantity and variety. This is a result of the ever-increasing rate of production of the documents themselves. There is a steady rise in the annual production of books. Micro documents are produced in millions each year. They are scattered in more than a hundred thousand periodicals. Some are found scattered in quite unexpected media. Some plead for this scattering at least to be stopped. In despair, some even cry "Halt", King Canute-like ! These wishes have not been fulfilled ! In the meantime, it is difficult for individual readers to keep track of all the documents, to locate the wanted ones, and to gain access to them. National economy demands some arrangement to meet this situation created by the world of documents. "Otherwise", warns the Fifth Law, "You will have to die in the midst of plenty !" One element in the arrangement to meet the situation is the provision of reference service in libraries. Reference librarians should keep themselves promptly informed of the new books coming out, the new micro documents appearing in every sector of the wave-front of knowledge, and of their respective host documents. They should also keep correlating these newcomers with the old occupants of the library shelves and cabinets.

151 Complexity of Library System

The Fifth Law drives libraries to have resort to reference service by its pressure in another sphere. The high rate of production of books and periodicals on the one hand and the inadequacy of funds for every library to own everything wanted on the other, lead to the necessity to look upon the reading materials in all the libraries in a country as if they formed a single pool. On this being realised to be a necessity, the Fifth Law comes forward with some further words of wisdom. It says, "Each library is like a unicellular organism in the world of living organisms. Biology has led these unicellular organisms to form colonies for their own efficiency. Loose colonies found it an advantage to integrate themselves into more organically knit multi-cellular organisms. Ultimately, giant organisms have been organised. They have thrown forth organs. These organs have specialised functions and specialised structures to suit them. This multiplicity of organs works in co-ordination. They work in co-operation. They work in harmony. Libraries have to emulate nature in this respect. The libraries of a country should integrate themselves into a library system. It is bound to be a complex system. Its members should specialise in order to gain efficiency in total performance". Many a reader will have to look for his documents among the several members of the national library system. It is frequently so in the case of a specialist reader. It is difficult for a reader to sense all by himself the particular library in the system likely to contain the particular document needed by him. Nor is it economical, from the national point of view, to make each reader do so. According to the Fifth Law, there should be specialisation of functions on the human side also. Some persons should specialise in the art of finding out, by personal discussion based on facet analysis, the kind of documents needed by a reader, locating them in the libraries of the national library system, and then arranging for their procurement for the use of the reader. This is a kind of personal service expected by the Fifth Law from the reference librarian. From the side of readers too, the request for such a location of the needed documents even in libraries other than his own service-library should come without any hesitation whatever. This is the wish of the Fifth Law [R30].

16 Deductive Approach

The preceding sections of this chapter have made an *a priori* approach to the emergence of reference service. They have presented reference service as a necessary implication of the Five Laws of Library Science. These are the normative principles regulating every aspect of library service and forming the starting point in developing Library Science. Reference service has been deduced from these normative principles. These normative principles or fundamental laws contain, in a latent form, all the ramifications of reference service—of the past, present, as well as future. They become patent as and when the needs of the community and the consequent obligations of the library put on new forms from time to time.

17 Documentation Service

During the last two decades, population pressure has increased beyond the capacity of natural and near-natural commodities to maintain the people. Therefore, these commodities have to be supplemented by artificial commodities, made by the chemical transformation of raw materials unfit for use or consumption in their native state. This transformation to get artificial commodities for food, shelter, and clothing calls for far more research output than in the past. This, in its turn, calls for the meticulous conservation of the research-potential of humanity. This calls for the rapid ploughing back into the research team of all new micro thought created from time to time. This, again, calls for intensification of reference service. To clinch this intensification of reference service, the term 'Documentation' has been coined in recent years. We are now in the documentation age of library service. Documentation service is reference service with emphasis on specialist readers and on nascent micro thought. This is a new ramification of reference service, made dominant by the social demands of the post-war period. We should expect other new ramifications in the future too.

18 Historical Approach

Apart from the *a priori* approach of this chapter, it is also possible to make a historical approach to the emergence of reference service. This approach should begin with the history of the very concept of library. It should trace the successive changes in this concept. It should trace also the successive changes in the functions of a library, caused by the changes in the concept of the library. It should then examine the diverse library techniques evolved from time to time in order to carry out these functions. This examination will lay bare the emergence of reference service. The remaining chapters of this part will be turned on such a historical approach.

CHAPTER 2

EVOLUTION OF LIBRARY

21 Place for Writing Books

The very definition of the term "library" has undergone a great change. It has had different meanings at different times and more than one even at one time. An early meaning, now obsolete, is "a place where books are written". In this definition there is no mention of readers, explicit or implied. Hence one cannot speak of reference service in a library in this sense.

22 Place to Keep Books

Another meaning, persisting from very old times, is indicated by the following passage in Chaucer's translation of Boethius (1374):

"The walles of thy librarie aparayled and wrought with yuory and with glass . . . in whiche I putte not whylom bokes, but I putte that that maketh bokes worthy of prys". [B7].

Here the term 'library' is used to denote a place set apart to keep books—a room in a house, or a building. Evidently, the term "Keeper of Books" to denote a librarian had originated from this definition of "library". It is used in the same meaning in the succeeding centuries right up to recent times, as shown by the following illustrative passages :

"1779. Camden's *Letters*—I there saw his library ; that is a room which contained his books.
"1854. Collin's *Hide and seek*—Zack descended cautiously in the book parlour which was called a 'library'".

Even here there is no mention of readers; and so reference service could have had no place whatever in a library in this sense.

23 Collection of Books

Another sense in which the term 'library' is frequently used, is "a collection of books"—merely a collection as such. Libraries in this sense have been formed at all times by royalties, noblemen, and even commoners. But readers did not form a necessary part of a library in this sense. Hence the problem of establishing contact between reader and book would not have arisen in it.

231 EXAMPLES

King Charlemagne, for example, is said to have been persuaded by his English librarian, the Alcuin of York, to 'collect a library'. But look at his use for it. The monarch expressly directed in his will that the collection should be sold and the proceeds given to the poor. According to Al-Makkari [M4], the inhabitants of the metropolis, Gordova, were renowned in the tenth century for their passion for 'collecting libraries'.

24 A Symbol of Respectability

Any man in power holding a place under government considered himself obliged to have a library of his own. He would spare no trouble or expense in forming collections of books, merely in order that people might say "such a one has a fine library". We have similar accounts of the passion for collecting libraries among the Muhammadans in the Eastern Kingdom. We have, for example, the story of a Persian nobleman paying a fabulous price for a book, not because he was concerned with its contents but because its size and its binding would just make the book fittingly fill and fillingly fit an awkward gap in his library. Some of the valuable private collections of North India, now sadly scattered throughout the world, owed their origin to this passion for collecting libraries, prevailing in the court of the Mughul emperors.

241 PRIVATE COLLECTION

Libraries in the sense of a 'collection of books' have been all along symbols of respectability [R18]. They have been mostly private-owned. In some cases, the owner might use them himself. But there could not have been in their setting any desire to make the people at large use them. Speaking about Gosselin who presided over the Royal Library at Paris from 1560 to 1604, Scaliger writes in his epistle of 1605.

> "I knew his way forty years ago ! Too ignorant to *use* the library himself and too jealous to allow others to use it".

Such a description may well suit many a librarian of the earlier days, but not, we wish, any one today ! Surely reference service is the very opposite of the needs of such libraries.

25 Public Institution

In addition to these definitions, the *New English dictionary* gives another meaning describing the library as a public institution or establishment. Certainly, this is the definition to be pursued by one interested in reference service. For reference service is a method of dealing with persons. There will be opportunity for such a method only in human institutions with functions including that of bringing them constantly into contact with persons. Let us see, therefore, what functions are ascribed by this dictionary to the library. Let us quote in full this promising meaning.

> "A library is a public institution or establishment charged with the care of a collection of books and the duty of making them accessible to those who require use of them."

This definition ascribes two functions to the library. Let us take them successively and explore the possibilities they offer for the advent of reference service.

CHAPTER 3

FUNCTIONS OF A LIBRARY

31 Function 1
Care of Books

The first function is "the care of a collection of books". This means protecting the collection from the ravages of the four enemies of books—fire, water, vermin, and human beings. Surely this task would have nothing to do with reference service. For a long time, this task was regarded as the main, if not the sole, function of a library. Accordingly the technique necessary for the due discharge of this function has been well perfected. And librarians had developed a great zeal in carrying out this function. Naturally the spirit dominating in them was janitorship or caretakership. Certainly it was not establishing contact with readers. The zeal of caretaker-librarians worked, on the contrary, in quite the opposite direction.

32 Function 2
Making Books Accessible

The second function is "the duty of making them (the books) accessible to those who require the use of them". It gave an opportunity for looking upon human beings, at least occasionally, as different from book-thieves. The duty of making the books accessible to those requiring the use of them was not, however, taken up at first with any great avidity. On the other hand, the age-long tradition of caretaker-librarianship, coupled with the absence of the necessary technique to deal with a large volume of issue-work, was militating against the due discharge of this second function. Indeed it appeared to be working at cross purposes with the first function. It took practically the whole of the nineteenth century to reconcile these two. Many of the library anecdotes of the last century show how often the second function had to give way. To quote but one example, there was the librarian of an American University whose unusually cheerful look on one day was explained by himself to be due to all the books being in the library except two which he was going to rescue from the hands of a professor ! [K2]

321 Library Attendants !

However, as the nineteenth century advanced and acts of compulsory education equipped an increasing number of people with the power to read, the second function had to be discharged at least in a literal way. That is to say, if anybody voluntarily came to the library and asked for a book, the library staff began to feel their obligation to produce it. But this was done mostly in a very mechanical way without any sympathetic human touch between the library staff and the reader. The work of the staff was at best comparable to that of a salesboy. In fact, the survival of the designations 'library attendant' and 'book lifter' is full of meaning. The unwillingness of many of our Library Authorities even to-day to change such a designation is significant. Obviously, they are still living in the nineteenth century atmosphere.

322 Gladstonian Pronouncement

By the beginning of the twentieth century, the library profession had developed enough technique to discharge the second function in a more satisfactory and efficient way. But an examination of this function, namely to produce books on demand, will show that the advent of the spirit of reference service was not one of its necessary concomitants. The spirit of reference service was not at all visible even in the libraries discharging the second function in an exemplary way. Look at the stricture implied in the remark passed by Mr Gladstone in 1859. As Chancellor of the Exchequer he told the House of Commons :

"The duties of the assistants in the British Museum Library are so easy and agreeable that their salaries might well be proportionately light."

323 Lingering into Twentieth Century

Unfortunately, in the India of even 1961, there appears to be many a nineteenth century man in positions of power and influence paying homage to this 1859 sentiment of Gladstone. Alas ! Even some librarians out-Gladstone Gladstone in this respect. No doubt, the second function of the library brought the staff into contact with human beings. But, with such a Gladstonian estimate or interpretation of the second function, genuine reference service could not take shape. The resistance to the advent of reference service was lingering well into the present century even in the West. Indeed according to James I Wyer [W3]:

"The theory of what passed for reference work a half-century ago was : Provide the books and keep out of the way of readers as much as possible."

"Make the books easily available in reading rooms so that the time of the librarian and his assistants may be economised for other labour."

324 Indian Institute of Science Incident (*Case Study* 1)

There was an amusing incident in India in 1947. It was in a meeting of the Executive Committee of the Indian Institute of Science in Bangalore. The Committee had accepted my recommendation to create posts of reference librarians and to place them in the grade of lecturers. The librarian pleaded for one of the old attendants on his staff to be promoted to one of these places.

Chairman : Can he do reference service ?

Librarian : Yes, sir. When somebody asks, say, for *Nature*, volume 49, he can produce it immediately much better than a new graduate appointed as reference librarian.

Chairman: That is not the reference service, described all this time by our friend.

As we moved on to the lunch room, the Chairman whispered into my ears, "Do not press your scale of salary for the librarian". He added, "We shall think of it later. Let us wait for this librarian to retire !"

325 Lurid Light of World War I

But a great change came over the phrase "reference work" in the train of a similar change that came over the definition of a library since World War I. This change in definition however does not find a place in the *New English dictionary*. Accordingly the phrases "reference work" and "reference librarian" are also missing in its pages. One has to remember however that the L volume of this dictionary was published as early as 1901. Hence, its definition is only descriptive of the functions of a library as they were understood in the nineteenth century. But we have had sixty years of momentous history since that definition was recorded. Two World

Wars had come and gone in the interval. The revolutions brought about by these wars in practically every department of human activity are well-known. Among other things, they gave a rude shock to the complacent manner in which most of the governments were spending phenomenal sums on universal elementary education--that is, on purchasing literacy for their citizens—without devoting a moment's thought to the necessary means of keeping up that literacy. The pre-war educational edifice of practically every country was like a mud building without a roof. The illiteracy and incompetence of thousands of so called educated recruits of the army served to disclose the huge waste of public money involved in a compulsory educational system not backed by a compulsory library system. As a result, country after country began to put a Library Act in its statute book after the close of World War I. After World War II, the newly awakening countries too are doing so.

33 Function 3
Conversion of People into Readers

As a consequence, libraries began to multiply in great numbers in most of the countries. They were all created by the legislature and charged with the definite task of arresting the educational wastage disclosed by the war. That means, a third and a new function is being assigned to a library. This new function is that of converting every person in its neighbourhood into a habitual library-goer and reader of books.

34 Time-Lag in Dictionaries

As stated elsewhere [R55] it is a matter for regret that the 1935 *Supplement* to the *New English dictionary* does nothing to take note of this new function and amend the definition of libraries to read as follows:

"A library is a public institution or establishment charged with the
1 Care of a collection of books;
2 Duty of making them accessible to those who require use of them; and
3 Function of persuading every person within its jurisdiction to accept and continuously use its service."

This giant dictionary exercises a giant's influence on lay Library

Authorities. This serious omission therefore greatly handicaps the implementing of the new and more human function of libraries. Surely, the British Library Association should take up this matter with the editors of the *Dictionary*.

35 What is the Sanction ?

Apart from giving suggestions to the learned editors of the *Dictionary*, we have now to examine the new function from our point of view and see how far it favours the advent of reference service in libraries. After seeing that conversion of every person in the neighbourhood of the library into a habitual reader of books is recognised as a necessary duty, we have to examine what methods are available for libraries to discharge it. Can they ask their parent legislatures to arm them with the necessary magisterial powers to penalise citizens that won't use libraries ? Even if such a sanction could be got, it can be easily seen how difficult it would be to enforce it. The penal clauses in the Public Health Act are cases in point.

36 Reference Service : The Only Means

The library profession realised the futility of the method of forced conversion. It unanimously decided on the humanisation of their duties—on the establishment of contact between the right reader and the right book at the right time and in the right personal way—as the only available and effective method of discharging the new function. This it calls "reference service". The profession cannot yet be said to have completely explored the full feasibility and ramifications of reference service. The exploration is being actively pursued. Every year new attitudes are being developed under the urge of the spirit of humanisation. The present attitude is that reference service implies "the provision of human beings as canvassing agents for books. Their business should be to interpret the books to the readers" [R34]. It is further required, quite contrary to Wyer's description, that the time of the staff spent on other labour should be minimised so that the greatest number of the most well-informed and efficient among them may be spared for reference service for the longest time possible.

37 Librarianship as Salesmanship

Canvassing agents for books ! Yes. Canvassing agents. That is the spirit of this new method called reference service. Indeed to use the most general term, an answer to the what of librarianship as understood today is found in the word "salesmanship". Perhaps that term might bring to one's mind greasy hands and oily loin cloth. Certainly no librarian will allow greasy hands and oily loin cloth in his library. Or to some, this word "salesmanship" may recall the picture of an aggressive, selfish, and self-willed fellow who would force some unwanted commodity on them. That kind of "salesmanship" is bound to be short-lived. At any rate, a library is not to gain much by associating itself with "salesmanship" of that sort. It is really trickery. Then what is the definition of "salesmanship"? It is certainly different from the two already mentioned. It is a definition that is coming more and more to the front in recent years not only in the commercial world but even in the sphere of governmental administration. We may start with a definition given by a town clerk of a big city in England. According to him,

"Salesmanship is the art of so presenting the advantages of a service or of a commodity that the prospective customer appreciates its benefit to him and is willing to pay the price asked" [W2].

38 Sublimated Salesmanship

For our purpose, we shall extend this definition a little further. We have to do it because there is no question of 'paying the price asked' by the individual customers in a library. One should not forget that a public library is a free library in the sense that it is free to all. The price of its service is not paid by each customer then and there or in proportion to the service he derives. On the other hand, the price is paid by the community as a whole in the form of a tax or rate; the amount paid being proportional to the length of the purse of the person who pays the rate. That is an aside however. All that we want to say here is that the payment of price is not at all to be made visible in the library atmosphere. Hence we would fix the meaning of the term for our purpose as follows:

"Salesmanship is the art of building up appreciation of the value or the desirability of a service, idea, or ideal, so that it is accepted and satisfaction follows its acceptance" [R52].

Reference service is salesmanship in this sublimated human sense.

CHAPTER 4

NEW LIBRARY TECHNIQUES

40 Evolution

This new outlook of sublimated salesmanship has made the library profession re-think its techniques. Some old library techniques have to be given up. Some others have to be re-designed. Above all, new techniques are being evolved from time to time.

41 Technique 1
Open Access

"Open Access" was the first technique to emerge. "Let the customers handle the books. Let them be allowed to go to the shelves without let or hindrance. No doubt this may result in additional damage to books and even in the loss of a few. Let us put that down as part of unavoidable overhead charges. Without sacrifice, we cannot attain an ideal. Remember Carnot's Law of Thermodynamics. Nature demonstrates that the transformation of one form of energy into another must necessarily involve the loss of some energy. So also in transforming the potential energy stored up in mute inert books into intellectual and spiritual energy that can activate human beings, some loss and leakage are inevitable. This law of nature—Carnot's Law—is inexorable." That is the insistence of "Open Access." And so the first effect of the assumption of the new third function by the libraries has been to recognise this law of nature, to take courage, and to forge the technique of "Open Access." To what extent this new technique has transformed everything in a library has been described elsewhere [R 23].

42 Technique 2
Ticket System of Issue

To eliminate the dangers of the incidence of impatience in the customers, the technique of "Book Ticket, Reader's Ticket" charging system has been invented. This has mechanised the issue system and almost perfected it [R33]. To-day the electronic charging system is being evolved to satisfy the Fourth Law even better.

43 Technique 3
Classified Arrangement

The third technique to emerge was a result of open access. Human mind in a state of search and enquiry proceeds essentially on systematic lines. Its tempo of search will be maintained without deterioration only if the books are arranged in a classified sequence. Otherwise many a reader, coming to the shelves, may go back in disgust without getting all the books needed by him. This accounts for the introduction of the classified arrangement of books in libraries. This has involved the libraries very deeply in the science and art of classification. This subject was once the close preserve of the specialists in logic and biological sciences. It is now being cultivated and improved beyond measure by the library profession under its new urge. Its vital role in communication has been examined in my *Classification and communication* [R 4]. Many new techniques are being evolved [R6]. Postulational approach, facet analysis based on five fundamental categories, zone analysis, and efficiency table are some of these techniques. We are far from finality in this matter. There are many unsolved problems [R49].

44 Technique 4
Analytical Entries

Books are complex entities. They often cover wide, and sometimes even, incommensurable fields. Classified arrangement is not sufficient to disclose their full value to customers. For, a multifocal book can be placed by a library classification only at one of its foci. A reader interested in any of its other foci will miss it. Even open access cannot give sufficient help in such a case. Hence the technique of subject analyticals or cross reference entries has been developed and practised in the building up of the library catalogue [R13; R60]. In particular, current issues of periodicals are promptly scanned. The nascent micro thought contained in their articles is fully displayed in closely classified documentation lists both on demand and in anticipation [R20].

45 Technique 5
Publicity

To attract new readers, the library profession has whole-heartedly adopted the technique of publicity. Publicity by individual libraries and by a central organisation like a National Library Association is no longer looked upon as too vulgar for the academic purpose of libraries. It is rightly argued whether the powerful technique of advertisement should be used only to cater to the lower urge in humanity and to corrupt its taste still further. It is rightly asked what is wrong in using its power to stimulate intellectual and spiritual cravings and thereby elevate humanity [M1; P1].

46 Technique 6
Stack-Room Guides

Having got Mr Everybody inside the library by publicity work in market places, streets, and homes, the new urge in librarianship engendered by the new third function has directed attention to the technique necessary to hold his interest and work on his curiosity. Some of these are the techniques of book display, shelf-arrangement, tier-guides, gangway-guides, bay-guides, and shelf-guides [B8; R36].

47 Technique 7
Reference Service

The latest technique to be forged is Reference Service. It is new. It is still being developed. In its turn, it calls for the intensification of some of the other techniques. Documentation work is one of the results. Depth Classification is another. Machine Retrieval is still another. Translation Service and Abstracting Service are still others. Our present interest is in Reference Service.

CHAPTER 5

WHY OF REFERENCE SERVICE

51 Danger of Mechanisation

The emergence of reference service is an inevitable implication of the third function of library. The other six techniques are no doubt necessary to convert all people into patrons of library. But they are not sufficient. There is a general reason for this. Most of the other techniques amount to mechanisation. Mechanisation involves the abstraction of the known from the unknown. It also implies the use of such things as will, in large measure, "stay put" once they have been abstracted. That is, their organic properties are such as can be held in check; ideally these would be completely destroyed. And the organic property, which is disregarded if not destroyed, is of course the living property. So it is that we say that mechanised things are "dead".

52 Dowering with Life Energy

Anyhow mechanised things are dependent things. They exist for use; and they are dependent upon use for beauty. A turbine at work is a thing of wonder and of beauty; but out of use, it is deader than it was before its elements were taken from earth. Because of this need for redeeming use, the multitude of mechanisms, surrounding us, may justly be regarded as appealing objects making persistent demand upon us. Nay. Because of their inanimation they threaten us with the sense of death unless they are continuously dowered with our own life energy.

53 Experience of Living

This pressing demand made by the mechanisms and the techniques amidst which we live compels from us a question of momentous importance. How much have we the desire and the strength to animate them before they become burdensome. When the material and technical activity and, still worse, red-tape activity, of conducting a library begin to take precedence over the experience of living and serving, sooner or later we shall have to pay in ennui and decadence [P3].

54 Human Agency to Redeem

Hence the need for introducing a human agency to redeem everything else by putting them to active use. When the reader comes amidst the library, there must be someone to say [T6]

"Take my hand;
For I have passed this way,
And know the truth."

55 Artificiality of Book

In addition to this general reason there are three special reasons for providing that "someone." First, books are after all artificial entities. Appreciation of their value does not come naturally. It has to be induced deliberately. This cannot be done except by personal methods.

56 Artificiality of Catalogue

Secondly, in the catalogue listing the artificial entities called books we reach a higher order of artificiality. This we call by the dignified name "Conventions." The cataloguing conventions are on the surface quite contrary to what Mr Everybody is familiar with. Therefore he needs personal initiation.

57 Psychological Need

Thirdly, the psychological tempo of Mr Everybody is such that we cannot retain his custom unless he is given prompt and exact service in a personal way. He is human and a human personality alone can keep him in good humour and make the appreciation of the value of books blossom in him and transform him into a willing beneficiary of the library.

58 Human Converter

If such a human personality is not provided, the potentially great plenty in the holdings of the libraries of to-day will be nothing but a mockery. Indeed the problem in libraries is no longer one of scarcity in any sense, except that of scarcity in the human converters of the potential energy of books, mouldering on shelves, into the kinetic energy of use by readers. This, in its turn, is due only to scarcity of initiative in high places and of understanding generally.

59 Insistence of Democracy

So far as knowledge is intuitive or hereditary, the need for reference service will not be seen. But with our present insistence on equality of opportunity for information, knowledge, and inspiration from the sublime thoughts of men of genius, reference service becomes essential to national progress and efficiency through democratic methods. There can be no true democracy without reference service.

CHAPTER 6

CLOSER VIEW OF REFERENCE SERVICE

Having thus traced the genesis and arrived at a formal definition of reference service and its relation to library organisation in general, let us now evolve the full picture of reference service in all its details with the holistic principles at the back of our mind. The filling of details will be facilitated if we consider it aspect by aspect. Remembering that reference service is establishing contact between reader and book by personal service, we may search for the essential aspects by taking the two factors—readers and books—in succession. We may recognise four categories among readers: the freshman, the general reader, the ordinary or generalist enquirer, and the specialist reader. Accordingly we get four aspects of reference service: initiation of freshman, general help to general reader, ready reference service to the ordinary or generalist enquirer, and long range reference service to the specialist as well as generalist reader. Initiation and general help will involve a practical knowledge of the psychology of readers. Ready reference service will require a good knowledge of reference books. Reference service for serious study will require a good bibliographical mastery and familiarity with the developments in the universe of knowledge.

CHAPTER 7

MESSAGE OF HOLISM

There is need for a warning at this stage. Reference service is but one of the many techniques to fulfil the third and the new function of the library. The several techniques should not be looked upon as independent of one another. No one of these techniques should be developed without relation to the others. Their holistic setting should not be lost sight of. As expounded elsewhere [R64] there is now-a-days division of function between Classification, Catalogue, Reference Service, Stack-room Guides, Issue Methods, and Open Access. None of these need any longer delude itself that it alone is solicitous for the man in the street. Each of these must be prepared to share its solicitude with the other factors of the library. Thus its own efficiency and the very justification of its individuality depend upon flexible co-operation with the others, based on a holistic view of library organisation. This is the message of holism.

Part C

Initiation of Freshman

CHAPTER 1

WHAT OF INITIATION

11 General Arrangement

According to the last part, a library is now a social institution. It should attract to itself all the citizens in its area. All the readers are to be admitted into the stack-room. They are to be allowed to browse among the books and help themselves. Let us remember the Fifth Law: A library is a growing organism. It grows both in its readers and in its books either by addition or by replacement. The very vastness of the book collection of the library will, in spite of a most carefully worked out system of placards and guides, be bewildering to many readers. At any rate, it will be so to the comparative strangers, the freshmen. Hence one of the first things to be done by the reference librarian is to relieve the bewilderment confronting a person coming to the library for the first time. The first step in the initiation of a freshman is to take him on hand and to show him round with sympathy and enthusiasm. He should be made to feel that the library is a human institution worth coming to. In this step, he must be made to understand the general arrangement in the library.

12 Classification Scheme

Let us take a closer picture of the reference librarian and the freshman walking round the stack-room. A good deal of their conversation centres round the arrangement of the books on the shelves. The freshman cannot but be struck by the helpful sequence of the subjects. This is announced by the gangway-guides and bay-guides following one another. The reference librarian leads him further into a closer examination of the way in which the books in a particular bay stand in relation to one another, as indicated by the shelf-guides. After crossing a few bays and when the freshman shows signs of having been acclimatised to the situation, the reference librarian invites his attention to the manner in which the books on a particular shelf cohere in a helpful filiatory sequence. In this, he enters the second phase of initiation—initiation into the scheme of classification in use.

13 Variety of Collection

Thus passing on to the freshman the secrets of the classifier's art in small enjoyable doses, observing with awareness the rate at which the freshman absorbs the scheme obtaining in the library, and taking care to heighten his curiosity at every step, the reference librarian probably finds it possible to tell him the need for the library arranging the books in different collections. He explains the contents of the main collection, the secondary collection, the tertiary collection, the special collection, the undersize collection, the oversize collection, and so on. He finds opportunities to warn the freshman that he will be missing much of the help of the library, if he confines his attention to the main collection alone. Of course the extent of the emphasis upon the different collections depends upon the standing—the academic or educational standing—of the freshman. For an ordinary reader primarily seeking recreation for leisure hours, the emphasis falls on the main collection. For a reader with research interest, the emphasis naturally falls on the periodicals collection and undersize collection. For a reader with antiquarian interest, more time is naturally spent in the elucidation of the secondary and tertiary collections. This is the third phase of initiation.

14 Use of the Catalogue

Perhaps by this time the reference librarian and the freshman have become sufficiently intimate and begun to understand each other. The latter should have also caught something of the enthusiasm of the former for books. That explains the two being doubled over some tray of the catalogue cabinet. As stated in section B56, a library catalogue is an artificiality of the second order. It has bewildering conventions. The reference librarian is trying his best to break the mask of artificiality and help the freshman to probe inside the trays. He is led to discover much of the helpful information found packed in the various cards. The freshman sees the different colours of the cards—some white, some green, some pink, and so on. He learns something of their significance. He asks in wonder why in the world such detailed analysis of the books is prepared. He is told that all that is done is to save his own time, and to help him to find his books promptly and exactly. He is told how he can spot out his books from whatever side he approaches it—subjects, author, title, editor, translator, commentator, series, etc. The familiarisation of the freshman with the structure and the use of the library catalogue is the fourth phase of initiation.

15 Library Rules

The last phase consists in telling the freshman of the personal service he could get and of the way in which he should reciprocate. The reference librarian has by this time become such a friend of his that he takes liberties with him even to crack jokes. Such a lighter vein is necessary to initiate the freshman in the details of the mechanism of issue work, to read with him the rules of the library, and to bring home to his mind the full import of the restrictive and penal clauses in the rules. A negligence of this side of initiation would result in unpleasant repercussions at a later time. There are cases of readers of ten years' standing expressing surprise at the provision of monetary sanction for enforcing return of books at proper time. Ignorance of the rule about sub-lending is usually brought to light after a most embarrassing experience at the loan counter almost leading to bitterness. Occasionally, the reader's ticket is even destroyed like a bus-ticket, in spite of its stiffness. Later, the reader is denied loan of books for non-production of tickets. Then he bitterly complains that he was never told at all that the tickets were to be preserved and produced in exchange for books. Whatever legal protection the library may have by the mention of all such information in its rules and on the tickets themselves, omission of explicitly and personally telling the freshman of the use and the importance of the readers' tickets is a source of irritation. This would be avoided by an experienced reference librarian with a human outlook.

This personal explanation of the mechanism of issue work and the clear emphasis of the duties and the privileges of a user of the library form the fifth phase of initiation.

CHAPTER 2

WHY OF INITIATION

21 Size of the Library

To-day, the library is an instrument of self-education. The Fifth Law of Library Science would make it a growing organism. In particular it grows in its stock of printed resources and in the number of its readers. Even a library, found to be small to-day, will become large very soon. On account of its size, a library has to adopt many complex aids and apparatus to make itself efficient as an instrument of self-education. Many of the reasons for a special initiation of readers in the use of the library and library apparatus flow really from its magnitude. A small library of a few thousand volumes will not show up the need for any special initiation of readers. The difficulties of using a library appear only when its size exceeds a certain limit, even as the problem of erecting a hall assumes a great complexity and requires the services of a specially initiated engineer if its dimensions—its width, length, and height—exceed a certain limit. Largeness of the library is the first reason for the need for the initiation of a freshman. The reference librarian should do it.

22 Specialised Sections

A modern library of any appreciable size has to organise its staff on a functional basis. Such an organisation into several sections is necessary in order to distribute the readers comfortably and to secure for them proper attention from the staff. A freshman has to be told about this.

221 Circulation Section

The Circulation Section has to deal with hundreds and thousands of visitors and members. It has to maintain an accurate record of all the use, whether in library or outside it, of all its resources. It is situated at the point controlling the only exit and entrance of an open access library. It has to attend to the stream of visitors coming in and going out continuously throughout the day. Therefore, the Circulation Section cannot devote more than a minute's attention to any particular reader. Still the readers seldom realise that any attempt on their part to get into discussion with the circulation staff holds up traffic. The freshman has to be told about this. He should also be initiated on the correct way of presenting his books for either charging or discharging. Otherwise, he will bungle. He will thus create an annoying congestion at the entrance or exit gate, as the case may be, though unknowingly.

222 Catalogue Room

There is then the catalogue room. This room is quite on the way of the reader to the stack-room. There is a large sign-board announcing its name. It contains an impressive battery of catalogue cabinets. Tell-tale sign-boards stand perched on them. In spite of all this, many a freshman asks "Where is the catalogue?" Of course, a shy freshman may not put this question. But he will simply look scared or fidget about with hesitation and fear. In either case he needs attention. The section of the library that can give him the necessary attention is the Reference Section.

223 Information Desk

Then we have the Ready Reference Section with the information desk. Its existence, the kind of service offered by it, and the right of the readers to take service from it are peculiar to a freshman unacquainted with modern library-outlook. He seldom believes their possibility. He should be told about them. He should even be given a regular demonstration. The information service of a modern library is unique. It is intimately personal. It answers queries. It finds out facts for readers, whether needed for public or private purpose. Its service is absolutely free. Anywhere else, the freshman is accustomed only to service on payment. The effect of this experience is too deep for a freshman to believe the offer of free personal service to be a serious one. Or he deludes himself with the idea that the special attention given to him is something peculiar to him and to that particular occasion.

2231 HEAD OF DEPARTMENT INCIDENT
(*Case Study* 2)

The head of a department of government called at the library for a piece of specialised information falling within the purview of his department. A member of the reference staff attended to him throughout the half-an-hour of his stay in the library—that is, until he got his information. He felt flattered by this special attention. He thought that it was all due to his official position. He, therefore, went into the librarian's room to render his thanks for it. But the librarian said that the staff had only done their duty and that it was done to every serious seeker after knowledge or information. On hearing this, the reader was surprised. He asked "Do you really help everybody like this?"

2232 LANDHOLDERS' ASSOCIATION INCIDENT
(*Case Study* 3)

An important tenancy bill was on the legislative anvil. The landlords were in a flutter. The agent of the Landholders' Association was desperately searching for some old enactments of an earlier century to collect data for opposing the bill. An earlier set was located for him by the reference librarian. He then felt the need for several other subsidiary data such as the speeches in the then legislature, the sequence of amendments upto the latest consolidated Act, the parallel data pertaining to other countries, and some theoretical exposition about the rights and duties of landlord and tenant. He was prepared to persuade the Landholders' Association to pay some smart member of the staff for help in tracing all such information. But the Reference Section had already anticipated a run for that kind of information. It had, therefore, prepared in advance a fairly exhaustive bibliography. This bibliography was put into the hands of the agent. He was agreeably surprised. He even became cynical and apprehensive of danger to his profession. For, he remarked, "If my principals know that libraries offer free service in this manner, we shall soon be losing our jobs!"

2233 ZAMINDAR AND SLAVERY INCIDENT
(*Case Study* 4)

A much more telling experience came our way. A rich zamindar (= Holder of Real Estate) was in trouble. He was driven from pillar to post by the paramount power. He was standing at bay. In his despair, he construed that all the actions directed against him amounted to making a slave of him. A brilliant idea entered his mind at this stage. "The League of Nations—of the enlightened nations—would have certainly adopted a convention against slavery. The government of my country is a member of the League of

Nations. Hence any such convention is binding on it. If only I could get the text of that convention!" In this mood, the zamindar rushed into the library one morning along with his private secretary. The reference librarian on duty did not know either that he was a zamindar or that he was a persecuted zamindar or that he had a bee in his bonnet. He simply took up the convention against slavery as a usual reference question. After a few minutes of search, he placed before the enquirer the pertinent volumes of the *International conciliation*, with the correct pages thrown open. The service was found by the zamindar to be precise. It was also prompt. Therefore, he instantaneously tossed a hundred rupee note. The reference librarian would not accept it.

"How grateful I am! Elsewhere I have spent hours on this without success. You have helped me after all. You have taken so much trouble. I must pay for it!"

"No. I have simply done my duty. It is part of my routine; and I am already paid for it by the Library Authorities."

"What, you have already been paid for finding out for me the convention on slavery!"

224 Free Information Service

Surely, the freshman needs enlightenment on the new functions taken over by the library to-day. He has to be told in particular of its free information service, The fundamentals of the organisation of the library is the second reason for the initiation of freshman. The reference librarian is the person to initiate him.

23 Open Access

Again the freshman has to be told about open access. It has been shown elsewhere how open access emerged as a necessity under the pressure of the inexorable Fifth Law [R29]. Every other Law has begun to uphold its value—each from its own angle. This new feature—open access—has thrown open to every reader the sanctum sanctorum of the library—the stack-room—hitherto completely hidden from his view and zealously guarded against his intrusion. The freshman does not easily shed his inherited impulse to withdraw himself involuntarily from the approach to it. For, it contains the treasures of the library. Anywhere else, the treasure room is a prohibited area. Even when persuaded to step in, he regards it merely as a privilege to gaze around. He is too nervous to touch the books and much more so to pull them out from their resting place. He often stands dazed. When he is encouraged to touch and handle them, he begins to read them standing. He does not find a place in the stack-room to settle down and read. And he is too afraid to take the books away from the stack-room. He needs to be told that the books may be carried by him to the reading room for study or even to his home after being charged at the counter, after registering himself as a member. All this initiation is in the interest of the freshman. But one instruction has to be rubbed in in the interest of the library itself. He has to be told that open access gives him the privilege of taking out books, but not that of replacing them in the shelves. He must be told that the books should be left on the reading room table or at the counter—whatever be the convention of the library. If the telling of this does not form part of his initiation, he invariably tends to carry the books back to the stack-room. And we know the chaos resulting from each reader replacing his books on the shelves in a large library. Open access is then the third reason for the initiation of freshman. The reference librarian is the person to initiate him.

24 Scheme of Classification

The open access system brings to prominence the necessity for initiating the freshman in the scheme of classification in use. For, under the pressure of the Laws of Library Science, an open access library arranges its books in a classified sequence in accordance with some scheme of classification. However logical the scheme may be, it cannot escape altogether an element of forcedness and artificiality. There is no unique system of natural classification even for the universe of knowledge in the abstract. When it comes to classification of embodied knowledge or books, many complications set in. There is little chance for any freshman, however gifted, to understand any scheme of classification naturally—that is, without initiation. And most readers have another handicap. This is partly due to the dominance of alphabetical arrangment in many affairs of life—witness the alphabetical sequence in which the names of children are read out from the attendance register, day in and day out throughout their educational career. It is also due partly to the still lingering tradition passed on to them by the earlier generation. As a result, most freshmen come expecting an alphabetical arrangement of books on the shelves. Many of them would have never heard of the possibility of a classified arrangement. They simply feel puzzled at the apparently chaotic sequence of the books on any single shelf. This reaction is likely to be very pronounced if the book numbers of the books in an ultimate class are based on the year of publication rather than on the name of the author. Nothing whatever is gained by leaving the freshman to struggle over this problem unaided. It is helpful to tell him even in his first visit something of the scheme of arrangement. Yes. Initiation of freshman should shake his mind free from alphabetical fixation. No doubt some people think that the necessary illumination can be vouchsafed for him by the supply of a carefully worded guide to the library, explaining briefly, along with other matters, the scheme of classification. But however lucid the guide may be, it is doubtful if an ordinary man can help himself by simply reading through it. Our experience is that a personal initiation made in the concrete setting provided by the stack-room and carefully adjusted to the capacity and the previous knowledge of the individual freshman is far more effective and economical. The question is which is the section of the library to which this personal service to the freshman would be most appropriately entrusted. Surely it is the Reference Section; for it forms the liaison between reader and book. Classified arrangement of books is, then, the fourth reason for the initiation of freshman. The reference librarian is the person to initiate him.

25 Library Catalogue

The library catalogue presents a bundle of conventions. It is even treacherous. For, it appears to be in a familiar, natural language. But, in reality, the language of the catalogue is an artificial one. The treachery is due to its using ordinary words. Its words are not morphologically or radically artificial. But its syntax is artificial. Its semantics too is artificial. The use of punctuation marks is not all orthodox. The words in a name-of-person are inverted. All these puzzle a freshman. The significance and use of its index numbers and call numbers are not obvious. A freshman picks up the index number from a class index entry and asks for *the book* with that number. How can he know that the number represents a whole class of books and not a single book. The cross reference index entries are another puzzle to him. It is not unusual for a freshman to pull out the catalogue card from the cabinet. He wishes to carry it with him, either to show it to the librarian or to use it for locating the book. The catalogue being in cards is itself strange to the freshman. He expects the catalogue in book-form. The freshman should be helped out of all such puzzles, even in his first visit to the library. The conventions of the library catalogue form the fifth reason for the initiation of freshman. The reference librarian is the person to initiate him.

26 Rules of the Library

Again it is necessary to make the freshman read the rules of the library. He should also be helped to understand the full implications. In the majority of cases, the copy of the rules given to the freshman involuntarily slips into his packet, without waiting to be read. We do not gain much by attributing this to faulty training. The fact is there. There is need to remind the freshman that the rules are to be read and understood in the first instance. All rules are artificial. Their details cannot be sensed instinctively. The Rules of the Library form, then, the sixth reason for the initiation of freshman. The reference librarian is the person to initiate him.

27 Special Rooms

Again the freshman has to be told of the use of the other parts of the library such as the newspaper-room, the periodicals-room, and the research-room. Sign boards there may be. A plan of the building there may be. And yet in the case of a large number of freshmen, they appear to become invisible to their eyes; or they do not deliver their full message. The psychology of the freshman appears to be really abnormal psychology. His hesitancy and shyness are best dissolved by the kind words of a sympathetic reference librarian. He has to be told of his privileges and his special duties and responsibilities in using those special rooms. He is best told these things by the reference librarian. Special rooms, then, form the seventh reason for the initiation of freshman.

28 From the Angle of Readers

281 Initiation of Children

Till now we have been pursuing the why of initiation from the point of view of the complexity in the structure of the library and the library apparatus, flowing from the Laws of Library Science. Let us next examine what light is thrown upon it if we view it from the side of the reader. There can be no doubt about the need for initiating children in everything regarding the library—open access, scheme of classification, conventions of the catalogue, rules of the library, and so on. For, the children have no chance to experience them anywhere outside the library. These cannot be learnt by imitating the elders at home, even as speaking, mode of dress, table manners, sanitary habits, and social etiquette are learnt imperceptibly. Initiation of children is best done in the school libraries.

282 Initiation of Adults

The need of initiation for adult readers may be questioned. But this is not valid. For, no two libraries are alike in its lay-out, services offered, extent of open access, scheme of classification, kind of library catalogue, conventions of the catalogue, rules of the library, and issue method. Therefore, even an adult freshman should be given some initiation, even as an adult guest or relative has to be initiated into the habits, hours, and conventions of the family and the lay-out of the house—position of the dining room, toilet room, switches, etc.

283 In India To-day

The initiation of adult freshman can be slight and quick, if the education of the adult had included instruction in all these matters. But we know how notoriously educational institutions—particularly in the India of to-day—leave them untouched. Even in the United States, the land of libraries, the first systematic code for the initiation of children in the use of school libraries appeared only so late as 1927 [S1]. But surely it is impossible that the moment such a code is published the adults of the community will become so proficient in the use of library apparatus as to make initiation by the reference staff redundant. It is no exaggeration when we say that it will take at least one generation before the members of the community would have their initiation in the use of libraries completed before leaving school—this is assuming that the library would have by that time been recognised as the heart of the school. But when we contemplate the lethargy still persisting in school authorities in their relation to the school library, it looks as if it will take a century before the library becomes the heart of the school. Hence we may safely assume that the initiation of adult freshmen will continue to be a necessary part of reference service in our libraries for several decades.

CHAPTER 3

HOW OF INITIATION

31 Geniality

Geniality is the first requisite in the initiation of a freshman by the reference staff. Except for passing by the circulation staff at the moment of entering the library, the reference librarian is the first human constituent of the library coming into close contact with the freshman. Hence, the first impression formed by him about the hospitality of the library is likely to be largely conditioned by the manner of the reference librarian. Therefore, if the work of the Publicity Section of the library is to be fruitful and result in permanent additions to its customers, the genial reception of the freshman by the rerefence librarian becomes a necessity. When the reader goes home, his memory should constantly tell him, "The bewitching smile of the gentleman at the library is still before my eyes. I love to go to the library as often as possible, even if it be merely to meet him."

32 A Walk Round

The freshman should be taken round the library. The various rooms open to the public, such as the general reading room, the periodicals room, the catalogue room, the special reading rooms, the librarian's room, the stack-room, the room for drinking water, and the public convenience rooms. He should also be shown the points where reference librarians can be found. He should further be shown the entrance and the exit points, and the way they are controlled. He should also be told about the formalities of entrance and exit, including the rule of the queue.

33 Open Access

While in the stack-room, the freshman should be told about the sequence of subjects, the formation of different collections, and the function of the different guides, such as gangway guides, bay guides, and shelf guides. In an informal way, he should be told about the open access system and its implications in regard to his obligations. Probably, he will see other readers enjoying the benefit of the open access.

34 Classification

A moment's talk with the freshman is sure to disclose the main subject of his interest. After it is sensed, the freshman should be taken to the part of the stack-room housing the books in that subject. While amidst the books congenial to him, a few further questions will elicit from him the specific subject interesting him at the moment. It would be best to begin by showing him the books in that specific subject and interpreting the numbers on their backs. The common class number and the varying book numbers are sure to attract his attention. This gives the opportunity to familiarise him with the idea of "ultimate class." [R16]. With this ultimate class as centre, his attention can be invited to the preceding and the succeeding ultimate classes. In this way, he can be made to see the helpful filiatory nature of the succession of classes. Without in any way embarrassing him by the use of the classifier's jargon, it should be impressed upon freshman's mind that apart from the books, placed in the ultimate class in question, information on his specific subject could also be found in parts or chapters of books falling within classes of greater extension. He can be helped to realise that they precede his ultimate class. He should further be told that information on some particular aspects of his specific subject could also be found in the books in classes of smaller extension than in his ultimate class. He can be helped to realise that they succeed his ultimate class. Taking larger strides on either side of the specific subject, forming his centre of interest, it must be possible to demonstrate to the freshman the helpful sequence in which the main subjects themselves fall in the scheme of classification in use. Speaking in general terms, the freshman can thus be made to sense and appreciate the Apupa pattern (Alien-Penumbral-Umbral-Penumbral Alien pattern) provided by the scheme of classification. [R5].

341 Grouping of Subjects

Apart from thus initiating the freshman in the general picture of the layout and the detailed view at close range on one or two specific subjects of interest to him, there is the necessity to acquaint him with the specific nature of the grouping of subjects produced by the scheme of classification in use in the library. No two minds, still less no two schemes of classification, may agree totally in the details of the grouping of subjects. Therefore, many questions may arise in his mind.

3411 SAMPLES OF MOOT QUESTIONS

Should meteorology go with physics or with geology or with geography? Should dynamics go with mathematics or physics? Should astronomy be an independent main subject or part of mathematics? Should astrophysics be looked for in astronomy or physics? Does biochemistry belong to chemistry or biology or medicine? Is veterinary science to be found with books on medicine or zoology, or with those on useful arts? Do plant pathology and plant breeding belong to botany or agriculture? What about wave mechanics, wave geometry, and wave functions? This string of questions can be lengthened *ad infinitum.*

3412 RANGE OF REFLEX ACTION

There can be no uniqueness in the answers to these questions. Whatever be the logical or psychological foundations claimed for each scheme, there is no escaping the fact that at bottom the grouping of subjects is a matter of convention. Therefore, the freshman should be told and repeatedly reminded of its details and results in succeeding visits. He should soon be helped to become familiar with them. He should be brought to the stage of believing them to be natural. At any rate, the grouping of subjects, brought about by the scheme of classification in use, should be soon brought within the range of his reflex action.

342 TERMINOLOGY

Next comes the trouble in terminology. The names of most of the sciences and subjects are seldom static. They change from generation to generation. They sometimes change even overnight. For this there may be various causes. These may be trivial and even partly comical. But the effect of the change on the relation between the freshman and the scheme of classification may be grave. One or two examples will do.

3421 ADVENT OF 'PHYSICS'
(*Case Study* 5)

The well-known science, physics, has changed its English name in comparatively recent years. Formerly it had a name which an anecdote will disclose. A young American went to Princeton College. He hunted through the library for some time. Then he said to the librarian, "You don't seem to have any books on natural philosophy!" This gentleman replied, "Young man, come with me!" He took the boy to an alcove, pointed to a word printed in large block type on white board and said, "We call it physics!" This happened in the later seventies, when the newer name was beginning to displace the old, as the story itself implies. For more than a century before that, the old name was universal in English-speaking countries. Men occupying themselves with mechanics and sound and heat and light were known as "natural philosophers." Would that they still were! It is a long and cumbrous title but less cacophonous than our present name of "physicists," with its three or four sibilants in three successive syllables—surely one of the ugliest words in any language. The continental contemporaries have escaped such a tongue-twisting name. This seems rather unfair. For it was they—or their forefathers, rather—who sent the word "physics" across the Channel and the Atlantic and round the Cape of Good Hope to displace the old English term. They had taken it from the Greek, of course; and they had been using it in about the present sense for hundreds of years. But during those same centuries, the English had gone to the Greek for the same root word and had used it to denote the art of medicine. This usage has not been completely ousted even now. The simpler and more natural personal form "physician" has gone with this usage. So, we have it from ill-luck with hazards of the history of language. And we should have ample cause for appealing to a court for a change of name, if only there were a court with sufficient authority. And still we have not told the chief of the linguistic misfortunes of the physicists.

3422 CHILDREN OF PHYSICS
(*Case Study* 6)

Not only has their science changed its name in the last one hundred years: it has failed to pass that name—either the old one or the new—on to its children. By the children of physics, we mean the several applied arts and sciences to which it has given birth. Let us illustrate. One boy goes to college and he graduates in geology; then he starts out into the world and makes his career by looking for oil or coal or gold; but he still calls himself a geologist and so does the world at large. What he writes is labelled geology. Another is graduated in chemistry; and he spends his life thenceforward in refining oil or making sulphuric acid or perfumes or dyes or vitamins or asphyxiating gas; but to himself and to the world at large he is always a chemist; and his books are labelled chemistry. But here is another who took up physics as soon as he came to college and continued it all through his student days; and his career consists in controlling and directing physical phenomena by his knowledge of physical laws, or in designing machines on the basis of physical principles. And what does he call himself and what does the world call him? An electrical engineer or a radio engineer or a designer of lenses or maker of turbines, or a naval engineer, or an acoustical engineer, or a mechanical engineer or an aeronautical engineer; and only the census tables could say what else! He has not departed from physics; but physics has lost the credit of his achievements. The colonies of this science have renounced the name of the mother country. And the emigrant has often the notion that, in settling in the fields of engineering, he is changing his nationality; whereas, actually, he has never left the empire of physics.

343 Conventions in Classification

"The Statute of Westminster" appears to be working at different levels in different empires. A scheme of classification is applied to reduce them to uniformity by force of conventions. Corollary: the reference librarian should initiate the freshman into these conventions by slow degrees.

344 Boundary Lines

The boundary lines between the empires of the classes in the map of knowledge shift as suddenly and as frequently as those of the political divisions in Europe and of the districts and taluks in the India of to-day. The Canon of Currency [R44] plays hide and seek with their jurisdiction. In a large library with several miles of books it is not practicable to revise and repaint their nationality on the backs of books and in all the associated records as frequently as the situation requires. The finance and the man-power required to do this revision work to the satisfaction of the capricious Canon of Currency are prohibitive. Hence, the libraries do the only sensible thing possible. They endeavour to carry on the administration without changing their nationality-register, until there could be a sign of permanent settlement. The freshman must be shown in slow degrees all such make-shifts that every library is obliged to adopt.

345 Classification by Cultural Epochs

This element in initiation will become even more difficult if the novel classification principle propounded by John J Lund and Martimer Taube is adopted. They recommend *A non-expansive classification system. . . . .period classification* [L5]. Its adoption would involve the splitting of time into several periods or "spans of years within which knowledge presents a unified structure which can be expressed in a system of classes and sub-classes. When such a system of classes requires extensive structural revision, namely, when the established system is no longer adequate for the classification of knowledge in books, a new period is inaugurated and with it a new system of classes and sub-classes. The following is a tentative list of periods.

1 Early civilisation of the Near East.
2 Hellenic.
3 Hellenistic and Roman.
4 Medieval (including Arabic to the thirteenth century).
5 Age of transition, Renaissance (Fourteenth, fifteenth and sixteenth centuries).
6 The seventeenth century.
7 The age of physical science (Newton to Darwin).
8 The age of "Progress" (Darwin to the last world war).

3451 RECONDITIONING ASSOCIATIVE MEMORY

If the classification is done on this principle, the work of the initiation of the freshman should involve the difficult job of reconditioning his associative memory into chronological and cultural compartments. The violence to the Canon of Reticence [R45], which this should willy-nilly involve, will spring back on the reference librarian in the form of revolt from many a reader. Even the meekest may be provoked to turn round and swear "D—n your classification! It is really too much."

35 Cataloguing

The conventions of cataloguing are even more unnatural on the surface. They reach the high-water mark of artificiality. They are many in number. Few readers absorb them all, if they are all propounded at one time and still less in their first visit. Hence, great discretion should be exercised in fixing the dosage and the time of administration. Some readers cannot absorb the instruction until they experience the idiosyncrasies of the catalogue to their chagrin.

Prophylactic treatment is not effective in such cases. Some readers may not need certain inoculations as they may never be exposed to certain types of entries. The technique of corporate-author heading, for example, need not be told to some. The use of analytical entries may never come in the experience of others. No doubt the postponement of attention till the accident occurs may result in some readers becoming delirious. But if the reference librarian knows how to handle such patients, initiation into certain cataloguing conventions can be made to go home most effectively at that stage than in the first visit.

351 Inversion in Name-of-Person

The now commonly current cataloguing convention changes the sequence of the words constituting a name-of-person. In a modern Western name-of-person the family name (surname) is promoted from the last to the first place. The personal name (forename) is denied even a "*see* entry". This is so much at variance with the ordinary experience of the freshman with name-of-person everywhere else. Therefore, he must be instructed in this matter in successive visits. This inversion may look natural to librarians. But it is really quite unnatural. The reference librarian should remember that even for the librarian it began to put on the garb of naturalness only after the bold venture recorded in Andrew Maunsell's *Catalogue of English printed books* [B2 and M5]. "They make their alphabet by the Christian name, I by the Sir name."

3511 Bernard Shaw Incident

(*Case Study* 7)

An under-graduate studying for the honours degree in English literature came one day with a cynical contortion of face and said:

"The law 'Every Reader His or Her Book' is preached by you *ad nauseam* from platforms. But it seems to be, like all precepts, for others and not for you."

"Why do you say that?"

"You are a university library; and still you don't have a single scrap of Bernard Shaw."

"Are you sure?"

"Yes, I have scanned every one of your blessed cards."

He went to pull out a tray in anger. He pulled out the B -tray.

He was then shown a whole battery of Bernard Shaw cards in the S-tray. Then, his cynicism took a new turn:

"Then if you are true to the Second Law, you have surely thrown the First Law overboard."

"How?"

"You say 'Books Are for Use and not for Preservation'."

"Yes, I do."

"But you have virtually hidden them away by filing the cards with S and not with B. We *naturally* expect them in the B-tray."

The principle of inverting the words in the names of personal authors had to be explained to him—not merely the fact but also the why. This experience raised him to a high pitch of curiosity. Then, even the abstract Canon of Prepotence [R8], behind this apparently artificial twisting of names, could be paraded before him. He was pleased to see it paraded.

"I never thought that there would be so much philosophy behind listing books. Your illustration of the addresses on post cards was most interesting. [R57]. I am glad I missed the 'Shaw' in 'Bernard.' I have learnt a new principle and a new outlook. Many things become clear to me now in the light of your Principle of Prepotence."

Indeed, a successful initiation at the ripe moment!

352 Coined Corporate Name

Books of corporate authorship baffle the freshman even more than those of personal authorship in respect of the choice, the rendering, and the style of writing up of the headings in their entries. For a book of personal authorship the title-page gives all the words making up the heading, though in a different permutation. Hence the freshman has a chance at least to recognise in the heading the words familiarised by the title-page. He has merely to accustom himself to the inversion. In other words, artificiality arises only in rendering the name in the heading. But a corporate-author-name is an altogether improvised one. Even the library profession has not yet arrived at a unique rule for its improvisation [R61]. The German practice differs from the Anglo-Saxon one. In fact, the artificiality arises in this type of entry not so late as the rendering of an ascertained name, but even as its very choice. Personal *vs* corporate author, government *vs* institution, charters, expeditions, civil actions and criminal trials, constitutions, laws, and statutes are some of the moot points. In respect of these, not only the different cataloguing codes disagree. But even one and the same code [R31] violates the Canon of Consistence [R9]. Hence the exasperation of a freshman seeking to help himself with the catalogue. But, it is not wise to raise all at once all the cloud of corporate-author entries. Initiation in respect of them should be delayed. The experience of the freshman should become ripe and make their use a necessity. Anticipatory theoretical instruction is positively futile and wrong in such cases.

353 "See" and "See Also" Entries

The "*See* Entries" lead to pathetic and even comical situations. Here again anticipatory instruction is not always of much avail. So also with the "*See also* Entries." To the freshman, with mind obsessed with the information or the recreation being sought, the typographical variations and the alignments and even the conventional colour of the cards, used to signify such entries, convey no meaning.

3531 *See also* Entry Incident
(*Case Study* 8)

A young man with a patient at home tumbles upon the catalogue entry "Ulcers *see also* Suppuration."

"That is what I want to know about" he says to himself, copies it on a slip of paper and begins to search for it in the stack-room. He is sensible enough to go to the medicine gangway. But after wasting some time, he comes to the staff and asks to be helped to the book *Ulcers see also suppuration*. Here are other misleading entries of that nature.

Wives *see also* Domestic relations;
Thieves *see also* Embezzlement;
Manufacturers *see also* Trade-marks;
Malays *see also* Headhunters;
Cowboys *see also* Ranch life; and
Authors *see also* Scientists.

3532 *See* Entry Incident
(*Case Study* 9)

Similarly a freshman just beginning the study of political science is pleased to find the entry "Vassals *see* Feudalism." He remembers his teacher mentioning "Vassals" in the lesson on feudalism. He copies it taking it for the title of a book and goes to the shelves, only to come back with disappointment. He asks the reference staff to pick out for him the book entitled *Vassals see feudalism*. Here are other misleading entries of that nature:

Adventures *see* Imposture;
Composers *see* Musicians;
Scottish marches *see* Borders of Scotland;
Sea kings *see* Northmen;
University settlement *see* Social settlements; and
Welfare institutions *see* Industrial betterment.

354 Class Index Entry

Preferably even in the first visit, the freshman should be introduced to the structure and purpose of a Class Index Entry [R12]. Perhaps, he may be asked to mention the subject of his interest at the moment. Its class index entry may be located along with him. He may then be made to appreciate the significance of the Index Number found in it. It may be interpreted for him. Its translation into words giving the heading of the entry may be shown. Then he may be shown the corresponding region in the Classified Part of the Catalogue. He will then enjoy the succession of main cards giving the names of the books on that subject. He may also be helped to see the panorama of the succession of the guide-cards carrying the numbers and the names of the classes filiated to the class he mentioned. Here he may be told that a class index entry has for its index number, a class number only, unaccompanied by a book number.

355 Book Index Entry

At that stage, the freshman may be helped to locate in the Alphabetical Part the author entry of one of the books, chosen by him from the Classified Part. He may be told about the Alphabetical Part containing not only class index entries but also book index entries such as the author entry. The presence of a book number in the index number of a book index entry [R14] may be pointed out. In this concrete manner, the difference between call number and class number, in structure and in function, may be brought home.

356 Right Time for Telling

It is desirable to inform the freshman about the conventions regarding such entries and demonstrate their use to him even during his first visit. But in most cases the proper impression is not formed. It is only when they land themselves in difficulties that a sure opportunity offers itself to rub them in. As Townshend would put it [T5]:

The experience that an individual needs for his development proceeds from within that individual.

Only in this case we are compelled to take part to both help and hinder.

If we help too little or hinder too much, or if we help too much or hinder too little, we damage the growing individual.

If we attempt to impose an alien or untimely experience from without, we inevitably botch a man or a woman.

357 Matter for the First Visit

The freshmanness of the freshman does not get exhausted readily. It takes a long time to wither out. The reference staff should remember the psychology of deferred initiation. But it may be asked if there is nothing in the catalogue that lends itself to anticipatory instruction or instruction during the first visit. There is plenty. He may be shown in a general way the parts of the catalogue and told what kinds of question will find an answer in its entries. Cutter's lucid analysis [C2], reproduced below, suggests what can be done during the first visit:

1 To enable a person to find a book of which either
  (A) the author, or
  (B) the title, or
  (C) the subject is known;
2 to show what the library has
  (D) by a given author,
  (E) on a given subject, and
  (F) in a given kind of literature; and

Means

1 Author entry with necessary references for (A and D).
2 Title-entry, or title-reference (for B).
3 Subject entry, class entry and cross-references (for C and E).
4 Form entry and language entry (for F).

358 Questions by Freshman

The reference staff should encourage the freshman to put questions that occur to him to test the ability of the catalogue to fulfil its objects. In tracing answers to these concrete questions, the nature and the names of the entries should be demonstrated.

In this way a good deal of ground can be covered. Particularly the structure of the main entry may be explained. Most of the types of book index entries can also be shown. They are the Author Entries, and various Collaborator Entries such as Editor Entries, Translator Entries, Commentator Entries, Compiler Entries, Illustrator Entries, Introduction-writer Entries, Foreword-writer Entries, and so on. So also some Fanciful Title Entries and Series Entries may be shown. Not that all these entries should be shown at once or to all the freshmen. The extent to which the field can be covered will depend upon each concrete situation—the interest, the general capacity, and the mood of the reader.

36 Rules of the Library

While the initiation of the freshman into classification and cataloguing has to be spread over several visits, practically everything about the rules of the library and particularly the mechanics of issue work should be explained to him during the very first visit. The first step is to see to it, by direct telling or by indirect suggestion in the case of refractory persons, that the rules are carefully read through by the freshman before personal initiation begins. When he announces having finished reading them, the facts about the holidays, if any, and the working hours may be reiterated.

361 Condition of Loan

Then they may be told about loan rules and particularly about the prohibited categories such as atlases, bibliographies, encyclopaedias, yearbooks, periodicals, and rare books. Other points to be covered are:

1 Number of volumes that can be borrowed at one time;
2 Period of loan;
3 Overdue charge, including conscience box; and
4 Sublending.

The vexatious, but necessary, rule about sublending must be told even now—that is before they break it unknowingly and try to wriggle out of it with stories bordering on dishonesty. The date label and its use may then be shown. In open-access libraries the freshman should be explicitly told that he will have to help himself with the books required for study.

362 Charging and Discharging

He should be asked to present the selected books at the counter with the date label thrown open and a reader's ticket placed on the date label of each book, so that the counter assistant can apply the date stamp without the necessity of having to turn it about. He should also be told that he should cross the wicket gate before he could take charge of the books. Similarly he must be shown the right way of presenting the books brought back from home at the entrance or discharging counter, the correct mode being of course presenting all the books with the date label thrown open and turned towards the discharging assistant. He must be told to claim a ticket of his in return for each book returned and to verify if the ticket bears his name and address. It is also desirable to impress upon the readers the great advantage there will be for all concerned if the rule of the queue is observed both at the entrance and at the exit gates.

363 Care of Reader's Ticket

The freshman should be told that no book can be drawn from the library without the surrender of one of his borrower's tickets in exchange. He must be asked to preserve the tickets with greatest care. There is no harm in suggesting that they are best kept in the purse and in warning against their being sent away to the washerman along with the coat! He should be further told the obligation to surrender the tickets while terminating membership.

3631 BITING THE TICKET INCIDENT
(*Case Study* 10)

The reader's ticket was made of thick cardboard and lined with cloth. One day, I saw a member in the corridor leading to the stack-room biting it with great difficulty.

"Why are you biting the ticket?"

"Look at this line on the ticket. It says 'You are responsible for every book borrowed on this ticket'. If I leave it whole, somebody else may borrow a book on it."

"But, what will you do to borrow the next book?"

"The library will give me a new ticket. Is it not so?"

364 Library Ethics

Library ethics includes:

1 Observance of silence, including silent reading and abstaining from conversation;

2 Spirit of living and letting others to live, including the sharing of library books with others without usurping them unduly for one's own use;

3 Using the books of the library with care, including abstinence from underlining, folding the corners, and using the book as a physical material for other uses such as head-rest or protection for head from sun and rain;

4 Resistance to the temptation to abuse open access, by means such as hiding or misplacing books to prevent their being used by others; and

5 Library hygiene, including avoidance of scattering scraps of paper on the floor, of spitting through the window, and spilling ink. A freshman should be inducted into library ethics. But it cannot be done effectively through precepts alone. Silent but firm correction should be made whenever there is a deviation from the right path. The atmosphere of the library should be so built and maintained that conformity to library ethics is spontaneous. Merely painting the word "Silence" on the walls of the reading room serves no purpose. Showing the "Silence" card board to a reader who whispers serves no purpose. The Temple of Silence can be built only by good example and various ineffable ways of building a good tradition.

3641 PRINCIPAL'S PLIGHT
(*Case Study* 11)

It was an afternoon. Fyson stepped into the Library. He was the principal of a local college. He was impressed by the solemn silence and perfect orderliness in the reading room. He shouted to me, "I find many of my students here. They are so quiet. But why are they so noisy in my college library?" I moved forward to him, clasped his hand, and took him to my room without uttering a word and without giving him a chance to speak out. I need not say what I told him. He apologized for having disturbed the silence of the reading room. "Yes", he agreed, "It all depends on the tradition we build up and on the example we set up."

CHAPTER 4

INITIATION IN COLLEGE LIBRARY

41 Opportunity for Initiation

A college library is an institutional library. Its freshmen are all students in the college. Their initiation need not all be casual. It need not be contingent, as in a public library, on the voluntary coming in of a freshman. On the other hand, the initiation of college students can be a planned one. They can be brought in for initiation at stated times in groups of stated strength. Their initiation will prepare them also as eventual patrons of the public library. Moreover, their initiation can be woven integrally into the college life of the students. It can be purposively correlated to classroom work and laboratory work. Thus, the college presents a splendid opportunity for initiation of freshman. To make the potential opportunity an actual one, the cooperation of the teachers is necessary. At any rate, their cooperation will make the students enjoy the library initiation and the formal instruction in the college holistically. In particular the method of teaching itself should make the students value work in a library and seek the use of books. Then, the initiation will become purposive in their eyes.

411 Wasted Opportunity

But the potential opportunity is still being wasted. The library is not yet made an integral part of college life. Sufficient public attention is not given to the fact that the universities and colleges are turning out hundreds of graduates who have never truly realised that books can be of help in solving problems. This may seem a bold remark as applied to a class of persons all of whom are presumed to have spent three to five years in absorbing the contents of books. Nevertheless it can be asserted with confidence that many students know only that text-books are prescribed for their course. But they do not know, at any rate in the practical sense—in the sense of acting on the knowledge—that books, monographs, and periodicals exist on practically every subject and further that it is necessary and helpful to consult subject-encyclopaedias, periodicals, and other sources. This is mainly due to a complete failure to realise what 'the literature' on any subject can do. It may also be due to faulty appreciation of the fact that if one desires to obtain information on any given subject, the surest method for the average man is to use a library and not to endeavour to obtain oral information. Oral instruction is doubtless the best when it is individual and when it is given by a first-rate authority with sufficient time at his disposal. But these conditions rarely coincide in actual life. Students do not realise that an alternative is to use books. They fail to realise that this alternative exists over the whole range of human activities and natural phenomena, whether for abstract subjects such as ethics or aesthetics, industrial subjects such as chemical technology and mass production, the subjects which adorn life such as literature and the classics, or finally even the modest but agreeable subjects such as gastronomy and toilet.

42 Aetiology

In considering the reason for the ignorance of students as to the possibilities of libraries and books, we are inclined to air a heresy and to suggest that our universities have gravely over-emphasised the importance of lectures. The ordinary lecture is as much of an anachronism as the wax-tablet and stylus. Further in their excessive respect for the lecture tradition, the universities and colleges have never fully grasped the fact that this tradition should be reconsidered in the light of the invention of printing. From the moment the printed text-book became available, the universities should have revolutionised their methods of teaching. It must be admitted against this that some students are aurals who absorb instruction better through the ear than the eye and are thus unlike the visuals. But for the latter at any rate, the ordinary lecture is a serious waste of time. The superstition that a course of lectures should take the place of a text-book should now be finally exploded.

43 Lasting Remedy

It seems clear that suitable text-books should be used for the greater part of the heavy work of instruction. The function of the lecture should be first of all to stimulate the student, then to prescribe reading and send him to the literature at once, then to show him how to read, and finally to comment on what he has read. The best lecture is that in which the student feels the impact of a forceful or fascinating personality. Such lectures must be few and far between. Surely it should be obvious that the main body of information should be obtained by the student from the books. The lectures should serve as a sentiment, as a guide, as a commentary, but on no account as a mere substitute. Whether this explanation be accepted or not, a study of the university system, coupled with some practical experience as student, as teacher, and as administrator, has satisfied me that the difficulty in using the opportunity, inherent in college life really exists and that the lasting remedy is as outlined above.

44 Experience as a Teacher

The formulation of this remedy was made out of the sheer necessity inherent in the teacher-student context. It was made long before I became a librarian or I ever dreamt of becoming one. It was based on experience as a teacher in the period 1917 to 1923. It was actually lived in those years. Little did I then dream that I would become a librarian. Indeed, I did not even know of the existence of the library profession. Purely as a teacher, I was led to realise the potency of a good library in stimulating the self-educability of the students and in helping each to develop along his own lines, at his own rate, and to his own fullness (see Chapter A2).

441 Coimbatore College Incident
(*Case Study* 12)

I was transferred to the Coimbatore College in 1920. I did not find the library of the college adequate. Therefore, I gave the Principal a list of the essential books to be bought. The list came back to me with the laconic remark "Extravagant". I then had the certitude and the fearlessness of youth; and so I wrote back that I should not be held responsible for the results, unless the books were provided. No doubt, I now realise what a rash act this should have been in a Government College. Through God's grace, the worst did not happen. The Principal sent for me. My trial began.

"Why do you want so many books?"

"For the use of the students."

"Do you really believe that your students are going to use them?"

"Yes, certainly."

"If they really read all these books, each of your students will become a Hanumantha Rao or a Ramanujam."

"Why not?"

"You are thinking of the students you first met in Mangalore. The students of this place are a poor lot. You can't make much of them."

"Give me a chance, Sir. I do believe that even the boys of this place will shoot up if only we give them their books."

"You are too optimistic. Anyhow I shall sanction your wish this year as a special case."

The year came to an end. I was transferred from that college. I went to the Principal to say "Good bye".

"When the Director was here a few days ago, he congratulated the college on the excellent results in your group—with the first in the presidency and 17 out of 19 passed! I told the Director that I should not be held responsible for the standard going down again in future years, as you would be no longer with us."

"But the library will still be with you and for the use of the boys. This phenomenal result is traceable largely to the books you were good enough to sanction."

K S Vaidyanathan, the Principal, and myself had a hearty laughter. He stood converted.

45 First Aid

However, a sudden revolution in the method of teaching in our universities and colleges is very difficult. For, the top management are inclined to be conservative. Much time and effort would be required before any far reaching change could be effected—before the library is made the heart of the college from which everything in the college radiates and by which everything gets irradiated. As a result, the initiation will have to be done solely by the librarian himself for some years. In spite of the absence of help from the method of teaching followed in the class-room and in spite of the work in the class-room rousing no curiosity whatever in students to go to the library and find out for themselves, the library should voluntarily attract the students. Each year it should give them practical instruction in the exploitation of the printed materials in the library. This first aid is a fundamental right of the students. The university and college libraries should give it to them.

46 Philosophy of the First Aid

The main body of university and college training is either cultural or vocational or both. For cultural training, it is immediately apparent that the student must learn how to learn in the future rather than aim at acquiring a body of fact-information. It is not so generally realised that this statement is also true for vocational training. If we are training a chemist or an engineer, our object should not be to teach a repertoire of professional tricks, but to teach the student how to learn in after-life, i e, during his professional career. It is impossible to turn out a chemist or an engineer with all the fact-information he will ultimately need. The 'camel theory' of education stands exploded. Hence the aim of the instruction should be to enable the student to learn for himself in after-life. In many cases this learning will be from books rather than from persons. College training should therefore include:

1 The obvious substratum of fact-knowledge and professional information;

2 A training in scientific method; and

3 Some explicit training in the use of books.

Further self-instruction must be largely derived from books. Therefore, the initiation phase of reference service should be an integral part of university teaching *for all students* and not merely for research and honours students. Although some teachers are inclined to think that the art of consulting books is innate, there does exist a real technique of which even an elementary knowledge is useful, and therefore such technique should be taught. This is the philosophy of the first aid proposed in section 45.

47 Scheme of Initiation

471 The Library

Function and use of library; facilities for general reading and special study. How to read; rapid reading; thorough reading; participative reading; thinking and contributing our own thought to the ideas of the author. Conducted tour of the college library in small groups. Library rules; routine in using books; the purpose of restrictive rules.

472 The Book

Make-up of the book; binder's title; half-title; title-page; varieties of the table of contents; varieties of index. Books in sets; generic and individual title-pages; distribution of index either in each volume or in several volumes or in a separate volume. Periodicals; index in each volume; cumulative index. The author; status; other works.

473 Classification

Why classification? Class number; a system of artifiicial language; translation of the name of the subject of a book into an ordinal number. Mechanisation of arrangement. Filiatory arrangement. Scheme of classification in use. Book number; its purpose. Call number; the various places where it is written; accuracy. Shelf-arrangement; different collections.

474 Catalogue

Questions answered by catalogue. Kinds of catalogue. Parts of classified catalogue. Kinds of entries; main or subject or call number entry; added entry; general entry; class index entry; cross reference index entry. Book index entry; author entry; collaborator entry; title entry; series entry. Nature of heading; personal author; corporate author; pseudonym. Arrangement in the classified part and in the alphabetical part; pitfalls in arrangement. Multiple heading. Consolidated entry.

475 Reference Book

Meaning of the term 'reference book'. Varieties as set forth in Part H of this book.

476 Bibliography

Classes of bibliographies; means of up-to-dateness; annual edition; periodical cumulation. Familiarity with the published bibliographies in the special subject of the student.

477 Notes-Taking

Bibliographical notes, Notes of subject matter. Stages of notes-taking. Mechanics of notes-taking. Equipment for notes-taking.

478 Number of Meetings

The initiation will have to be done in several meetings. The library catalogue and the reference books may each require three meetings. The others may each take one meeting.

48 Louisiana State University Library

(*Case Study* 13)

Two thousand freshmen and the library is the title of a stimulating description of library instruction in a western university which is worth perusal [A2]. Here is a summary:

481 Who Should Bell the Cat

Such a title sounds rather like 100,000,000 Guinea Pigs and at times the freshmen probably feel like guinea pigs. But in return the instructors have moments of wishing that people would stop having so many children! At Loiusiana State University, library instruction is presented in a one-semester-hour course required of freshmen. It did not begin as such, however. For four years a member of the library staff gave three or four lectures to all freshmen through the English department. The department was annoyed at having to give the time to library instruction; and the University was convinced of the value of it; so in 1936 an independent course was introduced. Three trained librarians are now employed to do reference service and to give the freshmen library instruction. From the academic view they have teaching and library experience. The course gives one-semester-hour credit and is on the same credit basis as any other course in the university.

482 Distribution of Pupil Load

With approximately two thousand students and only three instructors who have other duties, the problem of distribution of pupil load is solved by an equal division of the freshmen into fifteen sections each semester. This is not advocated where it is possible to give instruction to all students during the first semester, because at Louisiana State University they have observed the more immediate adjustment of those who have it first and they have a definite advantage over those who must wait until the second semester.

483 How It Works

The classes meet weekly with about fourteen lectures during a semester. The content of the course includes library regulations, the parts of a book, bibliography making, the card catalogue, indexes, encyclopaedias, and yearbooks. Three lectures are devoted to the catalogue, two to indexes, and one each to the other groups of reference books.

484 Student Chooses Subject

At the beginning, each student selects a subject in which he is genuinely interested, the only requirement being its representation in enough of the books to make it worthwhile for a bibliography. It may be the same one he uses for a term theme in English or for a paper in any other course. Throughout the semester he examines the card catalogue, the indexes, and groups of reference books for this subject. At the end of the semester he compiles a term bibliography from his notes which have been revised and returned to him by the tutor. This kind of practical experience in the library is similar to any other practical course.

In addition, during the study of the card catalogue, two problems are given to remedy natural mental confusion and to overcome handicaps presented by any card catalogue. They are prepared by the co-operative effort of the instructors and the catalogue department.

485 Topics for Examinations

As to test and examinations, a pre-test at the first meeting of the class usually shows them what they do not know. Each week a simple test at the close of the lecture covers the chief characteristics of the books discussed and previously examined, bringing out points usually brought out by the well-known 'problem' but not likely to be evident in every group of books for every subject chosen by the students. The final examination is built around a central topic (a tie-up with the bibliography subject idea) with a sequence among the questions as nearly as possible like the logical steps involved in locating material for term papers. For the examination last January the timely subjects of the Pan-American Conference and the new map of Europe were used. In May the subjects were San Francisco, New York, and the national parks, with summer vacations in mind. This type of examination is interesting to prepare and apparently fun to take.

486 Assignments

In making assignments, experimentation has shown that better results and deeper interest are gained by having the students examine reference books before the lecture relative to them; but the reverse method is more successful for the card catalogue and periodical indexes. Full explanation and discussion before an assignment are important. Putting library instruction across to freshmen requires every bit of showmanship and motivation through catching their interest and appealing to their intelligence that is possible. One highly successful trick is to have them bring to class from any two books in the assignment, two questions that might be used for the radio programme 'Information, Please.' Being allowed to read them in class, with the instructor selecting the person to answer, is a powerful stimulus, as is the popularity of the radio programme.

487 Complete Follow Through

Much of the value of instruction is lost without some one at hand to give assistance when difficulties arise in using tools studied. Since the freshman instructors are readers' advisers with desks in the lobby of the library there is a complete follow through. Someone is always present to meet these needs.

488 The Moral

A programme of library instruction for graduate students is being developed slowly at Louisiana State University. They have had enough real evidence of the value of the freshmen course to feel that it could be useful in other institutions. If it did no more than give the freshmen a feeling of ease in the library instead of one of incompetence, the effort would be worthwhile. But it does more. Each department of the library testifies to a greater and a more intelligent use.

CHAPTER 5

INITIATION IN SCHOOL LIBRARY

51 Right Stage for Initiation

Time and labour spent on initiation bring the best dividend if they are spent on children. Habits are best formed during childhood. This is a truism. And use of books is a habit. Even at the age of two, a child imitates its elders in picking up a book and 'reading' though still without the slightest notion of even a single letter of the alphabet. I myself remember a habit of mine at the age of three. My father used to read the *Ramayana* every day. It was a delicate fragile manuscript in palmyra leaves. When my father had gone out, I used to pick it up and 'read' it. This was reported to my father. He felt concerned about the safety of his fragile book. He, therefore, made for me a dummy sheaf of palmyra leaves. I was not satisfied as there were no scribbles in it. He then scribbled something on each leaf with his stylus. Then it became a book for me! I used to 'read' aloud from it every day. Similarly, use of library also is a habit. In Canada, Germany, Great Britain, Japan, Scandinavian countries, U S A, and U S S R, it was a joy for me to see infants below the age of five moving about in the libraries along with their elders and often quietly losing themselves over picture books. The result of this early library habit was visible in the children of the higher age-group. They could help themselves in the library. They could follow the classified arrangement of books on the shelves. They knew their pet regions on the shelves. They knew the use of book-tickets and reader's tickets. I had heard them discuss books among themselves. I had also seen them read out books to their infant brothers and sisters.

52 Right Place for Initiation

In reality, the right place for initiation in the use of library should normally be the school library. At the present stage in our country, our adults have had no school libraries in their childhood. The older adults have not had a library even at college. Public libraries are being established for their use just during the last few years. Therefore, three chapters of this book had to be devoted to the initiation of adults. I wish that the picture given in my *School and college libraries* [R53] and in my *Organisation of libraries* [R41] become a reality. About a generation or two thereafter, initiation in the ordinary use of library can be completed in the school library. A further course of initiation in the deeper and more involved use of documents of various kinds can be completed in the college and university libraries. There may not then be need for initiation in the public library.

53 Mode and Speed of Initiation

The first requisite to initiate pupils is geniality. Next it goes without saying that the librarian should have a clear grasp of all into which he should initiate them. He should be an adept in practical child psychology and in the methods of teaching children. He must know to make initiation absolutely free from boredom; nay, he must make it pleasurable. He should know to charge it with mirth and humour. He should be able to provoke laughter at intervals by narration of telling anecdotes. Indeed, the anecdotal aroma of the initiation should make them recall it even at the feeblest association. For, children learn anything far more effectively in a concrete setting than in an abstract one. Often, initiation has the best educational effect only if it comes after the pupils have come to the end of their own initiative and resources and are at the brink of giving up the pursuit in despair. There is need to emphasise that the psychological moment is always late in coming. Children normally wish to fight their battles all by themselves. Further, time does not count with them. Thank God, there are no hustlers among children at least! They go about their business in perfect ease, leisure, and geniality. They are not oppressed by the sense of the fleeting of time. They go about their work as if calmed and composed by the sense of the eternity of time. In this, they resemble realised souls and seers. But adults invariably become hustlers sooner or later. The school librarian should, therefore, control himself and abstain from offering help prematurely and hustling through initiation.

54 Formal Lesson

What is informally learnt by experience with or without guidance must be periodically clinched by spirited formal lessons. Sometimes such a formal lesson may even initiate experience. Formal lessons should be carefully distributed throughout the school course.

They are best organised in a concentric system. That is, the same problems should be repeatedly tackled in more and more intimate and complex ways as the experience of the pupils becomes progressively richer. Formal lessons do not mean lectures. The conduct of each lesson should be a participative one, rich in questions and answers. The pupils should thereby be ever kept in a state of alertness and awareness and not that of passive listening or of staring at the teacher with the mind vacant or switched off to something else as it often happens in lectures. The lessons of the first cycle will naturally be turned on very young children. It is good to intersperse them with appropriate stories and songs. There should also be plenty of demonstrations and opportunity for the pupils to verify and experience what they are told. The topics for formal lessons may be taken to fall into the three groups:

1 Library civics and hygiene;
2 Library technique; and
3 Reference book.

A syllabus is indicated for each group. The contents of each group may be covered in courses of three or four cycles.

55 Syllabus for Library Civics and Hygiene

551 Care of Book

Clean hand. Opening of a new book. Turning pages carefully. Use of book-marks. Taking out books from the shelf without injuring them. Putting books back on the shelf right edge up and back out. Putting books in a safe place at home. Avoidance of exposure of books to rain and sun.

552 Physique of Book

Paper used. Its varieties. Their wearing qualities. Binding. Spine. Sides. Corners. Hinge-portion. Sections in the body. End paper. Board. Covering material. Its varieties. Their relative strength. Demonstration with a partially bound book.

553 Library Behaviour

Queue system. Soft steps. Silence. Library as common property of the community. Live and let live. Preservation of books for succeeding generations. Respect for library rules. Restriction on period of loan. Restriction on number of volumes for loan at one time. Non-loanable books.

56 Techniques of the Library

561 Lay-out of the Book

Title-page and its contents. Distinguishing the name of author from those of collaborator and publisher. Imprint. Table of contents. Preface and conspectus. Chapter formation. Section formation. Maps and illustrations. Notes. Glossary. Index. Bibliography. Pagination. Page heading.

562 Stack-Room

Plan of the stack-room. Gangway guides. Bay guides. Shelf guides. Tags on backs of books. Browsing. Taking help from librarian. Recent additions shelf. Replacement of books not allowed.

563 Classification

Call number. Class number. Book number. Need for classification Main classes. Their filiatory sequence. Subdivisions of main class. Appreciation of the general effect of classified arrangement. Practice in arrangement.

564 Catalogue

Catalogue cabinet. Safety of the trays. Cleanliness of cards. Mode of turning the cards. Guide cards. Main entry. Added entries. Arrangement of entries in the classified part and the index part. Sections in each kind of entry. Questions answered by different kinds of entries.

565 Issue Method

Reader's ticket and its use. Book ticket and its use. Responsibility of the reader in each case. Date label. Significance of the date last stamped on it. Method of presenting a book at the charging counter and the discharging counter. Overdue charge. Conscience box.

57 Reference Book

571 Linguistic Dictionary

Lay-out of the dictionary. Guide words at the top. Key to pronunciation. Arrangement. Spelling. Syllabification. Pronunciation. Accent. Morphological forms. Part of speech. Diverse meanings. Phrases. Foreign words and phrases. Names of places and persons. Abbreviations. Signs for proof reading. Flags of nations. Other extraneous information. Comparison of different dictionaries.

572 Encyclopaedia

Encyclopaedia. Inclusive letters on the spine and the title-page of each volume. Arrangement of entries. Index. Year of publication. Illustrations. Maps. Bibliographies. Subject covered. Up-to-dateness. Comparison of different encyclopaedias.

573 Biography

Who's who. Only living people. Periodicity. Arrangement. Extraneous information. Who was who. Only people who died in the period shown on the title-page. Biographical dictionary. Only dead people. Supplements.

575 Year-book and Directory

Year-book. Current information. Recent statistics. World events. Sports information. Arrangement. Index. Subject covered. Area covered. Periodicity. Comparison of different year-books and directories.

576 Atlas

Atlas. Area covered. Area of bias. Location of places with the aid of the index. Recognition of physical features. Understanding the colour scheme. Material in addition to maps. Population. Gazetteer. Specialised atlas. Scope.

Part D

General Help to General Reader

CHAPTER 1

INTRODUCTION

11 Specificity of Reference Service

The title of this part is difficult to justify. In the first place, there is no general reader. Every reader is a particular reader. Similarly, there can be no general help. Any help can only be specific. In the last part, we examined the specific help to be given to any particular reader coming to the library for the first time. In parts F and J, we shall discuss how a specific enquiry or a specific problem brought up by a particular reader should be pursued.

12 Residual Matter

This part should, therefore, deal only with the residual principles and generalities, not readily falling within those parts. The residual matter will really be made up of odds and ends—non-descript types of problems, bound to arise in the day-to-day life of the reference librarian. But, even then, they will be concrete problems.

13 Case Study Method

Hence, the best and the most lively method of discussing them will be to open our note-book of case studies, containing the notes jotted down of all unusual varieties of situations, events, and readers. But we dare not cite all the cases recorded in it. That will draw out this chapter to a wearisome length; because all the cases taken together will require a good deal of explanation to give a proper setting.

14 Blakean Ratio

Therefore, as an alternative, we are obliged to work out the Blakean "Ratio" (=mental abstraction) of the actual readers as well as the concrete situations by rounding off most of the "individuating minute particularities." No doubt, such abstraction and generalisation will lead on to the "abomination of desolation." Blake has given this warning. In spite of his warning, we indulge in it and set aside most of the concrete case studies. And

From them make an Abstract, which is a Negation
Not only of the Substance from which it is derived,
A murderer of its own Body, but also a murderer
Of every Divine Member: . . . . [B5].

To escape from the curse of Blake to some degree at least, we have introduced pictures of actual situations here and there.

15 Way of Experience

Every reference librarian knows the joy flowing from contact with readers. He knows too the troubles besetting the daily task. He knows also, and knows it too well, the magnitude and variety of his task. They make it almost impossible to cope with every situation to his full satisfaction. The beginner in reference service is sure to have his store of experience built up in due course. The only sure way is to build up experience laboriously. It is no doubt a hard way. Our attempt in this part is merely to whet his desire for such experiences.

CHAPTER 2

DIFFICULT READER

20 Introduction

Perhaps we may first discuss the difficult reader. That is the person for whom all our routine is built up; he is the chap that keeps us up to scratch. We may first think particularly about him, get at the back of his mind, and in a personal way take a look at this business of reference service from his point of view. Is he a real person or is he a bogey of our creation? Can it be possible that those horrid irritable people from whose approach the staff flees as from plague are really decent folk at heart if dealt with in the right way whatever the right way may be? As a first step in finding an answer to such questions, we shall analyse the elements likely to make a reader a difficult reader.

21 Obsession

The misery of many is caused by obsession. It is a common mental ailment. A person has a pre-conceived notion. It is firmly fixed in his mind. It needs patience and tact to pierce through the obsession of a reader. The reference librarian should learn not to laugh at the odd behaviour of such a reader. He should offer him help in all coolness many a time. He should succeed in establishing communication with him.

211 Insurance Agent Incident
(*Case Study* 14)

It was quarter past seven in the morning. Only one reader had called. He was fidgetting with the trays of the catalogue cabinet. The reference librarian had just finished his morning routine of going round the stack-room. He saw him still struggling.

"Can I help you?"

"No. Thank you."

By that time another reader went into the stack-room. And the reference librarian went with him. He came back ten minutes later to find the same old man fidgetting in the same old way.

"Surely, I can help you. What can I do for you?"

"Get away. I know your class too well."

Another reader went into the periodicals room. And the reference librarian went with him. Again he came back to the catalogue room to find the same old man fidgetting in the same old way.

"You have wasted much of your valuable time. I am sure I can find out for you what you want."

"Out with you, eternal pest!"

"It is nearing eight. After eight, students will come in large numbers. I may not be able to give you as much attention as I can now. Please tell me what you are looking for."

And then the blow fell; he glowered and bowled clean, "Don't be a d — n fool. Who allowed you here?"

"What are you talking! I am the reference librarian in charge."

"Get away, you liar. Reference librarian! What a word! ! That is the way of your class. Do I not know you?"

A few minutes passed. A stream of freshmen came. They were hovering round the reference librarian. He took them to the stack-room; he brought them back to the catalogue and began to initiate them in its use. But the same old man was still fidgetting in the same old way. But this time he looked foolish. A new light was just dawning upon him. He waited till the students settled down in the reading room. He waited for an opportunity to find his old "pest" alone.

"I am really sorry. I took you for an insurance agent, pestering people everywhere—in the booking office, in the bank, and in the temple—offering all kinds of little services just to worm into us."

"Never mind. Tell me now what you want."

Presently they disappeared into the stack-room. After a while, the same old man came with half a dozen volumes in his hands and a profuse smile on his face.

"I never knew that an officer is spared full time to help us in this way—an officer who comes in so early as 7 A M, an officer who puts up with all such incivility from fools, an officer who moves on equal terms with these young urchins, such a learned officer. . . ."

22 Superiority Complex

The floor of a library is always believed to be a place of great equality. For, there we all meet at the same level in a world of thought and its records. But there may be readers who set this at naught. Such a reader has his mind fattened with superiority complex. He is a greater trial to the reference librarian than the man with obsession. The reference librarian should develop greater patience. Reticence, firmness, and ignoring the ugly complex will make him win ultimately.

221 ICS Officer Incident
(*Case Study* 15)

Occasionally a bumptious fellow, perhaps somewhere near the top of the ladder of bureaucracy, gaily glides along in company with his wife with all the consciousness of the power and pomp that attends him in office and out of office. Perhaps he is too fat and settles down under the fan. The lady is escorted by the reference librarian to the fiction shelf.

"That is too trivial. Take this—*Good earth*. It is so realistic and so human."

"I have not heard of this author. Oh, it is Chinese!"

"Yes. It is a lovely depiction of Chinese life. And its English is transparent. I have never seen anything like that. This is one of the best sellers of the year. They say that the Nobel Prize is assured for the author. Hav'nt you heard about her?"

The fat official under the fan clears his throat. He has evidently overheard this conversation. He booms out:

"Will you please not lecture my wife?"

Our courage in such situations should be drawn from the words of our national poet:

"Come friend, come my hero, give us courage to serve man even while bearing the brand of infamy from him." [D2]. The moral is, "No pestering." Some one has said you must beware of bludgeoning the mind into sensibility. That is advice worth remembering.

23 Inferiority Complex

At the other extreme comes the reader with an inferiority complex. He is afraid of being misunderstood, of being treated in an off-hand manner, and of being ridiculed obliquely. His fear has a general cause. Only in recent years, the general public have begun to get rid of the fear of the printed word and of the place housing it. Many do not yet know to look upon libraries as places that they have a right to explore. His fear is due also to a cause of his own making. He believes himself to be ignorant; and he is afraid of being made to show his ignorance. That is the mentality constantly met with. And that is the stuff of which many a difficult reader is made. Obviously the attitude, if not indeed the duty, of the reference librarian is to inspire confidence and to give satisfaction to such people.

231 "Ibid" Incident
(*Case Study* 16)

A shy research student meekly moves towards the reference librarian. He speaks in a low tone.

"The book *ibid* is often referred to in my book. Can you help me to find it?"

"Let me see your book. Kindly show me that reference."

"Here it is in this page. It occurs in many lines in this list."

"*Ibid* is not the name of a book. It means merely, 'in the same book, as the preceding one'. It is a contraction of the Latin word Ibidem."

The reference librarian should not betray any sign of ridicule, surprise, or superiority. Do that and even the slight disappointment in the reader's mind will be erased and he will respect you because he realises you are doing your best. Several such incidents will occur to all. Here is a more involved one.

232 Ouspensky Incident
(*Case Study* 17)

A hesitant reader waits for the reference librarian to be found alone. He expects his request to bring rebuff. He does not like to have it meted out to him in the hearing of other readers.

A book is wanted—no author, no title, no physical attribute by which it can be identified; but it has a religious, almost mystical, tendency and may be associated with Russia. May it be some work referred to in a modern Russian writer, something between Ouspensky and Dostoevsky? It might be; and there in the index to Ouspensky is found the clue that tracks down the book.

All very intricate and chancy, one may say. But that is the sort of detective work in all politeness, that makes for the permanent regard and respect for a library. We constantly come across such shy creatures, too afraid to betray their ignorance. But one day, by a fluke perhaps, we clear up some tangle or dispel a mist in a person's mind and we have made a friendly patron for life. And it is the peculiar character of reference service that this winning of readers has to go on every day. Then only, the Laws of Library Science will bless the reference librarian with supreme satisfaction.

24 Traumatic Complex

The floor of the library presents opportunities to come across all kinds of complexes. The reference librarian should meet them with an attitude appropriate to each—sympathy, non-interference, firmness, callous indifference, and so on. Otherwise he will mar the chance for satisfaction following the use of the library. For example, sincere and unostentatious sympathy gives a chance to serve the person with an inferiority complex. But one with traumatic complex may be irritated and almost scared away even by any manifestation of attention or officiousness. For the trauma is concerned with a complex of ideas and emotions. It can be described as a psychic wound. Everything touching this complex, however slightly, excites a violent reaction. It leads to an actual emotional explosion.

241 Freedom Movement Incident

(*Case Study* 18)

An excited reader walks into the librarian's room.

"Kindly sit down."

"Dogs like me do not deserve a seat."

"Don't speak like that. Please do sit down. Can I help you?"

"I have been wanting to speak to you about your men."

"Please sit down, what is the matter?"

"Why do your men shadow me like this whenever I go into the stack-room?"

"Surely, there is no question of shadowing in the library. The reference staff will no doubt be found moving about at all times."

"No, I do not refer to that. They always dog me and watch what books I browse, ostensibly offering their officious help. I am not able to stand it. I don't want any help. I can help myself."

This sensitive reader had been in the freedom movement for a good part of his life. This had brought on him a good deal of attention from the detective. Poor man. He cannot believe any personal attention to be possible without some ulterior incriminating motive.

Once bitten, twice shy. For one not capable of understanding traumatic complex, he may appear to be a difficult reader. The best treatment is to leave him alone. Let him see every other reader being "shadowed"—attended to personally. Let him see their getting satisfaction in that way. Let him see that so far from objecting, they welcome, nay, they seek such personal attention. His trauma will be healed in due course; and a time will come when he too will voluntarily ask for personal attention. Perhaps that time can be hastened by the librarian himself walking into the stack-room and helping him with kindness, whenever he is sighted in the library.

25 Mere Ignorance

"Surely this library isn't run as well as it used to be."

"What, you haven't got it in the library? Why, I thought you get every book."

The lawyer complains that law is neglected. The doctor complains that medicine is neglected. The engineer has a similar complaint. The idle rich complain that there is not enough detective fiction. The economist grumbles that mathematics is favoured too much. The philosopher makes a similar grumble against education. These attitudes can be met only by tact and good humour with, if necessary, an effort to explain the difficulties of funds, the standard of the library, the increase in readers, and so on. Sometimes we are able to convince; at other times, the confused mentality is made more antagonistic. The best we can do with this kind of difficult reader is to convey a feeling of sincere desire to help and to find out acceptable substitutes. With the person asking for the book, not published at all, we can do next to nothing. But here again, an effort to understand the enquiry may go far to soften the shock when he realises he was stupidly asking for the impossible.

26 Thief

At the other end of the scale, there is the doubtful reader. He shows great familiarity with the library; and he sends you away. At the proper moment, he peels off the stiff covers of the book to facilitate smuggling. He steals! The vigilance required to watch in open access stack-room is most trying. This type of difficult reader, the reference librarian hates. He is most unscrupulous. Any precautionary action taken makes him simulate righteous indignation; and he makes a scene to the chagrin of the library staff. He is dangerous.

27 Fraud

Perhaps a more numerous species is the fraud. He would abuse the freedom given to him by hiding away books. Whenever the reference librarian comes to him, he pretends intense seriousness which seems to say "Don't disturb me!" He skulks and loiters in the stack-room with all cunningness. The book in great demand has just chanced to come back. But he has not brought his ticket. Therefore, he waits for his opportunity for fraud. At the proper time he picks up the book and hides it a few thousands of feet away in some other region of the stack-room.

271 "Asia" Incident

(*Case Study* 19)

Lyde's *Asia* was in great demand. For, it was the eve of a competitive examination conducted by the Public Service Commission. The registrations went beyond the allotted limit. The library accordingly decided to declare it temporarily a reference book so that everybody might have a chance. But the book could not be found. The charging tray did not have its book card. Nor was it in the binding tray. A vigorous search was made. Half a dozen hands were put on it. Much staff time was wasted. Many readers had to be denied the reference aid, as *Asia* had to be discovered immediately—before the season would be out. But no success. All the members of the staff were looking at one another with a sense of defeat, shame, and helplessness, as we do after a clever theft in our home.

* * * *

Next evening at the rush hour, a nice looking young man presented Lyde's *Asia* at the charging counter. He was caught in a trap without his knowing it. Little did he imagine that all eyes were on the look out for *Asia*.

"From where did you get this?"

"Why, from the stack-room, of course."

"Did you pick it out yourself, or did somebody else help you?"

"Very queer questions! I had never been asked such questions till now. Why all this insult? Why these prying questions?"

"I am sorry. No insult was meant. I simply asked."

"*Simply* asked! I too *simply* say I took it out myself. I shall also *simply* tell the librarian about this insolence in the presence of so many readers."

"Yes, sir, do please go to the librarian."

"I have no time now. I know when to go to the librarian. Don't think that your coolness will make up for your insult."

But the wicket gate won't open.

* * * *

"Come and sit down. Will you? What's the matter?"

"The attenders at the counter are very rude."

"Really! I am so sorry. What's that book in your hand?"

"Lyde."

"I am sorry, young man, you have been caught red-handed. I don't propose to make any fuss about it. I shall forgive you. Tell me the truth. Where did you take the book from."

"I am sincerely sorry, sir. I had it hidden behind the row of *ZDMG*—those black German volumes in the second floor."

"Do you realise how detestable your action is?"

"I do, sir. I am very sorry. I promise I shall never hereafter be so selfish."

* * * *

"Well, there are a dozen registrations for it. If we lend it, everybody will not have a chance. So you must read it here alone along with others."

"Can you not allow me loan this time only, sir?"

"Be more reasonable. For your crime, I can withdraw all the privileges from you. I can cancel your membership. I may refuse to admit you into the library. But you are a young man. I want to help you. I don't propose to take such a drastic action. Behave better. Remember what a precipice you had been walking on. Live and let live. That should be your principle in life."

"I thank you, sir, for all your kindness. Please don't tell my father or my professor. I shall starve the whole of to-day to purify myself. Please bless me. I want your help."

So he sobbed and a soul was redeemed on the floor of the library.

Yes. General help to general reader in a library includes also the reclamation of nice-looking readers from selective criminal propensities.

CHAPTER 3

DIFFICULT MATERIAL

30 Introduction

The world of readers loves the world of books. Equally so, the world of books loves the world of readers. Still they do not always get on well with one another. A reference librarian is needed to smoothen their relation and sometimes even to establish contact between them.

Every reader wants his books. Equally so, every book wants its readers. Still they may not know how to find out one another. A reference librarian may be needed to help them find one another.

301 Match-Making

Their matches are not made in heaven; they have to be made on the floor of the stack-room. They are not made by Brahma, the creator; they have to be made by the reference librarian, the match-maker. Still the reference librarian is not a mercenary, like many a professional match-maker. Trickery cannot be his method. He cannot exploit the moment's impulse and slip out of sight for ever. He has to act like a wise parent. He has to choose on abiding and lasting grounds.

302 Idiosyncrasy

The readers, no doubt, present difficulties. But the books are by no means behind them in this respect. The idiosyncrasies of books and periodicals and their persistence even in spite of every device improvised to straighten them were explored by us of the Madras University Library in a set of five papers presented to the Second All India Library Conference held at Lucknow in 1935 [P4 and R32]. It is the pleasant privilege of the reference librarian to smoothen the difficulties on either side and match the right readers with the right books. It is amusing to witness them play all the pranks of lovers. But, we should not fail to step in at the moment of the pranks threatening to become strifes and to lead to prolonged estrangement.

31 Obliquity

Some books wilfully fix on their doors strange and misleading name-boards. God knows why they play this mischief. Is it merely to provide opportunities for the reference librarian? Whatever the motive might have been, they put the right lovers on the wrong track, and bring in the wrong ones who are obliged to withdraw in utter embarrassment after having opened the doors. Oblique titles are a problem to the general reader. They are also equally a problem to the classifier [R39] and to the cataloguer [R58]. But even after these have solved the puzzle and put up the correct class number or specific subject heading as the case may be, the readers often fail to benefit by them. They are of real and certain use only to the reference librarian. Readers stand bewildered unless the reference librarian puts them on the way.

311 "Calculus of Variants" Incident

(*Case Study* 20)

Greg (W W). *Calculus of variants*. 1927.

This book has played pranks on many a mathematical reader. It is intended for historical bibliographers engaged in the reconstruction of ancient texts from a number of conflicting manuscripts giving variant readings. But they are scared away by the term 'calculus'. The services of the reference librarian are necessary to find the right reader for this book and to save it from being ignored by him.

It is true that the author is candid enough to admit "The subject considered in the following pages, under the rather pretentious title of the Calculus of the Variants has been the central problem of textual criticism at any rate since the establishment of genealogical method" (*Extract from p v of the book*).

But this is not going to be of much help unless the reference librarian intervenes and brings it to the notice of readers.

312 "Reparation" Example

(*Case Study* 21)

Plus (Raoul). *Reparation*. 1931.

The title of this book recalls to the mind of most readers a subdivision of political science. But it deals with 'reparation' in the sense "to offer to God (to our Lord) compensation for the sins of others". (*Extract from p 29 of the book*).

Surely it is only timely intervention of the reference librarian that can avert the disappointment of readers as well as of the book.

313 "Co-Operation" Incident

(*Case Study* 22)

Durell (Fletcher). *Co-operation, its essence and background.* 1936.

This book was actually recommended for purchase by experts in economics. But the book lays down its aim as "to state in brief outline a general philosophy of life" and "to stress idealism and the spiritual values related thereto." (*Extracted from p* 2-3 *of the book*). Its chief concern is social ethics developed from the point of view of a particular "Value Philosophy." Many students of economics had to be warned by the reference librarian about the obliquity of this title. Equally many students of ethics had to be assured of the book really belonging to their field of study.

32 Partial Comprehension

Readers know that their new love often prefers to live amidst its own kith and kin—in joint families of enormous size. Hence when they do not find it alone, they go in search of it in such joint families—general treatises. But these joint families have the uncanny practice of having similar names and class numbers painted on their door front. The reader enters one of them in high hope. But to his disappointment all the sisters are there but not his own sweetheart. He has to withdraw with discomfiture and try the next one and the next one and the next one and so on. Sometimes continued disappointment overpowers him. Shyness comes on him. He then goes away in disgust, too dejected by too many failures. When the reader has to look up such partially comprehensive books even the catalogue will desert him [R48 and R59]. And it is only the human reference librarian that can be of any help. The reference librarian has to play the part of the old grannie. He should direct him with kind words like "She is in that family, living in that green house."

321 Example

Stewart (R W). *Matriculation physics.*

This book deals only with heat, light, and sound. It omits properties of matter, electricity, and magnetism. The generic term

"Physics" on the back of the book would mislead many a reader wanting information on electricity. He should be warned by the reference librarian.

33 Various Forms of Exposition

The books sometimes put on various kinds of dress. Like Sri Krishna some bewilder their lovers by surrounding them simultaneously in different dresses — catechism, case studies, source-books — and in the form of verse, drama, fiction, essays, and so on. Perhaps, they appear in so many dresses and so many forms presumably in order to increase their chance to please their lovers. But they are not easily recognised in such forms and dresses. They also forget to inform their lovers, in the cipher symbol carried by them, about the form or dress put on. Many schemes of classification do not indicate the form of exposition in the class number or the book number. Even when a scheme like the Colon Classification has found a device to indicate them, the reader is unable to decipher them. At best they are of help only to the reference librarian. And so the reference librarian has to choose the correct form for the reader. Sometimes the lovers (books) take the trouble to learn foreign languages to please their prospective wooers and try to speak in several tongues. The use of a strange tongue makes the reader take them to be alien and pass by them. He needs to be pre-warned about the language used. But, many schemes of classification fail to indicate, in the class number or the book number, the language of the book. Even when a scheme like the Colon Classification makes the book number announce the language in cipher symbol, the reader is unable to decipher it. It is at best of use only to the reference librarian. And the reader fails to choose correctly unless the reference librarian comes to his aid.

331 Rural Sociology Example
(*Case Study* 23)

Here are three books. Each of them deals with the rural sociology of India.

1 GANGULEE (N). *The Indian peasant and his environment.* 1935.
2 BRAYNE (F L). *Socrates in an Indian village.* 1929.
3 SLATER (Gilbert), *Ed. Some South Indian villages.* 1918.

In the first of these "some of the problems that confront the

Indian countryside and its inhabitants are discussed. . . . The extracts from my [author's] journal . . . and a *selection* of letters written to several persons . . . are now made available to the public." (*Extract from p xx of the book*). Thus the subject is expounded in the form of anecdotes and descriptions of concrete occurrences at particular points of time. Hence it is topical and highly human. But, however, it lacks the advantages of a formal exposition. It should be of particular interest to Indian readers. Many of the local touches and allusions may not have much meaning to foreigners.

The second of the above three books covers nearly the same ground as the first. But it is neither topical like it nor expository as an ordinary treatise or text-book. On the other hand it "represents. . . the actual record of conversations between the author and some of the Gurgaon villagers with whom he has been so intimately connected. (As a result) the book is lucidly and forcefully written" (*Extract from p vii of the book*). It is model of sublimated catechism.

The third book constitutes a collection of case studies in rural life made by a team of students working under the direction of the editor. He "drew up a 'Village Questionnaire' as a guide to the students in the investigation of their own villages". (*Extract from p 21 of the book*). The result is page on page of dry-as-dust data valuable for research students but rather scaring to the general reader.

332 Plato Example

(*Case Study* 24)

Here are three books dealing with utopias. Each of them carries the name of Plato on its title:

1 Nettleship (Richard Lewis). *Lectures on the republic of Plato*, ed by G R Benson. 1906.

2 Crossmen (R H S). *Plato to-day*. 1937.

3 Dickinson (G Lowes). *After two thousand years: A dialogue between Plato and a modern young man*. 1931.

The first of these books is a reproduction by his students of Nettleship's "Lectures on the *Republic*". (*Extract from p v of the book*). The lectures closely follow the text of Plato. They are virtually commentaries on the dialogues. They thus constitute a book on a book.

The second gives the substance of a series of radio talks in the series, "If Plato Lived Again". "When, therefore, I read again those gloomy scripts in the *Listener*, it occurred to me that it might be worthwhile to write a book in which, unhampered by the limitations of broadcasting, I should try to describe the attitude of Plato to our modern world. *Plato To-day* is the result." (*Extract from p 12 of the book*). Such is the author's description of the book. Thus though based on lectures, it has not adopted the lecture-style.

The third book covers virtually the same ground as the second. But instead of the expository style, it is in the form of Platonic dialogues.

333 Student Life Example
(*Case Study* 25)

Here is a third set of three books. Each of them deals with student life:

1 Gardner (Donfred H). *Student personnel service.* 1936.

2 Mackness (Constance). *Miss Pickle: The story of an Australian boarding school.* 1927.

3 Oakden (Ellen C) and Stuart (Mary). *Growing up: How one did it in different times and places.* 1930.

Though all these three books deal with the same subject, the first is virtually the report of a committee of investigation; the second is in the form of a novel; while the third is historical in form. Readers need the help of the reference librarian in evaluating them correctly and choosing that form of exposition which would suit their standard, temperament, and taste.

34 Style and Standard

Then comes the standard and style. All the daughters of the same family do not live in the same standard and style. Some live down to the level of the poorest. Some hover to the highest; their standard is too severe except for a handful of aristocrats. There is the whole spectrum of all kinds of intermediate standards and styles. They are so many. A reader feels bewildered. Neither the classifier nor the cataloguer is of any help even to the reference librarian. Each book has to be examined individually and sized up by the reference librarian. The bewildered reader is obliged to seek the discriminating help of an informed reference librarian and open his heart to him. He has to ask the reference librarian, "Which of these can I get on with, without discomfort, or at least without an incessant heart-break?"

341 Difference In Standard

Here are three books. They are quite divergent in style and standard; and yet they share the same title to the bewilderment of readers high and low. When the third of these titles was included in the book-selection list of a university library for the consideration of the expert adviser, it was scored out in red with the remark "Elementary on the face of it. Fit only for a school library!"

1 Seshu Ayyar (P V). *Elementary mathematics.* 1916.

2 Lagrange (Joseph Louis). *Elementary mathematics,* tr by Thomas J McCormack. 1898.

3 Klein (Felix). *Elementary mathematics,* tr by E R Hedrick and C A Noble. 1932.

3411 SESHU AYYAR

The first is an elementary text-book suited to the secondary school leaving certificate syllabus of Madras.

3412 LAGRANGE

The second is a translation of the lectures delivered in the year 1795 at the *Ecole Normale* by one of the greatest of modern analysts. "The originality, elegance, and symmetrical character of these lectures have been pointed out by De Morgan and notably by Duhring, who places them in the front rank of elementary expositions, as an exemplar of their kind. Coming as they do, from one of the greatest mathematicians of modern times and with all the excellences which such a source implies, unique in their character as a *reading-book* in mathematics, and inter-woven with historical and philosophical remark of great helpfulness, they cannot fail to have a beneficent and stimulating influence." (*Extract from pp v-vi of the book*). The first two lectures are on arithmetic. The second and the third are on algebra. They reach up to cubic equations and the general theory of equations. The last lecture gives a delightful popular exposition of the employment of curves in the solution of problems and discusses topics like the curve of errors, the circle and the inscribed polygon, and parabolic curves.

3413 KLEIN

On the other hand the third is addressed to the advanced student of mathematics. Its pages "constitute an invaluable work, serviceable alike to the university teacher and to the teacher in the secondary school. There is, at present, nothing else comparable with them, either with respect to their skilfully integrated material, or to the fascinating way in which this material is discussed." (*Extract from p vii of the book*). It reaches such advanced topics like quaternion multiplication, theory of small oscillations, and the proof of the transcendence of e and π. Klein states quite plainly in his introductory lecture "I shall by no means address myself to beginners, but I shall take for granted that you are all acquainted with the main features of the chief fields of mathematics. I shall often talk of problems of algebra, of number theory, of function theory, etc., without being able to go into details. You must, therefore, be moderately familiar with these fields, in order to follow me. My task will always be to show you the *mutual connection between problems* in the various fields." (*Extract from p 1-2 of the book*).

35 Hide and Seek

Books sometimes indulge in the play of hide and seek—for fun it may be to begin with; but occasionally they get hidden away and lost to their readers, unless traced out and rescued by a reference librarian of considerable alertness, experience, and industry.

351 Analytical Entry

Theoretically one should expect the analytical entries of the library catalogue to bring them to light if not to prominent notice. The *Classified catalogue code* devotes a whole chapter to this problem as applied to books [R13]. And as applied to periodicals it has worked out an elaborate set of rules to disclose books either marooned within them or hanging as an appendage sometimes capable of separation and sometimes not [R15].

352 Difficult of Realisation

But these rules constitute a counsel of perfection! For, even libraries, paying intellectual homage to such rules, find the actualities — staff, finance, "initiative in high places and understanding generally" —unhelpful, if not obstructive, to even a reasonable realisation.

353 Ulster of the Fifth Law

This phenomenon called for an examination of the philosophy of analytical entries in the *Theory of library catalogue*. In it will be found a detailed picture of how the Law of Parsimony drives a wedge amidst the Laws of Library Science and makes an Ulster of the Fifth Law so as to fatten itself—by the policy of divide and rule [R62].

354 Need for Reference Service

Even supposing that the Laws of Library Science stood united and triumphed over the onslaughts of the Law of Parsimony and the undermining of the mental inertia of the public, it is doubtful if a general reader could help himself in tracing out such hidden books without the help of the reference librarian.

Let us have a closer picture of the various forms of hide and seek.

CHAPTER 4

MODERN BOOK

41 Book Within Book

Among modern books, we occasionally have books within books.

411 Schrodinger Incident

(*Case Study* 26)

The English version of Schrodinger's *Nobel address* was eager. sought; but it wouldn't come out as a book by itself. What a relief it was to all concerned when the enterprising reference librarian dived into his *Science and human temperament* and brought it out from its depths for distribution to expectant students of wave-mechanics.

412 Abercrombie Incident

(*Case Study* 27)

Abercrombie's *Principles of literary criticism* was often out on loan. But there was a great demand for it. Many a reader was to have been sorely disappointed. But this was averted to his surprise by the enterprise of the reference librarian. For, he found this document mocking its suiters from its hiding place inside the capacious pages of W Rose's *Outline of modern knowledge.*

413 Familiar Hiding Place

The above examples illustrate unusual hiding places. But the familiar ones are collected works, omnibus editions, anthologies, symposia, fest-schrifts, and memorial volumes. The general reader is seldom able to look up and locate his requirement in such hotch-potch heaps. He should be helped by the reference librarian. And the reference librarian should have acquired an intimate knowledge of their ins and outs by the very process of helping readers.

42 Book within Periodical

Books within periodicals are even more trying if not more frequent.

421 Wells Incident

(*Case Study* 28)

A few years ago the local dailies featured prominently H G Wells' lecture at the Royal Institution on the *Idea of a world encyclopaedia.* Readers were accustomed to expect Wells' productions to come as books or pamphlets. This was the signal for a rush in the library. But they had to go away disappointed. In a few days, however, the eagle eye of the reference librarian made a discovery. The whole lecture was lying hidden in an unmutilated condition in the *Nature* of the year. The Second and the Third Laws were thereby propitiated. And the Library itself felt redeemed.

422 Regular Seducers

The reference librarian knows, but the general readers do not know, which periodicals are regular seducers. He maintains a list of them. He storms them systematically. They are thus made to make a confession. This work is beyond the power of the catalogue of an individual library. It may be attempted by a bibliography promoted by international effort; but it is yet to come. Reference service therefore happens to be the only means of rescuing such books from within periodicals, 'dowering them with our own life energy', and giving them away to their suiters. When engaged in such service, the reference librarian attains supreme bliss. His soul may very well be imagined to hum Janaka's words:

इय सीता मम सुता सहधर्मचारी तव ।।
प्रतीच्छ चैनां भद्रं ते पाणिं गृह्णीष्व पाणिना । [V3].

"Here is my daughter Sita (=picked up from the earth through its furrows).
She will help you in your life's pursuits.
Accept her. You will be happy.
Clasp her hand by your hand."

423 Periodicals for Rummaging

The *Transactions* of the Royal Societies of various countries, the *International conciliation*, the *Smithsonian miscellaneous collections*, the periodicals of the Field Museum of Natural History, and the *Pandit* are some of the notorious seducers. Every reference librarian should rummage them thoroughly for hidden books.

424 Examples of Seduced Books

Here are some examples of huge books or topical little books caught up in some of them.

4241 TABLES AND FORMULAE

(*Case Study* 29)

Two formidable tables lie hidden in the volumes of *Smithsonian miscellaneous collections*. The whole of volume 88 constitutes a most valuable set of physical tables. Here at least the back of the volume can take the subsidiary label *Physical tables*. But the *Mathematical formulae and tables of elliptic functions* are not allowed even that freedom as they form but one number of volume 74. A reference librarian with the necessary knowledge should salvage them. Otherwise, these compendious works would lie irrevocably hidden away to the annoyance of all the Laws of Library Science.

What is more tantalising, these works go through several editions but each edition persists in hiding itself in some volume of the same periodical. The general reader must be thankful that they are constant at least in the choice of their hosts.

4242 ELECTRIC LIGHT

(*Case Study* 30)

An interesting history of electric light occupies 95 pages of the *Smithsonian* volume 76. Perhaps, it is also the only history of the subject. It is not in the nature of a normal article in a periodical. Henry Schnoerder's *History of electric light* is beyond doubt a book within a periodical.

4243 SKELETAL REMAINS

(*Case Study* 31)

Alex Hrdlicka's *Skeletal remains of early man* occupies 380 sumptuous pages of volume 83 of the *Smithsonian*. It is an important book. It will be hopelessly missed by the general reader interested in prehistoric anthropometry. The reference librarian should come to his aid. It is beyond doubt a case of book within periodical.

4244 IRISH CONSTITUTION

(*Case Study* 32)

I remember the eager search by many a general reader for the text of the *Constitution of the Eire* (Ireland) (1938) and the *New Soviet constitution* (1936) when they were in a nascent state. I remember also the nasty strictures passed by some ignorant readers on the library. They called it ante-diluvian. I deliberately call them ignorant. Because they themselves confessed later to the stupidity of their remarks. In each case, they asked for the book immediately after seeing the news of its enactment in the local dailies. Within a month, they were served to their satisfaction by the reference librarian from the pages of the *Internationai conciliation*. The books themselves came much later. They then realised that even two months were too short a period for these constitutions to be embodied in regular books. These were cases of combines of difficult readers and difficult reading materials.

CHAPTER 5

ANCIENT WORK

51 Eastern Classics in Western Host

During the last one or two centuries many classics of Hindu, Buddhistic, Jain, and Islamic origin were ushered into the world of print. Till then, they were only in manuscripts. Due to economic factors, they could not be provided for to lead an independent existence in printed form. Most of them had to be billeted in oriental periodicals such as the *Journal* of the American Oriental Society, *Journal* of the Asiatic Society of Bengal, Z D M G, *Sitzumgsberichte* der Koninglich preussischen Akademie der Wissenschaften, *Archiv fur Mathematik und Physik*, and so on.

511 First Printed Version
(*Case Study* 33)

1 For *Sariputra prakarana* one must turn to the pages of the *Sitzungsberichte*. One will find there to one's delight even a facsimile reproduction of the palm leaf manuscript.

2 The general reader can get the following material only in v 4, 12, and 14 respectively of the *Journal* of the American Oriental Society. He has to be told about this by a well-versed reference librarian.

21 An English translation of Umapati Sivacharya's *Sivaprakasam*;

22 W D Whitneys' *Index verborum to the published text of the Atharvaveda*; and

23 The text of the *Kausika sutra of the Atharvaveda.*

3 E Burgess's translation of the *Surya siddhanta* made its first appearance in print in volume 6 of the same priodical.

4 Similarly the first embodiment in print of the text and W D Whitney's translation of *Taittriya pratisakhya* with its commentary *Tribhasyaratna* will be found in volume 9 of the same periodical.

It is true that independent editions of these works have now appeared. But those original versions have still a value. The general reader does find unusual satisfaction when the reference librarian brings them to his notice.

512 The Only Printed Version
(*Case Study* 34)

R Pischel's classical work on "Shadow plays" entitled *Das altindischen Schattenspiel* is generally applied for by the general reader as if it were a separate book. But it occurs only as a part of the volume for 1906 of *Sitzungberichte*. The reference librarian knows it; and he has to tell the reader about it.

513 Split Printed Version
(*Case Study* 35)

We have at least one case of a work being split in printed version.

The *Paippalada sakha of the Atharvaveda* stands dismembered. Its first thirteen books are scattered in several volumes of the *Journal* of the American Oriental Society. But the remaining parts were for long lying neglected. They have now emerged as an independent book. This illustrates the possibility of a part of the book lying within a periodical and the rest in regular book form.

514 Only English Translation
(*Case Study* 36)

Here is an example of a book within book, the container being a modern book and the contained an English translation of an ancient Tamil classic.

Some years ago an American institution was obliged to find for one of its members either the text or the translation of *Talavilasam*. After much of ineffective search the Society asked us for light. This request made us realise the darkness surrounding ourselves. How after all we got light will be described in its appropriate place in chapter 2 of part K. It was eventually found *in toto* in E Blatter's *Palms of British India and Ceylon.*

515 Complete Bibliography

All reference librarians know, but few general readers do, how many oriental classics lie caught up either in original or in translations not only in periodical publications but also in many miscellanies and collections. A complete bibliography of such Eastern Classics among Western Hosts should be prepared and published. It can form a doctoral thesis in Library Science.

52 Sanskrit Anthology

Ancient Sanskrit literature is very rich in anthologies. Several works, not existing to-day in entirety, have left behind them representative fragments in anthologies. Any attempt to list them would take us beyond the scope of this chapter. The general reader is in perpetual need of the help of the reference librarian in locating in print many a piece partially preserved in tradition. Why general reader? Even experts are no exceptions! An analytical documentation list of the fragments in Sanskrit anthologies should be prepared and published. It can form a doctoral thesis in Library Science.

53 Sanskrit Puranas

Post-Vedic Sanskrit has got a characteristic class of books named *Puranas.* It is usual to describe a *Purana* as an encyclopaedia. But, for those accustomed to the atomising tendency in modern encyclopaedias, such a description would be misleading. In our present context, a *Purana* is a conglomerate of several books within books, great and small.

531 "Puranas" a Conglomerate
(*Case Study* 37)

1 It may not matter for the general reader if he does not know that the universally known book of books the *Bhagavad gita* forms part of the great epic *Mahabharata.* For it has seen hundreds of editions, translations, and adaptations. It has attracted to itself hoards of commentaries and long-drawn-out hierarchies of sub-commentaries.

2 Nor does it matter for him—at any rate for the Hindu reader repeating it every day—that the charming book *Vishnu sahasranama* also forms part of the same epic.

3 But in the case of several works, marooned in the Puranas and not yet given an independent embodiment either in manuscript or in print or by oral transmission, the general reader is completely at sea. The numerous local histories or *Sthala puranas* are examples. So also are many *Gitas.*

4 The same book occurs in different *Puranas,* but not in the same form or to the same length. Confusion between them is a fertile source of controversy. The well known and oft-sought *Aditya hyrdaya* is an example in point.

532 Index to Puranas

These *Puranas* are without a complete index. We come across many pathetic situations when a reader is hard-pressed to find a particular constituent book and we ourselves feel helpless unless we are fortunate to have amidst us one widely read in the *Puranas*, and functioning as a living index. Recently, an index of some of the *Puranas* has been brought out by the University of Madras. It only amounts to spade work. A thorough index to all the *Puranas* with comparative annotations should be prepared and published. It can form a doctoral thesis in Library Science.

CHAPTER 6

PLAY WITH TITLE

61 Introduction

Another class of books causes difficulty to the general reader. It makes reference aid a necessity. The books in this class play with their titles. The play may consist of the following kinds:

1 A book appears with different titles in different countries. This is a case of incognito names.

2 A book appears with different titles in different editions. This is a case of rechristening.

3 Several books conspire to tease the reader by taking the same title. This is a case of homonyms.

62 Benefit of the Catalogue

No doubt it is the business of the Catalogue Section to bring them all to order and link them up by a suitable system of cross-references, whatever be the research involved. This it has to do lest the Order Section should father on it the responsibility for the frittering away of the funds of the library on unintended duplications. But the general reader is seldom able to benefit directly by the cataloguer's careful work. The catalogue by itself is not sufficient for him. The benefit of the catalogue can often reach him only through the reference librarian.

63 Incognito Name

This class of difficult books is particularly common in the English language. Is this a result of the English speaking people being spread over different continents? What is the psychology behind naming the same book differently in different countries? Is there a sufficient reason for this? Or, can it be a deliberate design to mislead? Here are some examples:

1 Normal Angel's *Peace and the plain man* (of America) appears as *Preface to peace* (in England).

2 J B S Haldane's (American) *Science and human life* becomes (English) *Inequality of man and other essays*.

3 L P Jack's *Constructive citizenship* (of America) walks the streets of England as the *Art of living together*.

4 The incognito name of a novel of Jacob Wassermann dramatically changes from *Etzel Andergast* to *Dr. Kerkhoven* while crossing the Atlantic.

In their case, there is nothing strange in the general reader calling for the help of the reference librarian to identify and equate the different names. This camouflage has made colossal dupes successively and successfully of a book-selecting expert, an experienced order-librarian, an alert classifier, a painstaking cataloguer, and a chief librarian believing himself to be omniscient!

64 Rechristening

Rechristening of books does not require even a linguistic stock living scattered in different continents. It takes place even in the same country. It appears to have been in vogue from time immemorial. It has no doubt served as a trap to humiliate vain frauds passing for scholars. But it is a real trial to the innocent general reader. Surely the reference librarian should help him in this matter even after being unasked.

641 Reasons for Rechristening

In the case of ancient books, the forces causing rechristening have been all forgotten. In the case of modern books, some authors take the trouble to explain the reason for rechristening. Some of them are also candid enough not to obliterate the old name beyond recognition.

642 Remainder Copy

But what is the general reader to do when a publisher or an author buys the remainder copies of an older book for a song, tears off the title-page, and sticks in a newly printed title-page leaving no trace whatever of the old title. Is it anything short of a criminal act? When decoloration has set in the old book and the pirate is not clever enough to select for the new title-page old paper to match it, the criminal act may become a clumsy one. Surely the help of the reference librarian is necessary to the general reader in such cases of fraud. It is particularly so in the case of his intending to buy a copy of his own. We are told that this piratical rechristening became an epidemic among Arabic and Egyptian publishers, after Kemal Pasha romanised the script in his kingdom and caused the old books in the old script to be cast away as waste paper.

65 Homonym

Apart from the same book having different names, we have also the converse problem of different books having the same name. Here too the help of the reference librarian becomes a necessity. Here are some examples of homonyms:

651 Homonymous Titles
(*Case Study* 38)

1 There are two books sharing the title *Loaves and fishes.* One is a novel by S Maugham. The other is by H Carrington. It gives an occult version of the life of Jesus.

2 Two persons have christened their books *Between two worlds.* One is an autobiography of J Middleton Murry. He lays bare in it his spiritual struggle. The other is a discussion of the social problems of to-day by Nicholas Murray Butler.

3 Another riddle giving occupation to the reference staff is created by two books being entitled *Riddle of the universe.* One of them is a summary, by "one of the most eminent and thoughtful men of science in Europe" (as Mallock describes Professor Haeckel of the University of Jena), of the position taken up by science and evacuated by theology. It is a translation by Joseph McCabe issued in 1903 by the Rationalist Press Association. The second is an independent work by the translator himself published in 1934, surveying recent advances in every branch of science, affecting or likely to affect one's philosophy of life. The 'to-day', added as a distinguishing mark at the end of the title of the latter, is mostly missed or forgotten by the general reader.

4 *Bhavaprakasa* is the name shared by two different books. One is an exposition of an Ayurveda (Indian medicine) book by Bhavamisra. The other is Saradatanaya's treatise on Alankara (Sanskrit poetics).

5 Bhoja has christened alike both a grammatical and an Alankara work of his. They both carry the name *Sarasvatikanthabharana.*

6 *Janakiparinaya* is the name of a poem by Chakrakavi and of a drama by Ramabhadra Dikshita.

CHAPTER 7

INTANGIBLE QUALITIES

70 Introduction

All the difficulties, discussed so far regarding the nature of materials, are concerned comparatively speaking with tangible qualities of books. They can be brought to some system and under objective treatment. They do not completely evade solution by classification or by cataloguing or jointly by both. In fact the tendency among classificationists and framers of catalogue-codes is to invent devices to solve them more and more satisfactorily.

701 Nature of Flavour

But the general reader is in need of books being sized up for him on the basis of certain other qualities as well. These qualities cannot be separated from the authors' fundamental perquisites of vigour, originality, humour, outlook, and personality. These qualities are intangible. They evade all attempts at systematisation. They depend essentially on the judgment of readers. They are of the nature of a flavour. No mechanical or objective norm could be set up to size them up.

702 Kinds of Intangible Qualities

The general reader has to lean on the reference librarian more in respect of these qualities than of the tangible ones. He has to seek his help in choosing the book of the right flavour. Three kinds of flavour figure frequently in such requests. Based on intangible flavour, books are of the following kinds [R39]:

1 Book with a message;
2 Book with flair; and
3 Orientation book.

The reference librarian recognises them from his own experience. Moreover, his unique chance to pool together the experience of readers adds to his competence. A more resourceful and genial reference librarian will get it reinforced by judicious participation in discussing the books with the readers.

71 Book with a Message

711 Literature and Sacred Books

The first intangible quality to be explored is the possession of a message by the books. Generally speaking, the main classes Literature and Religion (the sacred books mostly) abound in books with a message. Not that every book in those classes possesses one. But the density of books with a message is greatest in those classes. Ordinarily, the general reader is not able to discard from these classes the books without a message.

712 Other Subjects

But books with a message are not so abundant in the other subjects. Not that they are totally absent. That is impossible. For, there is progress in those subjects; and progress implies the existence of books with a message. But the ordinary prosaic books simply transmitting information are too many in those subjects. Therefore, the few germinal books with a message are virtually lost among them.

713 Business of Reference Librarian

The general reader usually lacks the flair to spot them out readily. No doubt he may hit on them by chance. But on account of their relative scarcity, the odds are very much against him. Or, he can arrive at them by the laborious process of trial and error. But the necessary patience and perseverance seldom go with the general reader. Hence there is the danger of his going without the book and the book lying neglected on the shelves for long. The business of the reference librarian includes averting such miscarriages.

72 Book with Flair

721 Qualities Spelt Out

Another class of books making the general reader depend largely on the help of the reference librarian is books rich in flair. Such books are personal in their method. They display much judgment in the selection of details. Their style is racy. Once we begin them, we are led from page to page; we don't like to be disturbed; they have an aroma of their own; they are alluring; our curiosity never wanes; on the other hand it ever grows; we want to finish them at the very sitting—even sitting up late into the night. Turning their pages is like turning the pages of life itself. They are illuminating books.

722 Favourite of Reference Librarian

It is such books that make reading popular. They provide a great leverage to the Publicity Department of the library. It is they that are most helpful in fulfilling the new function of the library, viz., conversion of every citizen into a library-goer and a lover of books. Much of the encomium, got by the reference librarian, is derived from the service of such books. Some self-confident, opinionative, superior readers often remark to the reference librarian with a quiet firmness, "I do not think much of the opinion you expressed the other day on the merits of the book recommended by you". Even such readers condescend to compliment him on his recommendation of a book with flair. It is therefore a favourite of reference librarians.

723 Line-Clear Treatment

The sheer sense of gratefulness should make everybody in the library do well by such helpful books. The book-selecting expert should never jettison out any of them on any ground. The order-librarian should be prompt in getting them. The classifier and the cataloguer should give them "line-clear" treatment. The Maintenance Section and the Accession Section should release them for use without a moment's delay. The reference librarian should give them a central place in their apperceptive mass. He should virtually hawk them about. They are the books to be given to everybody; and they are books which everybody loves to read.

724 Difficult to Spot Out

But the general reader cannot spot them out except by chance which is untrustworthy or by the laborious process of trial and error which is exhausting, repulsive, and likely to be given up before achieving the result. Hence the need for the reference librarian helping the general reader with such books even before being asked.

73 Orientation Book

Then we pass on to the third intangible quality in books. It is a quality, much sought by readers with a catholic taste. Books with that quality may be called orientation books. They owe their value to two conflicting factors. Specialisation gets intensified nowadays. At the same time the man of culture has the urge to know the inter-relation of the various branches of knowledge. It is hardly possible for him to sense this inter-relation merely by reading the specialised books; and they are myriads. About 300,000 books are said to be published each year. This makes one agree with Pope. He said,

> When so much is said,
> One half will never be believed,
> The other never read.

And so the man of culture wants to have books, showing explicitly the moorings of the present day progress in knowledge.

731 Difficult to Spot Out

But such books are few and far between. Their specific quality does not lend itself to be made obvious by the class number or the catalogue entries. Hence, they get buried amidst the hundreds of the books without that quality. It is difficult for the general reader to spot them out. Hence the need for the reference librarian's liaison service in their case also.

732 Widening of Interest

The library stands to gain generally by finding such books for readers. The gain will be much. They should also find readers for such books. For, such books widen the interests of those who are, by nature, conservative in their field of study. Once their curiosity is stimulated by orientation books, it can be kept up and even sublimated by feeding them with the books with flair. This process should be diligently pursued by a resourceful reference librarian. He will then find more willing readers for the few germinal books, capable of acting as lever. The reference librarian should remember this: The ultimate consummation of the purpose of the library lies in finding wide circulation for books of that quality—seminal books, as Geoffrey West [W1] calls them—which open horizons even wider than their ostensible subjects, stirring the imagination over the whole broad scope of life, skirting the deep unspoken impulse of religion, and constituting as it were the flow of life itself.

74 Examples

Let us illustrate. Here are three sets of four books each. The sets belong to three different main subjects, *viz.*, mathematics, biology, and economics.

741 Mathematics

1 RUSSELL (Bertrand). *Introduction to mathematical philosophy;*

2 HOGBEN (L). *Mathematics for the million;*

3 *Place of mathematics in modern education* forming the eleventh yearbook of the National Council of Teachers of Mathematics of the United States, 1936; and

4 BOWLEY (Arthur). *A general course of pure mathematics from indices to solid geometry.*

742 Biology

1 CRILLE (George). *Phenomena of life;*

2 WELLS (H G), etc. *Science of life;*

3 THOMPSON (J Arthur). *Introduction to science;* and

4 SCOTT (George G). *The science of biology.*

743 Economics

1 STEINER (Rudolf). *Problems of world economy;*

2 Cole (G D H). *The intelligent man's guide to the world chaos;*

3 KIRKPATRICK (E A). *Sciences of man in the making* and

4 THOMAS (S EVELYN). *Elements of economics.*

75 Book with a Message

(*Case Study* 39)

The first book in each of the above four sets is of a seminal nature.

751 Russell's Book

Russell's book was published forty years ago. It immediately opened a new vista of thought. As stated in the preface of that book, it turned the mind of mathematicians to a new direction altogether, namely, to the foundations of mathematics. Till then mathematics was supposed to begin with the natural numbers as its basic elements and proceed thence to the development of the various branches. Witness the famous dictum of Kronecker (1823-1891) [K3]. "The natural numbers were made by God, all else is the work of man." Russell's book contained the message that these numbers occupy only a middle position in the structure of mathematical science—with the older mathematical disciplines above and the new theory of the foundations below. His work really annexed to mathematics something, lying undeveloped under the sway of philosophy—general theories of relation, order, sets, and groups. The research output in this new field has been enormous during recent years. Special periodicals like *Scripta mathematica* and *Fundamenta mathematicae* have come into existence to record progress in this field.

752 Crille's Book

Crille's book was published only twenty-two years ago. But it is of a fundamental nature. It is the result of many years' patient investigation; this was originally stimulated by a clinical experience in a hospital. It opens up a new method of investigation into cytological biophysics. Indeed it is inspiring to read Crille's picture of the cells of a living organism as secondary cells, storing, and transforming the solar energy, the fountain of all the energy in life on earth. It is too early to say how much this book is going to transform future outlook on life or how long it will take to catch fire.

753 Steiner's Book

Rudolf Steiner's book on *World economy* embodies the inspiring lectures delivered in the last years of his life. As usual, the pundits of economics, whose *dharma* (= role in life) is to prevent onslaughts of revolutionary thought, would have nothing to do with it. But still to their embarrassment many things stated by Steiner in those lectures are coming to be true. His theory is of a fundamental nature. It is dynamic. It is bound to provoke new lines of investigation in the near future.

76 Book with Flair

(*Case Study* 40)

The second book in each of the above three sets is a book with flair. Hogben, for example, has written this most charming book on mathematics—a subject which is believed to be as dry as dust. Indeed this book has nearly beat all records as a best seller. He has written for the general reader. And he has been rewarded by reaching an unprecedented number of them. He has convinced the public that a mathematics book can be as interesting as any other kind of book.

The same remark applies also to the *S 'ience of life* of H G Wells and the economics-book by Cole. Both these authors are so well known for their flair. And they have written much. Everybody knows about them.

77 Orientation Book

(*Case Study* 41)

771 Eleventh Year-Book

The third book in each of the three sets of examples is an orientation book. The *Place of mathematics in modern education* meets a real demand. During the three years after its arrival, hardly a month has passed in the Madras University Library without some professor of mathematics coming and asking for an account of the way in which mathematics can water other fields of thought. This yearbook had been our mainstay in meeting such requests.

772 Thomson's Book

Thomson's *Introduction to science* appears in the Home University Series. It is a masterful contribution to methodology. It displays the whole spectrum of science. And it depicts therein the position of biology.

773 Kirkpatrick's Book

Similarly Kirkpatrick's *Science of man in the making* gives a systematic account of different branches of the humanities and their inter-relations. The chapter on economics defines the scope of the subject both by the enumeration of its special divisions and by the description of other subjects bordered by it.

78 Pedestrian Books

(*Case Study* 42)

The fourth book in each of the above three sets is an ordinary reproducing text-book neither carrying a message nor possessing flair nor giving orientation. They are all prosaic. They are all pedestrian.

79 The Problem of Choice

As has been already stated, the sizing up of the books in the different ultimate subjects, in accordance with the extent of their share of these four intangible qualities, transcends the capacity of catalogue and classification. A specialist in a particular subject may be able to size up the books in that subject. But the very same specialist will feel himself quite at sea when obliged to enter into some other subject either for recreation or for information. The general reader may feel equally at sea in all subjects. It would be nothing short of cruelty to leave them alone in a large library, with books of such different qualities mixed up indiscriminately. Surely, the Laws of Library Science have every right to protest against such cruelty to readers and to plead that no library should deserve that name if it does not provide the necessary human agency to pick and choose in a manner that will exactly fit the requirements of each reader. The very nature of books demands it.

CHAPTER 8

DIFFICULT REFERENCE LIBRARIAN

81 Self-Complacence

There are no doubt meek readers, ignorant readers, loiterers, and wasters of time. Unreasonable, irritating, pompous, insulting readers drift into the stack-room. We reference librarians too are sometimes tarred with the same brush. As individuals we each fancy ourselves as "easy to get on with." We go on thinking so quite simply and sincerely. One day a good friend, perhaps the wife, says, "You know you are a difficult person at times, perhaps just a wee bit selfish." Then, we shed our self-complacency. Then, alone, we realise, all on a sudden, that our self-satisfaction is largely based on the fact that we usually get a good deal of our own way. True, we can, by seeing the faces of readers, gauge the depths of their experience. But, let us not forget another fact. Our face too speaks volumes to them. How quick we are to see the weaknesses and the faults of others! How blind we are to our own! !

82 Coming to Terms with Readers

The readers could tell tales of their difficulties with reference librarians. How often a stammerer voluntarily banishes himself from the library, because an inexperienced reference assistant burst into laughter. As for the long-suffering unemployed visitors, what could they not say of the minor rebuffs and little discourtesies encountered in their search for solace from libraries. May be the fact of reference librarian's superior familiarity with books blinds some of us to the difficulties and to the points of view of the readers. To know or to try to know the facts relating to readers would make a sensible difference in our attitude. Pugnacity, that prolific source of all kinds of warfare, would give place to geniality. Let us admit it. We too are difficult. Bricks of fair size could be exchanged in a battle of complaints, and one day it may be worthwhile staging a show of the kind.

Let us have no illusion as to the perfectibility of human nature. Let us be sure that the readers are our good friends and partners in the enterprise of bettering humanity with the aid of books.

83 Trial of Temper

Even experienced men lose their temper when overworked and exhausted. Reference service is a new idea. The amount of physical and mental strain it involves is not yet realised by those in power. It may wear out temper. Trial of temper is a common experience of a reference librarian.

831 Mira Bai Incident
(*Case Study* 43)

"Where can I find information on Mira Bai?"

"Go to the history shelves."

"I have seen all those books there."

"Then why do you ask questions as if you don't know anything?"

"No, I want to know if you can suggest any other source of information."

"Try the encyclopaedias: say, *Britannica* and *Religion and philosophy*. You may also try Baldwin's *Dictionary of philosophy*. Look up also the *Dictionary of national biography*. Also Chambers' *Encyclopaedia*, Nelson's *Century*, . . .Why, what is the matter? You seem to smile or. . .?"

"No, no. I do smile. Go on! Exhaust your list of encyclopaedias."

"Don't be cynical!"

"Don't think you are talking to a child!"

"No, I am conscious I am talking to a scholar! I beg your pardon —a professor who has read all the books in the history shelves!"

"There is a limit to everything!"

"So, there is! Don't think that you alone can distinguish a child from a professor."

* * * *

The pitch was rising rapidly. The building had awful acoustic properties. The reverberation had reached a senior's ears. He arrived. The junior withdrew with reluctance, his eyes still glistening —but his anger slowly settling into sullenness.

* * * *

"I just want to have one point cleared up."

"Perhaps I can help you. I am not sure. I shall try."

"Is the story about Mira Bai accepting a pearl necklace from Akbar authentic?"

"Perhaps this book may help you—*Bharatiya charitambudhi: a dictionary of Indian classical characters*."

"I don't read Hindi."

"Never mind. I shall read it for you. Here it is! This very question is discussed. Akbar was 122 years posterior to Mira Bai. That settles the question."

"What a relief! Something in me told me that it should be a myth. I had been worrying myself about this for some months now. I had exhausted every book on history. No light. I was really worried. I am ever so. . . ."

"No, no mention."

"I knew that this was the only place for all such difficulties!"

"I am glad you are satisfied. Please forget what happened a while ago."

"Oh, it is nothing! It is an exception. I know he didn't mean anything. Probably he is overworked and tired. Everybody here is quite nice. . . ."

832 Good Temper for Two

And the recipe for such miscarriages? Is there one? One really can't say; because we all go on doing our job to the best of our ability learning from actual experience—and then find our knowledge has come a trifle late for practice. Life batters us into shape. We are examples and spectacles to the young at our heels. There is a modern craze for sharing. May be the sharing out of good temper—witness Henry James' four words "good temper for two"—would help to solve the problem of facing readers. Let us try.

84 Square Man in Round Hole

Knocks received from the public may by degrees batter up an otherwise competent reference librarian into shape, not allowing overwork or exhaustion to betray him into bad temper. But the situation is quite different if the initial recruitment itself is faulty.

841 False Philosophy

There are moments in the history of any society when a false philosophy guides recruitment. About a century ago, for example the community of the New World believed that man was intrinsically a Jack-of-all-trades and that there was no such thing as individual aptitude. This really led to the adoption of the spoils system in politics and the principle of rotation in office. It led to a readiness to change from one occupation to another and to a lack of confidence in the expert in any field. Equalitarianism of the extreme crude variety was asserted by the collective will of the community in order to expunge outright all possibility for the persistence of the principle of petrified privileged classes. The principle of division of labour, indicated everywhere in nature, was thrown overboard along with the privileged classes. For, that principle itself was believed to have created the privileged classes. Such an epoch of irrational equalitarianism may coincide with that of the introduction of reference service, whose success depends so largely on personal qualities. Then, the odds are very much against the furtherance of reference service.

842 Undoing the Mischief

When a misfit is recruited the additional strain on those of the right variety is not merely that of having to do the work of that misfit, but also that of undoing the mischief, done to the reputation of the library by the misbehaviour of the misfit.

843 Chesterfield Incident

(*Case Study* 44)

A young undergraduate was new to the library. He chanced to seek the help of a misfit in the Reference Section. He was stretching himself to his full length in a chair, not assigned to him. He was a new recruit. But he was middle-aged. He had seen many trades. But nowhere could he find satisfaction. He, therefore, learnt something of library management.

"Sir, can you give me Chesterton's letters?"

"Bring the call number", boomed the misfit, still stretched to his full length in the usurped chair.

The young undergraduate was puzzled. He wondered what call number might mean. He went back to the entrance, turned through the pages of the gate register and finally came back and said "112".

"No, that can't be."

"It is correct, sir, I went to the entrance and verified it, sir."

"What did you verify?"

"That is the number against my name in the gate register."

"Ha, ha, ha! Wonderful! Is it call number? Go to the cabinet, man, look up the author index entry and bring. . .the call number."

These were the words, escaping in driblets in an articulate form amidst the laughter of the misfit. He had regarded himself utterly superior on account of the knowledge of the library jargon picked up by him a few months back.

The young undergraduate was smarting under this mixed shower of jargon and ridicule. For a few minutes, he stood motionless with his eyelids heavy with unshed tears and his throat choked with a lump.

* * * *

A senior chanced to come that side. The misfit skulked away to a distant gangway. But the young undergraduate was still motionless, though his eyelids were now nearly dry and his throat, clear.

"Can I help you?"

"Ye-es, please, if you can. I want Chesterton's letters."

"Chesterton's letters! Let us try the catalogue. Perhaps you are new to the library."

"Yes, sir."

"Never mind, I shall help you. You will soon learn these things. Here, you are. This is the index. Here you find the clue. The number for Chesterton is O:3M74. Let us now look at the classified part of the catalogue. Here it is. But we have no "Letters" of Chesterton."

"But my father recommended it."

"Look at this huge book. It is called the *Reference catalogue.* It mentions all the English books in print. Let us look into this and verify if such a book exists at all. . . . No, it does not exist."

"Thank you for your kindness. I have taken too much of your time."

"Never mind; I am only sorry I am not able to help you with the book you want. Are you sure of what your father mentioned?"

"Yes, sir. I am sure. He mentioned 'Chesterton's Letters to his godson'."

"Letters to his godson '. . . . ..to his godson'. . . .Can it be Chesterfield's Letters to his godson?"

"May be sir, I quite remember 'Letters to godson.' Perhaps

it is not Chesterton. . . . . It may be Chesterfield. Will you try?"

*   *   *   *

"You were right, sir. It was Chesterfield. When I took the book home my father was very pleased. He read it with me once. Then I read it over again all by myself. The whole of last week, I had been enjoying it."

"I am glad, you had what you wanted."

"May I go into that room where books are kept?"

"Yes, certainly. Why should you have any doubt?"

"Will he be there?"

844 Right Philosophy

There is no greater sin than scaring away readers. Some are endowed by nature herself with such unsocial and detestable qualities as to make them permanently unfit for any job involving contact with the public. Reference service depends ever so much on the geniality, self-effacement, and untiring energy of the reference librarian. Nobody should be recruited to the reference section without a thorough test by one with experience of reference service and its requirements. That is the right philosophy. No extraneous consideration, political, or personal, should set it aside.

85 Group Qualities

The stuff of which the staff is made, the relations of the staff, and the staff atmosphere will affect very intimately the service of the library. If these relations are bad, neither good buildings, nor good collections, nor efficient methods will be of use

The members of the staff should be on the most cordial terms among themselves. There should not be the least trace of jealousy or envy. Self should be suppressed. Every member should be prepared to pass off all work as anonymous. Maeterlinck's picture of the work in the bee-hive [M3] contains the most vivid and accurate description of the spirit, necessary in the reference staff, in order to function with maximum efficiency.

86 Coming to Terms with Books

We have to try one other thing. We should try to understand books. We should come to terms with them as much as with the readers. Perhaps this requires a much greater determination because the readers, being of our species, can participate with us in understanding one another. It may be that they appear to rub us on the wrong side; but even that will ultimately prove to be a good in disguise.

861 Muteness of Book

But the books are mute. They are not participative as the readers. Compared to readers, they are rigid. It looks as if either we understand them or we do not. There does not seem to be much scope for diplomacy, tact, or negotiation in the ordinary sense. All preparation to come to terms has to be totally on our side. Even the move for finding peacemakers has to originate from us. Their ultimate choice also falls entirely on our shoulders.

862 Split Mind

Still it is as necessary to know the books as it is to know the readers. It is no longer sufficient to know their backs. To establish contact between reader and book in a personal way, we must know each party intimately. Reference librarians have to understand books not for their own sake. Perhaps nobody does so. Nor have they to understand books for the direct personal use of the knowledge brought by understanding them. The readers understand them for that purpose. Reference librarians have to understand them in relation to their users—present and prospective. In fact as the eyes of a reference librarian race through the pages of a book, his mind has to split itself into two. One part has to be told to receive and assimilate what the eyes draw from the book. The other part has to be kept sweeping the world of readers to find out individuals or classes—with whom contact could be established. Still the acquaintance to be cultivated by the reference librarian with the world of books has to be as intimate as for those who put them to direct use. For, when he is face to face with a reader, his mind has again to be split into two. One part is to be told not only to record, associate, and integrate what the eyes and ears pick up from him, but also to psycho-analyse him. If the reader were an extrovert, this part of the mind of the reference librarian should keep him in good humour by engaging him in a pleasant way till his book is found. All the while, the other part of the mind of the reference librarian has to be wandering among the books to pick out those which will fit the reader best. Thus it looks as if the reference librarian can at no time give away his whole mind to books. However much he may throw the blame for this on the nature of his work, he should always be on his guard against the revenge which the books may spring upon him for such divided attention. They may escape re-collection if the acquaintance he made with them during the physical absence of the readers had not been intimate and thorough.

863 Medium Size Library

This business of coming to terms with books is most burdensome in medium size libraries. In small libraries the new books come in small numbers. They are usually very little varied. The reference librarian can therefore manage them individually without much strain. Big libraries will have an army of reference librarians. Hence, in spite of the number of their weekly accessions being formidable, and the range of knowledge covered by them being vast, the strain on each individual reference librarian can be kept within comfortable bounds by a balanced scheme of specialisation. A reference librarian of a medium sized library, on the other hand, does not have either of these advantages. He has to undergo all the ordeals of the proverbial man between two stools.

864 Potent Danger

He has to be conscientious. He should, without any prompting from outside, persist in getting a mastery of the documents with which he has to serve readers. He has to attain a high pitch of awareness and industry. Otherwise, the necessary intimacy with the books cannot be got.

Result: A low tone of reference service, poor opportunity to win the good will of readers, low chance for strengthening the staff to raise the tone, and in effect, heading towards increasing inefficiency and inanity. That is the potent danger.

865 Preventive Measure

The only means of averting the danger: Hard work, long hours, sincere effort, and a high pitch of awareness of the books coming in and of the interests of the readers. That is the only preventive measure.

Part E

Mystic Picture of Reference Service

CHAPTER 1

INTRODUCTION

11 Purpose-Complex of Library

A library is a social institution. It is a multi-purpose social institution. Some of the many purposes in its purpose-complex are:

1 To serve as social memory; and for this purpose,

2 To assemble, organise, preserve, socialise, and serve all expressed thought embodied as manuscripts, books, periodicals, their constituent documents, however minute, and every other similar document produced as a means for communication; and by this means,

3 To help in the transmission of the knowledge of the earlier generations to the later ones; and by this means,

4 To help in the cumulation and the further building up of knowledge from generation to generation; and in a similar way,

5 To help in the contemporary development of knowledge without any wastage in the building of knowledge, by the unintended and purposeless repetition of effort and the consequent wastage in the research-potential of humanity; and further,

6 To conserve the research time of humanity by the separation of literature-search from positive research; and also

7 To help in the perpetual self-education of one and all; and further,

8 To collect together all available recorded information — particularly in the form of reference books, and to socialise and serve freely all such information to each according to his needs at the moment; and by all such means

9 To increase the economic resources of humanity to the extent necessary to maintain the ever-increasing population, in comfort and free from want of any kind; and also

10 To help in the mutually understanding, mutually co-operating, and mutually tolerant peaceful co-existence of individuals, communities, and nations; and further

11 To help in the elevating, self-dependent use of leisure with the aid of freely served books, pictures, sound records, and other similar materials; and also

12 To help in increasing the opportunity for the spiritual awakening of one and all of the members of humanity.

12 Medium for the Achievement of the Purpose-Complex

The medium normally available to a library, for achieving the several purposes in its purpose-complex, is the printed document. It may be in the form of pictures, diagrams, and record of expression in a language. The dominant form is record of expression in a language. The record is in the form of phonetic symbols. Each primary symbol represents only a phoneme or a primary sound.

13 Primacy of Literacy

For the library to achieve its several purposes, through recorded medium, the people should have the capacity to read by reflex action the complex of phonetic symbols constituting a document. This capacity is literacy, in its elemental sense. The library may, as a temporary expedient, achieve some of its purposes by engaging literates to read out to illiterates. But, the normal and convenient method is to serve literates. The primacy of literacy in the well-being of society is now beyond question. Dandin, a literary critic of medieval India, clinched this idea in the epigram,

Literacy is the Cow giving anything wished for.
गौ: गौ: काम-धुगा ।

14 Primacy of the Library

Granting universal literacy, what is the next need in the scale of primacy? Library giving free service. The nineteenth century librarian, Melvil Dewey, clinched this idea by a pun on "A L A". It is the initionym of the "American Library Association". Dewey officiated at the foundation of that Association. It was in 1876. At that time, he punned on its initionym, expanding it into "Ask Library Anything".

15 Oversimplification

But the epigram of Dandin and the pun of Dewey, however picturesque, were oversimplifications. Literacy may be necessary. But it is not sufficient. By itself, no phoneme has normally any semantic significance. An intelligible combination and permutation of phonemes alone can convey a concept. To convey a complex of ideas—and this alone counts—a combination of words into sentences, a combination of sentences into paragraphs, and a combination of paragraphs into a whole piece of composition are necessary. Reading a document is not by itself equivalent to absorbing its thought-content. Over and above this, documents—*qua* documents—create difficulties of their own. This has been illustrated in chapters 3 to 7 of part D. It will be further illustrated in part H. Again the organisation of the documents in a library and the organisation of the library itself create several additional difficulties of their own. This has been shown in part C.

16 Too Many Factors

Thus, the number of factors causing difficulties and the number of difficulties themselves, standing in the way of the full benefit flowing from a library to one and all, are too many. The intellect can analyse them. It can prescribe the means to get over each difficulty severally. But a combination of several difficulties cannot be got over by the mere combination of the respective means of getting over each component difficulty. This is a familiar experience in life. The problem of Three Bodies in dynamical astronomy indicates this. So it is in all situations. The library situation is no exception.

17 Primacy of Personal Help

The presence of too many difficulties makes personal help to readers a necessity. A new class of specialists has to be formed to pull readers through the complex of difficulties. This special class of specialists are the reference librarians. A reference librarian too cannot do his best by intellectual training alone. No doubt, a good intellectual grind is necessary as a start. But, it is not sufficient to meet all situations. Ultimately, it is all a matter of flair, we say. What is flair. It is a subconscious solution found for getting over difficulties. There is perhaps the help of a dash of intuition. Flair is an intensely personal quality. It has to grow in an individual. Some may be borne with it. It transcends analysis with the intellect. It transcends mechanisation. It transcends even standardised thinking. The personal help of a reference librarian, with an abundance of flair, is often necessary to make the library achieve its complex of purposes, social and individual.

18 Entity-Dependent Comprehension

In this book, reference service is described intellectually. It is analysed by intellect. Chapters 3 to 6 of part F and of part J are typical of such analysis. Each of them brings out Preparation, Service, and Assimilation as the major or first-order clumps resulting from the break-down made by the analysing intellect. This is no doubt a convenience provided by the atomising intellect. But, in reality, it distracts attention from the wholeness of reference service. Indeed, reference service is ineffable. Its details are inexhaustible. Its aroma is indescribable. It is intangible. It is the wholeness of the reference work that does the work. But its whole picture is beyond the intellect. Still more so, it is beyond the senses initiating and feeding the work of the intellect.

181 Testimony of the Vedic Mystics

The Vedic mystics of India used the term 'Comprehender-Dependant' to denote comprehension mediated by the senses and the intellect. It is 'Kartru-Tantra' in Sanskrit. Comprehender-dependant comprehension is an artificial construct by the intellect. It is only partial. It is not the total comprehension of the entity — that is, thing or concept — in its entirety or wholeness. The mystic's comprehension is direct. It is unmediated by the senses or the intellect. The Vedic mystics of India used the term 'Entity-Dependant' to denote such a direct comprehension of the entity as a whole. It is 'Vastu-Tantra' in Sanskrit. Entity-dependant comprehension is that of the entity in its pristine wholeness. Because of his capacity for the direct comprehension of the whole entity, a mystic is called a 'Seer'. The term means 'one able to see rightly and fully and not partially'. A true poet is a seer or a near-seer.

182 Mystic's Communication

But the mystic's whole comprehension is not easily communicable to an intellectual. For the language, meaningful to an intellectual, is itself an intellectual construct. It is naturally fitted only to communicate the intellect's partial comprehensions of an entity. At best, it can give only a series of partial comprehensions, even as a cinema reel does when viewed in a still state.

183 Testimony of a Modern Mystic

This explains Sri Ramakrishna's saying that the words fail him in communicating his whole experience gained in his state of *samadhi.* This is the state in which the senses and the intellect are totally by-passed and pure intuition or mystic vision is in full play and comprehends entities in themselves as wholes.

184 Testimony of a Poet

This explains also the statement of poet Goethe that a divine language is necessary to communicate the mystic and whole experience of a poet. 'Divine language' means language other than and transcending the ordinary language of intellectual construct.

185 Medium of the Mystic

Therefore, the words of a poet, a mystic, or a seer are charged with undertones and overtones. His words are scintillating. He uses analogies. He uses word-pictures of profound qualities. His words, his analogies, and his word-pictures appear to struggle to communicate the whole in itself and by itself. Their suggestions are endless. They admit of layers and layers of meaning, without end. Each ordinary reader is, thereby, enabled to have a peep into a layer, just below the level of his unaided intellectual comprehension of an entity.

186 Seminal Quality

A truly mystic communication in word-picture stems from the seminal level. At the seminal level, many entities of the phenomenal level coalesce. In other words, a picture drawn at the seminal level can manifest itself in a variety of forms at the surface level. It can truly represent and communicate several phenomenal entities. Therefore, the same word-picture of a poet, a mystic, or a seer can yield a fuller comprehension of different entities when viewed in different subject-contexts. That is why a profound mystic text, such as the Vedas, admits of nearly consistent interpretation, as if it were at once a text on each of several subjects, such as Library Science, Astronomy, Geology, Anatomy, Music, Psychology, Education, History, Political Science, Economics, Sociology, or Law. It is not credulousness that reads a variety of communications in mystic utterances. A variety of communications is inherent in mystic word-pictures.

187 Full Picture of Reference Service

It may, therefore, be of value to reproduce here some mystic word-pictures, admitting of being taken as if they were word-pictures of reference service—its purpose, its emphasis on personal or individual service, the qualities to be developed by a reference librarian, his preparation internally within himself, his preparation in relation to documents, his devotion to service without flirting with fruits, and above all his geniality and his sharing with readers their problems, their struggle, and their ultimate joy of achievement. The succeeding chapters of this part make mention of some mystic word-pictures admitting of interpretation from the angle of reference service.

CHAPTER 2

LIGHT FROM THE VEDAS

The reader-guest is supreme to you.

Give him service with all attention and in all sincerity.

Give him service to the entire capacity at your command.

Give him service in all modesty and in full freedom from any touch of prestige or ego.

Give him service in full measure lest there should be any offence to the Laws of Library Science.

Acquire the best of knowledge and information for giving him in your service.

This is the import of some of the passages in the Vedas. These passages occur in the Taittiriya-Upanishat [T4]. Their obvious context is the exhortation given to a student completing his course of formal studies and entering life. But they equally fit in as an exhortation to one practising as a reference librarian. Here are the passages in Sanskrit:

अतिथि देवो भव ।

श्रद्धया देयम् ।

श्रिया देयम् ।

ह्रिया देयम् ।

CHAPTER 3

LIGHT FROM VALMIKI

31 Satisfying Specific Want

In the *Ramayana* of Valmiki, there is a word-picture of the entertainment of king Visvamitra and his retinue by sage Vasishta. The sage invokes his Cow. She could give him anything wished for.

O! Potency in perfection!
Come, come immediately and listen.
O! Cow giving anything asked for,
The result of all my penance,
Shower forth expeditiously unto each
All that each individually wants
From all the best in the six-fold essence [V2].

एहि एहि शबले क्षिप्रं श्रृणु च अपि वचो मम ।
यस्य यस्य यथा कामं षड्सेषु अभिपूजितम् ।
तत् सर्वम् कामधुक् क्षिप्रं अभिवर्षं कृते मम ।

32 Ideal of Reference Service

The ideal of reference service is pictured here. The collection in the library should have copies of all the documents created. It should be able to give any information or knowledge sought. Its organisation should be perfect. Its potency for service should be supreme. It should be easy to select whatever is of the highest value. The instant a reader calls, all that can satisfy his specific want should be given to him expeditiously, exhaustively, and in plenty.

33 Detailed Picture

There is another word-picture, in the same work, of the entertainment of prince Bharata and his retinue by sage Bharadvaja [V4]. It gives a more detailed picture of the plenty to be provided in a library and the variety to be provided in it. It gives also an elaborate account of the requisites in a library: A charming setting with flower trees and a green lawn, pleasant rooms, comfortable seats, sweet mellow composing hum of music, bright genial persons here there, and everywhere, offering hospitality to one and all. All this paints the ideal atmosphere for a library meant to give mental treat to all visitors. An interesting detail in the description concerns the attention to be paid to the visitors. Some are attended to individually. Some others are attended to in groups of seven or eight. It all depends on the needs of the various visitors. All this points to the ideal to be reached in the rendering of reference service.

34 Four-Fold Attributes

The main theme of the *Ramayana* is the descent of God as humans amidst humans, for cleansing the hearts and minds of the humans and establishing peace and order in the world. God appears as the four sons of king Dasaratha. The sage Vasishta, the premier and the high priest of the kingdom, names them Rama, Bharata, Lakshmana, and Satrugna respectively. These names admit of allegorical interpretation.

341 Satrugna

Satrugna denotes the control of the inner enemy—the little ego. This little ego is the root of selfishness. It makes one do the least and seek the most. It disables one from sailing on the steam of one's own conscience. Therefore one under its spell shirks work behind the screen. It makes one anything, if at all, to have limelight turned on oneself Therefore, the little ego should be constantly and vigilantly controlled.

342 Lakshmana

Lakshmana denotes service. It is service for its own sake. It is not service coupled with flirting with fruits. It is service without expecting any reward. Nor does it allow of accepting even a reward thrust on one. Lakshmana had served Rama through thick and thin in the worst of days. On the turn of good days, Rama offers him the position of being his deputy as king. But, he declines it firmly and without any hesitation.

343 Bharata

Bharata denotes patient, silent, persistent bearing of burden. In the *Ramayana*, he is marked out for the temporary task of rescuing and cleansing the people of the kingdom from the ills of continued prosperity and affluence. He is asked to bear the burden of the state. Though knowing that he will be at the head of the kingdom only during the fourteen years of Rama's exile, he accepts the call. He shuns pomp; he does not put on any symbol of royalty. He is ideally efficient in administration. The wealth of the state increases ten-fold. But, the moment Rama returns from exile, he steps out quietly in full joy. He is reticence incarnate. The poet describes him as "deep as the ocean." He talks little. Satrugna is his constant companion.

344 RAMA

Rama denotes geniality, charm, accessibility, helpfulness, and modesty *par excellence* and competence of the highest order. He shuns formality and prestige. He mixes with people freely. He puts them at ease by voluntarily opening conversation. And yet, he is measured in his talk. He is equable in temper. He is equally unperturbed by joy and sorrow. He is free from attachment to anything. And yet he is efficient and thorough in all his work. He is liked by all. He is sought by all. Lakshmana is his constant companion.

35 Model for Reference Librarian

A reference librarian has models for himself in this four-fold picture painted by Valmiki. He must emulate Bharata in hard work sailing on the steam of his own conscience and in knowing thereby every document in the library, so as to make the library yield ten times more result than it would otherwise. This he must do, not for his own private purpose, but for the good of others. To be able to live such a life, he must emulate Satrugna in continually controlling the little ego in him. He should emulate Lakshmana in serving readers efficiently and without any eye on reward or praise or even a word of approbation. He should emulate Rama in geniality, charm, ease of accessibility, freedom from any sense of prestige, equableness of temper, love and respect for readers, willingness to share their problems, their difficulties, and the joy coming on them with the solution of the problems and, above all, in attaining competence of a high order.

CHAPTER 4

LIGHT FROM THE "MOTHER" OF AUROBINDO

41 Trinity in Library

A library is a trinity made up of books, readers, and staff—particularly the reference staff. We have a library only at the moments of all the three factors standing integrated. The reference staff are the power mediating between reader and book and stimulating integration.

411 Attention to Reader

While on floor duty the reference librarian should not look up to men because of their riches or allow himself to be impressed by the show or the power of their influence. His attention to the reader should be conditioned not by any of these factors but by the extent of effort necessary for effecting contact between reader and book.

412 Self-Giving

All stain of egoistic choice, of hankering after personal profit, and of self-regarding desire must be extirpated from him while effecting contact between reader and book. There must be no demand for fruit and no seeking for reward; the only fruit is the fulfilment of establishing contact between books and readers; the only reward is a constant progression towards the attainment of the ideals set up by the Laws of Library Science. The reference librarian should allow nothing to creep in to stain the purity of the self-giving. His only object in action should be to serve, to fulfil, and to become a manifesting instrument of the Divine *Sakti* in her works. There must be no pride of the instrument, no vanity, no arrogance. The books constitute *Purusha* as *Akshara Brahma* (= scriptal form of God). The readers constitute *Prakriti* manifesting itself as *Manushya Prakriti* (= human manifestation of nature).

42 Cosmic Trinity

Truly, the part of the reference librarian is not unlike that of *Sakti* in the Trinity,

1 *Purusha* = The Divine Unmanifest;

2 *Prakriti* = Nature standing in need of enrichment by *Purusha*; and

3 *Sakti* = The Energising Principle activating the descent of *Purusha* on to *Prakriti* and the ascent of the latter to the former.

The *Purusha* seeks fulfilment in enlivened *Prakriti* and the consummation of the *Prakriti* consists in realising *Purusha*. The descent of *Sakti* on *Prakriti* transmutes the latter. The sublimated *Prakriti* reaches out to the *Purusha*. *Sakti* uses the reference librarian as instrument. He should value this opportunity.

He should strive to acquire the necessary wisdom, strength, harmony, and perfection to function as an instrument of *Sakti*. The aspects of *Sakti* corresponding to these four attributes are *Maheswari*, *Mahakali*, *Mahalakshmi* and *Mahasaraswati* according to Indian tradition. The following description of these four aspects of *Sakti* extracted from Sri Aurobindo's *Mother* gives an idea of the ideal to be sought by the reference librarian. [A10]

43 Maheswari (Wisdom)

She is the mighty and wise, one who opens us to the treasure house of knowledge. Tranquil is she and wonderful, great and calm for ever. Nothing is hidden from her that she chooses to know. A strength is in her that meets everything and masters. She deals with men according to their nature. Partiality she has none. To the wise she gives a greater and more luminous wisdom; those that have vision she admits to her counsels; the ignorant and foolish she leads according to their blindness. In each man she answers and handles the different elements of his nature according to their need and their urge and the return they call for, puts on them the required pressure and leaves them to their cherished liberty. For the truth of things is her one concern, knowledge her centre of power and to build our soul and our nature into the divine Truth her mission and her labour.

44 Mahakali (Strength)

There is in her an overwhelming intensity, a mighty passion of force to achieve, a divine violence rushing to shatter every limit and obstacle. She is there for swiftness, for the immediately effective process, the rapid and direct stroke, the frontal assault that carries everything before it. When she is allowed to intervene in her strength then in one moment are broken the obstacles that immobilise it or the enemies that assail the seeker. She is loved and worshipped by the great, the strong and the noble; for they feel that her blow beat what is rebellious in their material into strength and perfect truth, hammer straight what is wrong and perverse and expel what is impure and defective. But for her what is done in a day might have taken centuries. To knowledge she gives a conquering might and imparts to the slow and difficult labour after perfection an impetus that multiplies the power and shortens the long way. It is by grace of her fire and passion and speed if the great achievement can be done now rather than hereafter.

45 Mahalakshmi (Harmony)

She throws the spell of intoxicating sweetness of the Divine; grace and charm and tenderness flow out from her like light from the sun and wherever she fixes her wonderful gaze and let fall the loveliness of her smile, the soul is seized and made captive and plunged into the depths of an unfathomable bliss. Magnetic is the touch of her hands and their occult and delicate influence refines mind. The world's riches are brought together and concerted for a supreme order and even the simplest and commonest things are made wonderful by her intuition of unity and the breath of her spirit.

46 Mahasaraswati (Perfection)

She is *Sakti*'s Power of Work, and her spirit of perfection and order. The youngest of the four, she is the most skilful and nearest to physical nature. She presides over the details of organisation and execution, relation of parts and effectual combination of forces and unfailing exactitude of result and fulfilment. The science and craft and technique are her province. Always she holds in her nature and can give to those whom she has chosen the intimate and precise knowledge, the subtlety and patience, the accuracy of intuitive mind and conscious hand and discerning eye of the perfect worker. This power is the strong, tireless, the careful and efficient classifier. Her action is laborious and minute and often seems to our impatience slow and interminable, but it is persistent, integral and flawless. For the will in her works is scrupulous, unsleeping and indefatigable; leaning over us she notes and touches every little detail, finds out every minute defect, gap, twist or incompleteness. Nothing is too small or apparently trivial for her attention. In her constant and diligent arrangement and re-arrangement of things her eye is on all needs at once and the way to meet them and her intuition knows what is to be chosen and what rejected and successfully determines the right instrument, the right time, the right conditions, and the right process. When her work is finished, all is solid, accurate, complete, admirable. She is ready to face an eternity of toil if that is needed. Therefore of all the Mother's powers she is the most long-suffering with man and his thousand imperfections. Kind, smiling, close and helpful, not easily turned away or discouraged. A mother to our wants, a friend in our difficulties, a persistent and tranquil counsellor and mentor chasing away with her radiant smile the clouds of gloom, fretfulness and depression, reminding always of the ever-present help.

47 Source of Inspiration

Such then are the attributes of the four aspects of *Sakti*. These should inspire the reference librarian in his reference service. This inspiration should embrace both his external doings and inner adjustment. The inner adjustment is that of self-discipline and self-perfection. It should help him to get illumined knowledge, to lose himself in universal love and delight, and to establish himself in supreme self-mastery and all-mastery. Perfection will come with the advent of the feeling of his being an eternal portion of the consciousness and force of *Sakti*, the being of her Being, the force of her Force and the ananda of her Ananda. When this condition is entire, knowledge, will, and action will become sure, simple, luminous, spontaneous, and flawless, and an outflow from the Supreme.

CHAPTER 5

LIGHT FROM SANSKRIT

51 Granthālaya

In Sanskrit, merging is denoted by 'laya'. And 'ālaya' denotes perfect merging, integration, at-one-ment. It can also mean merging to the limit of the achievement of the purpose sought. 'Grantha' denotes expressed thought or work. The term for library is therefore 'grantha-ālaya', coalesced in to the form 'granthālaya'. Semantically, it means the merging of mind and grantha to the limit of the achievement of,

1 Enrichment of memory;
2 Elevation of emotions;
3 Stimulation of intellect;
4 Increase of knowledge; and
5 Release of intuition.

It can also mean the total set-up helping such a merging of mind and grantha.

52 Pustakalaya

A derived degenerate meaning of 'ālaya' is the point marking off the end of merging—the place of total merging. Moving a little further, it means the abode of the entity to be merged. A place cannot be the abode of mere grantha or expressed thought. Because, it is abstract, and place is concrete. To make it abide in a place, the expressed thought should be embodied. The physical embodiment of grantha is denoted by 'pustaka'. It is the Sanskrit equivalent of 'book'. Combining it with 'ālaya' in the sense of place, we get 'pustakālaya'. The term denotes 'library' in its Chaucerian sense of 'place for keeping books'. (*See* sec 22 of part B.)

53 Granthālayi

'Granthālayi' denotes a person helping in the merging of mind and grantha to the point of achievement of enrichment of memory, elevation of emotions, stimulation of intellect, increase of knowledge, and release of intuition. To be of efficient help in this, the granthālayi has to use many techniques. He should keep continuously sharpening them. These include organisation, administration, classification, cataloguing, personal help in the choice of granthas pinpointedly, exhaustively, and expeditiously, and service of the granthas chosen. Thus, the sanskrit term 'granthālayi' is more expressive than the term 'librarian'. 'Library Science' has 'Granthālaya-Sastra' as its equivalent in Sanskrit.

54 Pustakālaya-Pala

The term 'pustakālaya-pāla', or 'pustaka-pāla,' or 'granthālaya-pāla', or 'grantha-pāla' can at best mean only the protector of books. It may also mean the janitor of the library. In 1959, I saw in the Lenin Library in Moscow, two sets of persons constantly moving in all the parts of the library—the stack-room, the reading rooms, and all the other rooms. They were the security police and the men of the fire brigade. Their duty is to protect the books. The term 'grantha-pāla' or any of the others of its set can only denote a security man and the man of the fire brigade on duty in the library. They are all necessary in a library. But they are not librarians. None of them is a granthālayi. They all protect only the abode of granthas —the books—and the abode of the books—the library.

55 Anu-Laya-Sevi

The term to denote 'reference service' is 'anu-laya-seva'. It is a truly expressive term. Its semantic significance is 'service in the merging (of works, granthas) in the sense expressed in section 51, by working with the reader and not on the reader. The prefix 'anu' emphasises respect to participativeness with the reader. It emphasises also full respect to the 'individuating particularities' of each reader, as William Blake would put it. It thus expresses every element emphasised in the preceding chapters while describing reference. The term to denote reference librarian readily follows. It is 'anu-laya-sevi'—a truly expressive term.

Part F

Ready Reference Service

CHAPTER 1

WHAT OF READY REFERENCE SERVICE

11 Time Test

Ready reference service is reference service finished in a very short time—in a moment if possible. In other words, time is of the very essence of ready reference service. Usually the section of a library, specialising in it, is called Information Desk. This term emphasises an aspect of it; the staff meets an enquirer face to face and answers his enquiry immediately.

12 Source Test

It is usual to describe ready reference service as Fact-Finding service or Information Service. The published source normally used in ready reference service is a reference book of one kind or another. It is not planned to be read through like an ordinary book. It is expected to arrange small slices of information in its concerned field, in a way admitting of easy location and ready reference. The stock of reference books in a library is often supplemented by its file of ready reference cards. Each such card usually contains the information hunted out from diverse sources in the course of long range reference service. But the reference books form the main sources for ready reference service. They are described in Part G of this book.

13 Nature of Library

To fill up the details in the picture of the what of ready reference service one approach is from the side of the enquirer. Perhaps it is more appropriate to call it the side of the dominant type of enquirer. He will vary with the nature of the library. Hence, it is helpful to approach the question from the side of the nature of the library. From the point of view of ready reference service, we may recognise three classes of libraries:

1 Business library;
2 Academic library; and
3 Public Library.

14 Business Library

Business libraries include commercial libraries, industrial libraries, and libraries of the Departments of a Government. Their main function is to furnish information either on demand or in anticipation. The furnishing of information on demand is ready reference service. Finding information in anticipation is usually of the nature of long range reference service. The clientele of a business library are busy persons. They cannot find time to hunt up for information by themselves. Nor it is economical to make them hunt for information. Their time is all required in the pursuit of their specific business. The library department of a business house owes its genesis to a realisation of the need for a division of labour. Fact-finding or information-furnishing is the labour falling to the share of the library department. Thus, ready reference service in a business library is the furnishing of the exact information sought by the enquirer. He is, no doubt, a member of the business body. But his specific work lies elsewhere. In a business library ready reference service should not stop short of finding and serving out the exact information to the reader. It should not end merely with establishment of contact between the enquirer and the right book. The very economy of a business library rules out any such form of ready reference service. Thus business libraries demand an extreme form of ready reference service; they expect the reference librarian to go the whole hog.

15 Academic Library

At the other extreme we have the academic libraries. School, college, and university libraries constitute that class. We are here concerned with the majority of their clientele. They are the students. An important function of such libraries is the education of the students in the use of ready reference materials. They function as laboratories to learn the art of fact-finding by actual practice. Hence, stimulation of self-help is of the very essence of such libraries. The ready reference librarian should not import into such libraries the practice of business libraries. He should not himself find out facts for the enquirers. Doing so would amount to thwarting the very purpose of such libraries. In them, proper reference service would consist mostly of helping the enquirer to help himself. He must be lead by a chain of dextrous suggestions to the right reference book. He should thereafter be made to locate and abstract the requisite information by his own effort. It may not be out of place to take an active interest in the reader's pursuit of facts, without producing an impression of over-solicitude or undue curiosity.

151 Watt's "Dictionary" Incident
(*Case Study* 45)

A new research student wanted full information on cotton. He was started on Watt's *Dictionary of economic products of India*. He was not aware of the terms used, entry words in that dictionary being technical and not popular ones. Therefore, he looked up the 'C' volume. He was disappointed. At this stage, a suggestion was thrown to him about the desirability of first looking up the index volume.

There he picked up the reference "Cotton, Indian arboreous G. 382." He was perplexed for a while about the significance of the letter 'G'. Then he examined the set. Volumes 3 and 4 bore the letter 'G' on their spines. He pulled out volume 3. On opening page 382, he got 'Fishes.' Feeling embarrassed by this find, he tried volume 4, page 382. But this gave him 'India rubber.' Embarrassment gave place to disgust and impatience.

This was the right moment to give him further help. And so he was told about the significance of the numbers given in the index. They denoted the commodity numbers shown in the margins of the pages. They did not denote page-numbers. With this information, he again examined volume 3. But the last commodity-number in that volume was only 380. Volume 4 did give 382. But the commodity covered by it was "Chaulmugra oil". It was not "Cotton."

Now he was asked to read the prefaces to the several volumes. He was also helped to find the errata given in the preface to the last volume. It contained the following passage:

"The numerical references are to the series of numbers entered in the margin of the dictionary and commence afresh with each letter of the alphabet. . . . Attention has been drawn to the fact that an error runs through volumes III, IV and V of the dictionary when the consecutive numbers of Letters G and L, in passing from volumes III to IV and from volumes IV to V respectively, have been duplicated. . . . It is suggested that those who possess the uncorrected volumes should adopt a similar course making the first reference in volume IV, G.381 and in volume V, L.379. Reference to letters G and L in this index must be taken subject to the above erratum."

This passage led him to the equation

G.382 = Volume 4 G2.

At long last, he got his information. In the process, he learnt how to use this reference book.

152 Education in the Use of Reference Books

Suppose the enquirer was a member of the staff of a business library or a casual visitor to any kind of library. Then the proper form of ready reference service would have been to have traced the particular page for him. But in this case, the library in question was a university library. And the inquirer was a young graduate just then registered as a research student of the university. In his case the duty of the reference librarian was not merely to find out the fact for him; that was only secondary. The primary duty was to help him to educate himself in the use of this reference book among others. He would have to consult it frequently. Another duty was to make him realise the existence of dictionaries, differing in arrangement from the linguistic dictionaries. As an undergraduate, he would have been accustomed only to linguistic dictionaries.

153 Delicate Step

One may go to the extent of satisfying oneself whether the enquirer has got the right fact. This extreme step in ready reference service in an educational library is a delicate one. Only an experienced ready reference librarian can take that step without going beyond the limits of decorum. It should never be done in a way giving even the slightest occasion for the enquirer to suspect that the librarian doubts his capacity to find out facts correctly. If the manner of the librarian gives rise to such a feeling in the enquirer, it will lead to a very unpleasant reaction. If the enquirer is of an aggressive type, he may become rude. If on the contrary he is of a mild nature, he may become too shy to come to the library any longer for such help. Whether the ready reference librarian has acquired the necessary flair and is able to take this extreme step or not, the aim of ready reference service in an educational library is mainly, if not solely, the establishment of contact between the right reader and the right book.

154 Exception

However in a school, college, or university library all the enquirers may not belong to the category described above. Such a library will also be obliged to function as a business library in relation to the management. Perhaps, it may have to do so even in relation to the academic staff to some extent. Surely, it would be absurd for the ready reference librarian of a university library to refer his vice-chancellor to the *Who's who* when he urgently wants the address of a professor in some other university for completing a memorandum. So also it is doubtful wisdom to refer a teacher to the year-book when he wants a note to be sent to his class regarding some data suddenly required in the class-room. No doubt, it is quite possible for an unscrupulous member of the faculty to transfer to the shoulders of the reference librarian much of the load to be borne legitimately by himself. This is a delicate situation requiring tactful handling. It is better to err on the side of furnishing the actual information in doubtful or difficult cases.

16 Public Library

From the point of view of the what of reference service, a public library partakes of the nature both of a business library and of an academic library. Its clientele are made up of the entire public. Therefore, they are of a mixed variety. Experienced businessmen as well as immature students will turn up at the enquiry desk of a public library. Therefore, the ready reference service of a public library cannot be of a homogeneous type. For some enquirers the actual information will have to be found out. For others the proper thing will be to establish contact with the right kind of reference books.

161 Find Out the Fact

A lady might just step out of her car and ask for the address of an official of the town. She is best served by looking up the telephone directory and giving her the exact address. It may not be polite to ask her to help herself. Somebody has to send out an urgent telegram. He asks for telegraph rates. Perhaps the man at the reference desk can furnish that information even from memory. Surely, in such a case there is no need to pass the telegraph guide on to the enquirer, so obviously in a hurry. A trader may ask for the earliest date of sailing to Singapore, and he may not be interested in wading through the pages of the *Traveller's gazette*. It is not against the spirit of ready reference service to furnish the exact information in such cases, even in public libraries.

162 Simply Establish Contact

On the contrary, when the younger folk seek facts at the ready reference desk, it would be more beneficial to them if ready-made facts are not furnished. They might have been asked by their teachers to search for the facts as a piece of exercise — as a means of learning the use of reference books. The very purpose of their pursuit of the facts will obviously be lost, by the ready reference librarian straightaway dictating the information to them. In their case, ready reference service should really consist of eliciting from them in a heuristic way the path to be pursued by them and the reference books to be consulted by them, in order to arrive at the facts sought.

163 Burma-Shell Incident
(*Case Study* 46)

A young man came with a list of the following words:

Allergy	Debunk
Pathography	Nazism
Clambake	Pedology
Comintern	Safe period

Totalitarian

He wanted their meanings. He was suspected to be an addict to cross-word puzzle. Therefore, help was denied to him. He soon realised that he was misunderstood. Then he took pains to convince the reference librarian of the more serious purpose of seeking the meanings of these words. Then he was asked to consult the dictionaries. They occupied six bays of shelves in the reference collection in the reading room.

* * * *

"It is a very tiresome job. I have looked up several volumes. But these words are not all found."

"You must have patience, my dear young man."

"When I was at school my teacher told me that the people here in the library would help us readily in all such matters."

"Yes, it is true. But we only help you to help yourself."

"I want the meanings urgently. Will you please find out the meanings for me this time as a special case?"

"Why? What is the urgency? Do you want them in the next five minutes?"

"No, no. I can stay on till the library closes."

"Then, why don't you search for them yourself?"

"I want to be the first in finding out the meanings."

"What do you mean by 'first'?"

"Our officer has set this problem to several of us on the staff."

"Why?"

"He is an enthusiastic officer. He wants us to be ever increasing our general knowledge. He asks us to go to libraries and learn to use and enjoy books."

"But why has he set you these puzzles?"

"For several days he asked us to go to the library. But few of us did. We are all employed in the Burma-Shell Company. Now he has offered a prize to be given to the person, bringing the meanings of these words earliest."

"I see! I have no objection to find out the meanings on one condition. You should allow me to inform your officer of the exact extent to which you and I exerted ourselves in this matter."

"No, no. It is no good for me. Then he would not give me the prize."

"It is very interesting! Why does he do all that?"

"He wants us to learn the use of books."

"If I find out for you the meanings of these words, will it not defeat the very purpose of his setting these problems?"

"Yes, I quite see. It was really silly of me to have thought of this short-cut."

Then the young man was told that these words came into existence very recently and that he should look up the latest supplements to dictionaries or the latest editions.

164 Tact and Discretion

There may not be much harm in going a step further in the case of freshmen and helping them to understand the scope, arrangement and structure of the reference book to be used. But the ultimate location of the fact should be left entirely to the enquirer. Even mature people may have to be treated in this way under certain circumstances. Surely, when they are eager to help themselves, the ready reference librarian should not officiously thrust his services on them. On the other hand, his policy should be to avoid giving an opportunity to mature persons, having the leisure but being too idle to exert themselves, to exploit unduly his willingness to locate the facts sought. In fact, a good deal of tact and discretion should be used by the man at the enquiry desk of a public library in deciding the most appropriate form of ready reference service, suited to each enquirer. It cannot be reduced to a rule of thumb. It is a matter of flair. A wrong man at the enquiry desk may create for himself many embarrassing situations.

CHAPTER 2

WHY OF READY REFERENCE SERVICE

21 Introduction

In examining the what, some light has already been thrown incidentally on the why of ready reference service. However, it may be well to examine it *ab initio* in all its aspects. The answer to the why of ready reference service is best sought along three lines of enquiry. The history and the nature of reference books can be said to make ready reference service a necessity. The nature of the clientele of a library also contributes its quota. A still other consideration, justifying ready reference service, involves an examination of national economy.

22 Nature of Reference Book

221 Artificiality

A book itself is an artificial entity. But, a literate person gets accustomed to it from his school days onwards. Due to frequent use, familiarity wears out its artificiality in his case. A reference book has a higher order of artificiality. It is artificial even to a person, seeing no artificiality in an ordinary book. For unlike an ordinary book, a reference book is not planned to be read through. Further, educational institutions do not accustom the student to their higher degree of artificiality. Therefore, not only children, but even adults need aid from a reference librarian to know of the reference books. They also need help in making their way through the reference book and succeed in finding the information sought. For example, I left college in 1916. Till then, I had never been told about any general encyclopaedia. I was not an exception. Nor was my college an exception; it was one of the foremost colleges in the place. Eight years later, I became a librarian. My library was under the same roof as a much older public library. Here is a scene witnessed by me within a few days.

222 Encyclopaedia Incident

(*Case Study* 47)

A medical graduate, older than myself, became a city-father.

The water supply of the city was then a vexed problem. Cynics used to speak of it as 'Malony Mixture'. For, an officer of the Corporation of the City, Malony by name, was widely believed to have ordered the mixing of filtered and unfiltered water in order to meet the short supply of filtered water. The medical graduate had heard of the appointment of a university librarian. He therefore came to me for help. But, to my dismay, there was no book on the subject either in my library or in the other library under the same roof. I thought of the *Encyclopaedia Britannica*. But to my greater dismay, my library did not have it. But fortunately, the other library was said to have it. The medical graduate was, therefore, sent to that library.

"Please give me the *Encyclopaedia Britannica*."

"Which volume?", boomed a voice across the high counter-table. The medical graduate was puzzled. After some thought, he asked for the first volume to be brought for him. It did not shed any light on his problem. He then asked for the second volume. There also he drew nothing.

"Please give me the third volume," were the polite words of the medical graduate.

"How often am I to ascend up to the third tier?", shouted the giant sitting on the high throne within the counter-enclosure.

"Then bring all the volumes at once", pleaded the medical graduate.

"Am I made of steel to carry down all the 24 volumes?" was the thunder from the giant, reverberating from end to end of the long reading room.

There was no reference service in any library in those days. A library was manned mostly by persons with just the ability to read the backs of books.

223 Arrangement of Information

The arrangement of the information in a reference book varies widely and even wildly. It may be alphabetical at one extreme. It may be classified by subjects at the other extreme. Alphabetical and classified arrangement may be blended in any proportion. The arrangement may even be chaotic. Again the arrangement varies from one reference book to another. The arrangement is not similar even in similar reference books. Sometimes, the arrangement of the successive editions of the same reference book even is found to be different. In these circumstances, is it a wonder fo. the patience of the reader to run out completely before finding the information? But the helping hand of a reference librarian would enable him to travel through the reference book with profit. Even 'alphabetical arrangement' does not mean exactly the same arrangement in all reference books. No universal standard is possible for alphabetisation. It has to vary from language to language. Even within one and the same language, it is not easy to arrive at an agreed standard. All-through alphabetisation is one extreme. This was attempted in India as a standard. We have the Gestalt Arrangement at the other extreme [R63]. I had tried it out for some years. The helpful form appears to be somewhere between these two extremes. This was the finding of the Documentation Section of the Indian Standards Convention of 1957 [K1]. Readers feel puzzled by such varieties in alphabetisation. They long to lean upon ready reference service to wade through such varying alphabetical lists in order to get their information out of them.

224 Bombay Firm Incident

(*Case Study* 48)

A haughty Officer of the Indian Civil Service entered the library.

"I want the address of a firm. It is . . . ".

"Come along. Let us go to the reference shelf."

The latest volume of the *Asylum Press almanac and directory of Madras and Southern India (including Nizam's Dominions, Mysore, Travancore and Cochin)* was being pulled out.

"Of what use is it? I want 'Bombay'; and this is 'Madras'."

"Let us try it. Nothing is lost by trying."

"Your time and my time will be lost. I have a copy of this on my table. It does not give the address wanted by me".

"Is it so? It may perhaps behave better in the hands of a librarian! Let—me—try. . . . Here it is!"

"What a d—d fool I am! I tried and tried through all its pages. But I could not put my fingers on this page."

"No, it is no mistake of yours. The arrangement here is too involved and too inconsistent for any—shall I say—but a reference librarian!"

225 Entry Word

The entry word in a name-of-person puts another pitfall in the way of a reader looking up for information in a reference book. In the case of a name-of-person of a Western cultural group, some standard has come into vogue. The family name is used as the entry word. Even then, there is an appreciable percentage of multi-worded or compound family names, beyond the capacity of a reader unaided by a reference librarian. In the case of a name-of-person of an Eastern cultural group, — in a Hindu or a Muslim group — there is no standard to help a reader to an equal extent. The function of the successive words in a name-of-person varies from cultural group to cultural group. In some, the first word is the personal name. It is so in a Marathi name. In others, the last word is the personal name. It is so in a Tamil or Telugu name. Some have removable attachments. Others have irremovable attachments. Ayyar, Mudaliar, and Pillai are examples. Still others have both. What is a removable attachment in some name becomes an essential word in others. "Sastri" is such a word. "Sri" is another such word. The same name-of-person is put under different entry words in different reference books. All this is equally true in the case of names of corporate bodies. The entry sought may be missed by many a reader, if left unaided by a reference librarian.

226 Time Coverage

Another attribute of reference books calling for the help of a reference librarian concerns the focus in its time facet. Some begin their information from the farthest known period of antiquity and come down to their respective dates of publication. Some truncate this full range of time at both ends, to any degree chosen by them. Some others truncate it at any one end of the range only. This is true in the reference books in all subjects. A library gets at all times readers, not familiar with the period covered by the reference books to be used by them. Readers come across such pitfalls frequently in biographical reference books. A reader may look up the *Who's who* of the year for an account of a person dead long ago. He will go without his information but with bitterness against the reference book and the library itself, unless helped and made wiser by a reference librarian. As if to balance such a case, another reader may look up a retrospective biographical dictionary for an account of a living person. He too will go without his information but with bitterness against the reference book and the library itself, unless helped and made wiser by a reference librarian. The

British *Dictionary of national biography* is a reference book in point. The case study 118 given in section H211 illustrates the why of ready reference service, as viewed from the angle of the time coverage of reference books.

227 Subject Coverage

The varieties of subjects having reference books of their own are not well known to readers. Terms such as 'encyclopaedia', 'directory', 'yearbook', 'who is who', and 'atlas' bring to the mind of most of the readers 'generalia reference books' only. They do not expect corresponding reference books in subjects of small extension. The availability of more extensive, more ample, and more specific information in the reference books covering a single narrow subject only, than in generalia reference books, is not known to readers. There is therefore need for a reference librarian to put a reader on to the right reference book in the right specific subject. Some subjects involve a geographical facet. All reference books in such a subject do not cover the same country or region. Some cover the entire world. Some do not. Some cover only a particular country. Some others cover only a particular county or district. Many cover only a single city. And yet the title of many a reference book does not disclose the geographical area covered. This also proves to be a pitfal to many readers. The reference librarian has to help them through.

228 Account of Reference Books

Part H examines in some detail all such variations in reference books, in respect of arrangement of information, time coverage, and subject coverage. Students of Library Science should get a realistic sense of the matter by handling as many reference books as possible. They should study their peculiarities in respect of all their features. They should practise describing each reference book in a systematic way. A skeleton scheme for such a systematic description is given in chapter 8 of Part H.

23 Nature of Enquirer

We can get some more light on the why of reference service by approaching it from the side of the nature of the enquirer. From this point of view, the enquirers fall into the three groups.

1 Absentee enquirers;

2 Casual visitors; and

3 Regular customers.

Every one of these classes of enquirers makes ready reference service in a library necessary for a different reason. And all enquirers will fall into one or another of these three classes. Let us now examine the answer given by each of these classes to the question on hand.

231 Absentee Enquirer

2311 ENQUIRY BY TELEPHONE

The telephone is now a normal equipment of the enquiry desk in a library. And the furnishing of information on telephonic requisition is recognised as a legitimate duty of a library. No doubt practical convenience will rule out the use of the telephone for getting whole passages being read out or dictated. Only facts requiring a few words should be allowed to be sought through the phone. Now helping an enquirer, not present in the library, to help himself is out of the question. Therefore, a library should have a reference librarian to look up information on behalf of this class of absentee enquirers.

2312 NEWSPAPER OFFICE

Newspaper offices loom largest in this class of enquirers. The load of telephonic enquiry from the source is heaviest in the library in a metropolis. Here are some examples stimulated by the European war.

1 Can 'aerodrome' be used in the sense of 'airship'?

2 We have an astrological article on the course of the current war. The words 'cumbust' and 'trine' occur there. Are they approved 'astrological terms'?

3 Would you please locate for me some sumptuous information on the 'Maginot line'?

2313 GOVERNMENT DEPARTMENT

The government departments come next in order of frequency among telephonic enquirers in a library. Here are some examples.

1 The Board of Revenue is just working out the financial implications of the Tungabhadra Project. "What is the rupee equivalent of the Osmanic sicca?"

2 The Public Works Secretariat rings up for urgent attention.

It asks for the address of the American Institute of Radio Engineers.

3 The Speaker of the Legislative Assembly rings up for information regarding the legislatures of the world beginning their daily work with a prayer.

2314 PRIVATE ENQUIRER

Taken as a whole, private enquirers use the phone as often as the government and the newspaper offices. Here are a few examples.

1 I find the two following words occurring frequently in the newspapers this week. Can you let me know their correct meaning: Blitzkrieg and Weltanschauung.

2 I am reading a novel of Tagore in Hindi translation. Its title is *Ankh ki Khirkiri*. Is there any English translation of it?

3 I had conversation with some spirits on the ouija board this morning. A stranger spirit announced itself as Blanco White. According to him, one of his sonnets had been published. But his best had not been published. That was his grievance. He wanted to dictate it over the ouija board on a later day. Was there ever such a poet. If so when did he live?

2315 ENQUIRY BY POST

Another class of absentee enquirers is not on the phone; but they use the post. In a country like India libraries are as few as telephones. Therefore postal medium looms large in linking up absentee enquirers and libraries. As in the case of telephonic enquirers, postal enquirers too necessitate the maintenance of a reference librarian to locate the information on behalf of each correspondent and transmit it to him.

232 CASUAL VISITOR

Any library, well known for its service, is sure to attract casual visitors. In a well organised community of to-day, members are accustomed to look to their local libraries for information of all kinds. It, therefore, becomes almost a second nature of any person to call at the library of any place visited by him, to get his information. But, the Indian community has not yet been accustomed to a system of country-wide library service. Therefore, the habit of going to the library for information may not be perceptible in it. But, in our experience, most of the foreign visitors to Madras coming from Western countries, be it America or France or Germany or Russia or Czechoslovakia, invariably made a call at our library almost on the first day of their arrival. Various are the questions put by them. Some wish to look up a map of Madras, others wish to get a list of the historical spots and their location. Some ask for the gazetteers of the neighbouring districts; others ask for the names and addresses of the leading persons of Madras in the spheres of life of interest to them. A few spend some hours in the library pursuing some topic of local history or current local affair. Usually they want to equip themselves with all the necessary information as rapidly as possible before beginning to do the city. India too will, before long, become library-conscious. Then Indians too will appreciate and enjoy the value of a nation-wide net work of public libraries in their social economy. Then casual visitors to a library, from other places in India itself, will get considerably enlarged. They will even become dominant in number. Because any day the number of visitors to a town from within India will be far greater than that of foreign visitors. Surely there can be no question of a library including within its legitimate duty the work of educating such casual visitors in the use of ready reference material or in self-help of any kind. From the library point of view, the most economical way of serving such birds of passage is to make its reference staff feed them promptly with the exact information wanted. "Why should the local library feel obliged to do this kind of reference service for outsiders?", it may be asked. There is at least one answer to this question: Reciprocity. Do unto others as you would like to have it done to yourself, is a perfectly human motto. Hence the need for reference service to casual visitors too in all libraries open to the public.

2321 BUDAPEST TRAVELLER

(*Case Study* 49)

A European traveller called at the library at 10 A M on the very day of his landing at Madras. Whosoever came his way heard him utter the words:

"Parlez-vous Francais? Sprechen Sie Deutsch? Kya tum Hindustani bolte?"

Evidently he could not speak English. The word Hindustani made a member of the staff take the help of a Muslim peon on duty as an interpreter. But in no time the conversation took both of them beyond their depths. The traveller because his Hindustani vocabulary was too meagre to express anything beyond the elemental material requirements of a foreign tourist; the Muslim peon because his intellectual and literary equipment was too poor to follow the thought of the traveller. However, the peon was tactful enough to suggest to him that after 11 A M some members of the staff who could speak his language would turn up. "Accha" said the traveller and settled down in a chair.

* * * *

Eleven A. M. An experienced member of the reference staff came. He was immediately put on to the traveller. But he was soon staggered by the fluent French with which he was greeted and addressed. Not a syllable could be made out. Hence he asked the traveller in Hindustani to commit his requirements to writing. He did so. But his calligraphy was not easily deciphered. However something could be made out. He belonged to Budapest. He had programmed to stay in Madras for three days to prepare himself to tour South India. He would like to read French or German books on places like Mahabalipuram, Srirangam, and Madura.

He was started on *Larousse universel*, 2 t and Jouveau-Dubreuil: *Archaeologie de sud de l'Inde*, 2 t. Little by little he was led on to various other archaeological books and periodicals. The pictures in them instructed him where the language failed him. It was a pleasure to help him with fact-giving materials. He too expressed immense pleasure and gratefulness for the ready reference service given to him.

233 REGULAR CUSTOMER

2331 NEW CUSTOMER

In discussing the what of ready reference service we had indicated the extent to which even the regular customers, personally appearing at the enquiry desk, have to requisition the services of the ready reference staff. There is first the freshman. He is new to library apparatus of any kind. In particular, he is a stranger to ready reference books. He does not know the structure of most of them. He cannot readily size up their scope. He cannot evaluate the information contained in them without aid. It is the duty of the library to educate him in all these matters. After a few visits, a particular freshman may gain the ability to shift for himself without the help of the staff. But if the library is popular at all and if it does not rest on its oars until every person in its area becomes its regular patron, every day will bring its own quóta of freshmen. There must therefore be a full-timed ready reference staff to meet this perennial inflow of new comers.

The veteran visitors may ordinarily help themselves with the ready reference books. But on occasions, even the most considerate of them will be either hard pressed for time or will find themselves beyond their depths. In either case, the library should offer them the help of its ready reference staff. If the library is busy at all there is every probability for this class of readers adding their own quota to justify the maintenance of an enquiry desk manned by an adequate number of reference librarians.

24 National Economy

Justification for ready reference service can also be found on grounds of national economy. In any community the ready reference questions, brought to the library by its readers, are largely of a repetitive nature. There are certain patterns of questions arising quite often. Certain pieces of information become topical at certain moments. Even abstruse questions, requiring a carefully worked out chain of investigations, recur though at longer intervals. Let us imagine the absence of a ready reference staff. Then each enquirer will have to find out the same facts for himself, put forth all the necessary energy and spend over it all the necessary time. If we integrate the man-hours spent by a community in the course of any considerable stretch of time, the wastage of man-hours involved will be found to be very great. On the contrary, if we have a ready reference staff, any fact found for one reader once can be passed on to any other reader seeking it, without any additional expenditure of time either on the part of the staff or of the enquirer. It is immaterial from the community point of view whether the first man who spent the necessary time and energy to get at the fact was the enquirer himself or a reference librarian. But once the fact is got, the reference librarian can clinch it and keep it ever on the surface so that it can be passed on to every other seeker. It can function as the community's agency to pool together the results of all the ready reference efforts, no matter who the contributor was. From this point of view, the establishment of an enquiry desk manned by an adequate staff in all the important libraries of the community amounts to a measure of national economy.

241 WIDELY SOUGHT INFORMATION

Moments arise when the same fact is sought by quite a number of people in quick succession. At such moments it may not be possible for a library to produce enough copies of the necessary ready reference books to all the enquirers; nor is it an advantage to make every enquirer of the community go through the whole hog of dressing out the information for himself. It is distinctly conducive to general economy if there is a ready reference staff which can furnish by word of mouth the information so widely sought. Here are some examples:

2411 LUCAS ENQUIRY
(*Case Study* 50)

The morning newspaper announced the death of E V Lucas. The reference librarian immediately looked up the *Who's who*. He also began gathering together the books by and on Lucas. While assembling them, there was a ring on the telephone. One of the newspaper offices asked for some details about Lucas. Almost every other minute, there was a similar ring from other newspaper offices. All the newspaper offices were fed with the same information.

In the meantime the works of Lucas had all been assembled in a special shelf. In addition the following books on Lucas were also brought together with them:

1 Dilly Tante, *Ed. Living authors: a book of biographies.* P 235-236;
2 Gosse (E W). *More books on the table.* P 209-215;
3 Lucas (E V). *Reading, writing and remembering*;
4 Marble (A R). *Modern novel.* P 205-207;
5 Swinnerton (F A). *Georgian scene: a literary panorama.* P. 244-245; and
6 Waugh (A). *Tradition and change.* P 292-298.

A bibliography was rapidly stenciled. It included the following references not available in the particular library but perhaps obtainable in others:

1 Adcock (A). *Glory that was Grub street.* P 191-201;
2 Bennet (A). *Books and persons.* P 150-154;
3 Gosse (E W). *Books on the table.* P 103-110;
4 Hind (C L). *Authors and I.* P. 182-188;
5 Overton (G M). *Cargoes for crusoes.* P 212-231;
6 Schelling (E F). *Appraisements and asperities.* P 9-14; and

7 Walkley (A B). *More prejudice.* P 52-56.

As anticipated enquirers begain to pour in one after another for information about Lucas. As every possible preparation had already been made in anticipation, the crowd of enquirers was handled quite easily; and nearly everybody was given satisfaction.

2412 TWEEDSMUIR ENQUIRY

(*Case Study* 51)

One morning, a Reuter telegram stated that the condition of Lord Tweedsmuir, Governor-General of Canada, was serious. The most enterprising of the local newspapers immediately sent one of its representatives to the library to collect information about him. In addition to the *Who's who*, which equated him with John Buchan, the following three references were located:

1 Adcock (A St John). *Gods of the modern Grub street: impressions of contemporary authors.* P 43-50;

2 Dilly Tante, *Ed. Living authors: a book of biographies.* 2 columns; and

3 Johnson (R Brimley). *Some contemporary novelists.* P 183-192.

The first two books contained also a picture of Buchan. One of them was borrowed by the reporter for reproduction and quick return.

In the evening, news of his death had reached all the newspaper offices. Naturally, they all felt obliged to back the news with some biographical data. Some sent their reporters to the library; and others rang up for information. As every thing available in the library had been located and brought together earlier in the day at the instance of the enterprising newspaper, all the enquiries could be immediately disposed of. Thus the fruits of the labour of the ready reference librarian of the library reached the public that very night.

2413 BILDERBECK ENQUIRY

(*Case Study* 52)

James Bourdillon Bilderbeck was a local celebrity at Madras about the end of the last century. He was a professor and principal in the Presidency College, a government institution.

One afternoon the office of the Director of Public Instruction wanted details of his career. They were found in the *History of services of gazetted and other officers in the civil department serving in the Madras Presidency corrected up to 1st July* 1906 (the year of retirement of Bilderbeck). As the reference librarian began to read out from it, the man at the other end of the wire said:

"It is all too much for me to transmit. I shall ask the newspaper men to go to the library direct."

Quite a number of them came within the next few minutes. The office of the Director of Public Instruction had its own copy of this publication of the Government. But there was no reference librarian in that office. Nor was there any one with ready wit to look up that publication. But, it was almost a reflex action for our reference librarian to look it up.

2413 GIVING THE INFORMATION

In these three cases, nothing could have been gained by making every enquirer trace out the information for himself. The right thing to do was to place the ready-made facts in the hands of the enquirers on their arrival at the library.

242 CONVERSION OF LONG RANGE INTO READY REFERENCE

It may happen that some information requires prolonged investigation and search. In fact it should be classified with long range reference service. But if it is of topical interest, several inquirers will come for it in rapid succession. And the best way of serving them is to convert it into ready reference service and give the information outright without attempting to make them help themselves.

2421 BUCK ENQUIRY

(*Case Study* 53)

The award of Nobel prize for literature in 1938 to Mrs Pearl Sydenstricker Buck was the occasion for a rush of inquirers. The *Who's who in America* gave only four inches of information. Two other books were known to devote some pages to her.

1 Kirkland (W M) and (F). *Girls who became writers.* P 39-52.

2 Lawrence (M). *School of femininity.* P 311-318.

But these were not available in the library. However, the practice of the reference staff of perusing and mentally noting outstanding facts appearing in periodicals came to our rescue. It was recollected that some information about her had occurred in the *Wilson bulletin.* A search of its file disclosed that volume 6 (1931-32) contained six columns of biographical information with a picture and that volume

9 (1934-35) contained two more pictures. From the moment this reference was located, the problem changed over from long range to ready reference service.

2422 EDWARD VIII'S CASE

(*Case Study* 54)

King Edward VIII's abdication produced great pressure on the enquiry desk. It required some prolonged search to get some information on his abdication and "morganatic marriage." Ultimately the following books were found to be of some help:

1 *Encyclopaedia of the laws of England.* V 13. P 47-48. *Royal marriages.*

2 Halsbury. *Laws of England.* V 6. *Constitutional law.*

3 D'Auvergne (Edmund B). *Some left handed marriages, misalliances, irregular and secret unions of royalty.*

4 Cheiro, *Pseud. World predictions.*

5 Shaw (George Bernard). *Apple cart.*

After the references were located, this problem was converted into a ready reference one. For some days, the information was passed on merely by word of mouth.

243 LOCAL EVENT

In the above mentioned two cases certain world events led the reference staff to anticipate enquiries. They could complete the process of long range reference to face a stream of inquirers positively expected to come. Sometimes, a local event too may lead to a similar result. A long range reference service to an influential individual may induce several people to peruse the materials supplied to him. In that way also a long range reference service may later become ready reference service.

2431 RAJAGOPALACHARI INCIDENT

(*Case Study* 55)

There was an invitation on the librarian's table. According to it, Sri C Rajagopalachari, the Chief Minister, was to deliver the inaugural address of the Mathematical Association of the Presidency College.

The telephone made a tremendous noise. The librarian had to take up the receiver in hand:

"Have you got Pott's *Algebra*?"

"I have not heard of it."

"I am not surprised. It was a text-book half a century ago when I was at college."

"Is it so? In that case some of the older libraries in the city may have it. I shall try and let you know."

* * * *

"I have tried all the important public libraries. None of them has it."

"Did you try the Presidency College ?"

"No. To-day being Sunday its library is not open. But I know practically all the mathematical books of that college as I was once teaching mathematics there. I had never seen 'Pott's *Algebra*'."

"It is a pity. It was a beautiful book. It gave some interesting historical information about mathematics in ancient and medieval days."

"If you are interested in that kind of subject, perhaps I can give you some helpful material."

"I don't think anything can equal Potts. Don't trouble yourself."

"Why not you give me a chance? So much has been done in that field during the last fifty years."

"Is it so? But will it not be too much of a trouble for you?"

"Not at all. We are paid just to do such work. We are only sorry that people are not giving us opportunity to justify ourselves."

"In that case will you just prepare for me a select list of books on Hindu achievements in mathematics and send it on with two or three books of your choice?"

"Mathematics is a vast field; we have a good deal of literature? Do you want every branch to be covered?"

"Perhaps I wouldn't trouble you if it is so much".

"Excuse me. If I am not over-inquisitive, I presume you want this for your inaugural address day-after-to-morrow."

"Quite so! I wonder how you knew about it."

"I shall send you just one or two books to suit that purpose."

"Thank you. But perhaps it may be as well if you can send me the list which you mentioned."

* * * *

"The other day the Chief Minister addressed our Association. He said that you could give us quite a number of books on Hindu mathematics."

"Yes, here is a list. It gives the call number of every book. You may go to the mathematics gangway and look them up."

This recurred in the library for quite a number of days after the Chief Minister's inaugural address to the Mathematical Association. Thus the long range reference service of a sunday reverberated itself as ready reference service throughout the succeeding week.

CHAPTER 3

HOW OF READY REFERENCE SERVICE

31 Introduction

The questions what, why, and how are all only different facets of a single concrete experience. They are merely mental abstractions made habitual by the intellect's inherent urge to analyse and atomise. But, we should not allow the intellect to mislead us into a false belief. For the facets created by its atomisation are not independent entities. They do not exist in mutual exclusion. To change the figure, the what, the why, and the how are only fractional distillations into the atmosphere of conception. The holistic nature of the thing-in-itself is profound. We can never succeed in separating them out thoroughly. We cannot have a pure what, a pure why, and a pure how of ready reference service. The discussion of the what and the why of ready reference service is therefore charged with traces of the how of it. The how lies imbedded in it at various levels and in various associations, but always in a subordinate position. We shall now have it sifted and brought to the surface. We shall also give it our thought on its own primary right.

32 Three Processes

This we shall do by considering in succession three processes in the how, *viz*, preparation, service, and assimilation. Of these, preparation and assimilation are processes behind the screen. Service is the vital stage of the flowering and fruition of reference service in the open. The physical presence of the reader, or his voice through the phone, or his script sent from a distance are the vitalising factors. They fertilise and make ready reference service complete. But the reference librarian has to begin his preparation even before they arrive. And, even after the service is done, he has to continue the work of the assimilation of the results of contacting them and finding out their information. Thus assimilation and preparation take place largely in the presence of only the 'thought' of the readers. Further, they are convertible into one another.

33 Telescoping of the Stages

What is assimilation in relation to the past enquirers is also preparation in relation to the future enquirers. Moreover, the service itself contains preparation and assimilation in a latent or potential form. The stream of enquirers is continuous in a busy library. Therefore, the three processes will stand telescoped in actuality.

CHAPTER 4

PREPARATION FOR READY REFERENCE SERVICE

41 Classes of Preparation

Preparation for ready reference service falls into three classes. These classes correspond to three kinds of reference materials. They are,

1 New reference book;
2 New edition of a reference book; and
3 Fugitive material.

42 New Reference Book

New reference books come into the library from time to time by purchase, donation, or collection from heaps discarded elsewhere. The reference librarian should familiarise himself with each of them immediately on its arrival in the library. All the points discussed in the Part on the Nature of Reference Books should be borne in mind in this process. A novice may find this work uninteresting, boring, and almost impossible. But a reference librarian, with experience in contact with enquirers, will find it not only absolutely necessary but also absorbingly interesting. The greater the experience the greater will be the zeal for this kind of preparation. For, every item of information found in a book will recall to his mind the Ramu, the Seenu, and the Yogu as the fittest persons to be served with it at the earliest opportunity. Thus the preparation will get humanised and become pointedly purposive and, therefore, thoroughly enjoyable. After reaching this stage, preparation will become as involuntary as breathing.

43 Inner Urge

It will take time for the aspirant for reference librarianship to reach this stage. Till then, he should mobilise all his will and determination, and turn them on his work of familiarising himself with the reference books. Resentment is the ready shield usually improvised by ignorance. A new reference librarian should, therefore, beware of his proneness to misunderstand and misinterpret the solicitous suggestions of seniors. Where the staff is large, this devilish proneness will go to the extent of organising the never-do-wells and invoking trade-union tactics to thwart every chance for good sense to prevail. This state of affairs may even corrode a shaky senior. When his sound example has no effect on the new-comers, sullenness may set in on him. Ultimately, it tempts him to regress to the inaction and complacence of those very misfits under the fire of their cynicism of self-defence. There are instances of this happening even after several years of pleasant co-operation among the staff, as the result of a mischief-monger being thrust into the staff and deliberately egged on by the top-management itself to spoil the atmosphere. In such an extreme case, there may not be any means of preventing the spirit of the library perishing along with the reference service. But, normally the intensity of will to participate in the healthy life of reference service can avert such a tragic trend. There can be no effective external sanction to enforce on a reference librarian preparation of this kind. For, the reading public seldom knows its rights. From the very nature of things, it cannot anticipate the extent of help to be rendered to them by the reference librarian. It is particularly so in India at present. For, its adult population is not accustomed to receive help from libraries. Under these circumstances, the only incentive has to be the inner urge of the reference librarian himself to live up to his highest ideals.

44 New Edition of Reference Book

The second class of preparation for ready reference service consists of the work of skipping through the new editions of each reference book as and when they come. The reference librarian should acquaint himself with their outstanding new features. Various causes will introduce changes in a new edition. The march of events in the world at large is relentless; and a reference book has to introduce in its pages all the consequential changes. Accuracy of information is of the very essence of a reference book. Here we have to remember a factor in the organisation for the production of a reference book. It has to be produced on a grand co-operative scale. Hundreds and thousands of contributors and correspondents have to furnish revised data. All of them may not be equally alert. Some may not furnish their quota of information in proper time; and it may not be possible to hold up the issue of the revised edition for their sake. Thus all parts of the new edition may not be equally up-to-date. Often there may be "stop-press" appendices, incorporating late information. They should all be looked for and brought to attention. Again reference-book-production is an ever-growing art. New features are therefore continuously introduced from edition to edition. A large library will have to take many reference books. Therefore, this work of skipping through new editions will form a considerable element in preparation work. The details, featured in the standard for the description of a reference book, should be borne in mind and studied at the stage of preparation.

45 Fugitive Material

The third class of preparation for ready reference service is the maintenance of the cabinet of fugitive materials. Fugitive materials consist of newspaper-cuttings, magazine-clippings, loose prospectuses, folders, and similar ephemeral materials. These may be of value. Perhaps they may often prove to be the only source of information for the time being. They have to be located, collected, mounted whenever necessary, classified, filed in proper sequence, and periodically destroyed. This class of preparation assumes considerable magnitude in business and school libraries. With the back of the mind charged with the kind of questions of topical interest usually turning up at the enquiry desk, the requisite materials must be located by a perusal of newspapers and periodicals and by an alert look-out for folders and prospectuses. The materials thus collected must be expeditiously prepared and inserted into the appropriate folders.

451 Weeding Out

In a library manned by resourceful reference librarians, such fugitive materials will accumulate with uncanny rapidity. Unless periodically weeded out, the quantity may become an obstruction. Hence, this class of preparation should include a weekly or monthly review of the cabinet of fugitive materials and removal of out-of-date ones. This review is best done if coupled with the process of filing. For each new piece filed may suggest the old pieces to be removed because of their having become obsolete.

CHAPTER 5

SERVICE IN READY REFERENCE SERVICE

50 Kinds of Service

We shall next turn to the core of ready reference service. This is service to the enquirers. It will be convenient to recognise three kinds of service:

1 Training the enquirer in fact-finding;
2 Setting the enquirer on the right track to help himself; and
3 Furnishing the exact information.

The mode of service will be different in these three kinds. The time to be devoted, the attention to be paid, and the devices to be employed to keep the enquirer in good humour will all be different. The quality of the ready reference librarian needed most will vary with the kind of service. A sympathetic teacher's outlook will be necessary in one case. The capacity to keep oneself in the background will be necessary in another. Promptness and exactness will be required in still another.

51 Training in Fact Finding

Persons, coming to the library for the first time and likely to become regular visitors, stand in need of being instructed in the use of ready reference books. This is necessary as much in the interest of the ready reference staff as that of the enquirers. The policy of the staff should be ultimately to transfer as much of the effort as possible to the enquirer himself. The most economical way of doing it is to take him on hand at the earliest possible opportunity and demonstrate to him the method of locating facts in ready reference books. Formal instruction is out of the question. The ready reference librarian cannot 'lecture' to the reader; nor can he collect a number of new-comers and expound the art of factfinding in a theoretical manner. These methods savour of the class-room. These cannot be adopted in the library. In fact at no moment should an enquirer be made to feel being instructed. The correct attitude of the reference librarian should be the one described so delightfully in the words of Sita to Rama [V5]:

"स्नेहाच्च बहुमानाच्च स्मारये त्वां न शिक्षये।"

"I do not instruct; I only remind you out of my love and regard for you."

It is necessary to have this attitude even in the case of children.

52 Work with the Enquirer

The information should be sought in company with the enquirer at the speed determined by his capacity and previous knowledge. The passage from one book to another and the turning from one page to another should all be done in a way most natural and assimilable to the beginner. The superior skill and the great flair, acquired by a reference librarian through experience, should be muffled consciously. They should be prevented from giving, at any moment, a momentum or speed incommensurable with the capacity of the enquirer. As the investigation proceeds, many opportunities will present themselves to make him observe some of the peculiarities and to warn him against some of the pitfalls characterising the reference book in use. A resourceful reference librarian will also have the awareness to detect the setting in of tedium on the enquirer. He should ward it off with gentle humour.

53 Stages of Service

We may recognise three stages in the fact-finding pursuit in company with a new enquirer:

1 Precise enunciation of the information to be pursued and found out;

2 Chalking out the line of pursuit; and

3 Final spotting out of the information.

We shall study each of these stages.

54 Exact Enunciation

541 Oblique Enunciation

In most cases, correctly stating the problem to be pursued is half the battle. Various causes prevent an enquirer from stating his question in exact terms. He might have, in his own way, partially solved his problem and reduced it to a secondary one. At the enquiry desk, he will therefore mention only his secondary problem. The reference librarian will thus hear from him only an oblique enunciation of the problem to be pursued. The line of pursuit suggested by it may altogether be clear of the primary problem. It may even carry the enquirer to a point of annoyance. Several wrong paths may have to be pursued. By such trials and errors only, either party may discover the real problem being different from the secondary one stated explicitly by the enquirer. An experienced reference librarian could have developed the flair to sense the secondary nature of the problem. Then, he may elicit the primary problem in exact terms expeditiously. This will save a good deal of trouble for the enquirer and for himself.

542 Glass Industry Enquiry
(*Case Study* 56)

A middle-aged gentleman called at the library.

"I should like to have information on glass industry."

"What aspect?"

"Aspect? Some data and a brief survey."

He was directed to the *Encyclopaedia Britannica* in the first instance. Ten minutes later, the reference librarian went to him.

"Do you get what you wanted?"

"I have just perused the articles on 'glass' and 'glass manufacture.' They are historical and technical."

"You don't want them?"

"No, I am rather interested in the economic aspect."

"Then try this article on 'glass and pottery industry' in this volume of the *Encyclopaedia of social sciences*."

Half an hour later, the reference librarian again asked him if he got his information. He could not say. He would ask for additional help if necessary after perusing the whole of the article. Another half an hour passed; and the enquirer approached the reference librarian:

"This is nearer to my point."

"I am glad."

"But it gives only twenty lines on the problem I am pursuing."

"What is that problem?"

"Look! this article speaks of 'industrial hazards.' It is something like that."

"Did you look up the cross references to 'industrial hazards and sanitation?"

"Yes, I did. But it is all too general."

Then only his problem got enunciated in exact terms. To meet it directly *Occupation and health: an encyclopaedia of hygiene, pathology, and social welfare* published by the International Labour Office was brought to his notice. The article on 'glass industry' extended to twenty-one pages: ten pages were on the technique; and eleven gave statistics, and dealt with pathology, hygiene, and legislation. The enquirer was delighted with it. He got from it all his information. He left the library fully satisfied.

543 Prohibition Enquiry

(*Case Study* 57)

A parliamentary secretary ascertained by the phone if the library had books on prohibition. He arrived in the library a few minutes later. He had been a professor before becoming parliamentary secretary. He was shown some books.

"These discuss for and against prohibition. I don't want them. Show me some books on the social aspect of the problem. Where are they kept?"

"Here! In this section 'social pathology—drink evil.' There are just a few books here on the prevention of drink evil."

* * * *

"Even these are not to my point. Have you anything on prohibition law?"

"Yes, here are two books."

* * * *

"These too are no good."

"What is it exactly that you want?"

"Have you any books on the administration and enforcement of prohibition policy?"

"Yes, here are a few."

* * * *

"No, no! These are no good. They only deal with smuggling, bootlegging, and so on."

"Perhaps we may be able to find ou something helpful if you can say what particular problem you have in mind."

"I want information about exemption from prohibition law. In the acts, you simply come across the phrase 'unless' exempted."

"I expect that the details about exemptions will be found in the rules framed under the acts. They will be mostly executive orders and may not find a place in books."

"The *poojarees* (=priests in the temples of village gods) insist that wine is necessary for temple worship. You know that it is the thin end of the wedge. I want to know how similar problems have been met in other countries."

"Ordinary books are not likely to go into such details. Perhaps the annual reports on the working of the prohibition act or reported cases may give some information."

544 Iron Works Enquiry

(*Case Study* 58)

A telephone message from the head of a government department read "I am sending my peon to the library. Send through him one or two books on steel and iron works." The peon came; and two books on the subject were sent.

* * * *

Half an hour later the personal clerk of the official returned the two books and said:

"My officer does not want these technical books. He wants some books describing old iron works."

"Is he interested in the use of iron in antiquity?"

"Perhaps so. He mentioned 'Iron works of olden days.' That is all I know."

"Then take these books. They are all of antiquarian interest."

* * * *

The personal clerk returned again within another half an hour and said with some emotion:

"No sir. He asked me to return them immediately."

"Why?"

"I don't know. He is fretting and fuming. He wants me to bring other books."

"What exactly does he want?"

"I don't know."

"Ask him by phone, now."

"No. He is very angry. You may ask him yourself."

* * * *

It was 5 P M. The official came in person. He was an elderly English gentleman. In fact, he was a senior member of the Indian Civil Service.

"I thought my fellow only was a fool. Your fellows too are like that."

"Why, what's the matter?"

"I want some pictures of old iron works—say of the Moghul period. They send all sorts of things."

Presently some illustrations appearing in the *Memoirs* and *New imperial series of the Archaeological Survey* of India were shown. He was not satisfied with them. The assistants were asked to collect more such illustrated memoirs and the officer was taken into the librarians' room.

"This is the first time, I come here after you moved into these buildings."

"You like the buildings!"

"Yes, they are lovely."

"Where do you live now?"

"I am just now changing my residence. I have taken a new house. There is a big hall in it. My wife wants to have it partitioned. She has taken a fancy for an iron door and iron grating."

* * * *

He was taken into a deep conversation. In a few minutes a few recent bound volumes of architectural periodicals arrived with bookmarks in some advertisement pages. The old official examined the pictures in those pages. He was immensely pleased.

"It is just this kind of thing that I wanted. I shall ask my wife to come and have a look at them."

"I am glad you have got what you wanted."

"Not 'I wanted' but what 'my wife wanted!' But why were they not able to get them this morning?"

"Because you did not tell them that you wanted these!"

"Nor did I tell them now."

"But you told me that you were changing your residence etc. etc. This slip went to them, and they gave up the pursuit of *Archaeological memoirs* and looked up these advertisement pages!"

"I am sorry I called your men fools. Now I realise who was a fool! I am glad that you asked me to make a personal call. I am glad I came. I enjoyed your library. I shall bring my wife along tomorrow this time. I am sure she will enjoy it too."

545 Deliberate Distortion

An accurate enunciation of what exactly a reader wants is not easy either for the reader or for the staff; it takes long to shape; it is half the battle in most cases of reference service. In the above mentioned patterns, the enquirers were quite genuine. But it is also possible for the enquirer to make his questions oblique quite consciously and deliberately. Shyness, inferiority complex, or unwillingness to lay bare his cards may make him do so. It is shyness in most cases. It calls for a sympathetic handling by the reference librarian. A shy reader should be put at ease by kind words and participative manners. Once confidence is established, the correct enunciation of the question will become easy. But the position will be very difficult in the case of a brave enquirer, purposely withholding or distorting his exact problem. Even there, the geniality and the sincerity of the reference librarian may act as a corrective. Anyhow the obliquity of the question should be reduced as much as possible before chalking out the line of pursuit. Often, even this class of enquirer comes to terms in slow degrees, while working together.

55 Chalking out The Line of Pursuit

Having got as correct an enunciation of the question as possible, the reference librarian has to think out immediately the reference book likely to be of use. Without any air of instruction, he should readily show the enquirer its scope, arrangement, etc. A good plan will be to read the preface or introduction rapidly with him, with brief commentaries by way of emphasising special points or elucidating abstruse passages. It is also desirable to invite the attention of the new enquirer to the index and its nature. By this time, the reference librarian should have established a good relation with the new-comer. He can put the book into his hands and ask him to look it up, keeping himself in the background. It may happen that the enquirer is not satisfied with the information which he is able to find. Then the reference librarian should discuss with him what is wanting in the information got and show him in a friendly way how it can be amplified either from some other part of the same book or from some other book related to it. While proceeding along these lines a good deal of opportunity will arise to widen the experience of the enquirer in handling reference books without any formal instruction. In this way, the enquirer in a library must be made to learn more by doing than by listening.

551 Helping into the Right Track

Next we shall turn to regular customers and strangers, already familiar with fact-finding methods. They usually require the least time of the reference librarian. They mostly help themselves. But now and then the facts pursued are too elusive for them. Reference books do not yield them if pursued in the normal way. Then, the self-helping enquirers may get stranded They may show signs of discomfiture or disappointment. At that time, the reference librarian should come to their aid. The offer of help in such cases should be made most tactfully. The enquirer himself may ask for help. Then it must be complied with without betrayal of any air of superiority. The difficulties of the enquirer may be due to his not having a clear enunciation of the information wanted by him. If so, his problem should first be given the correct shape. The method will be similar to the one adopted in the case of new-comers. But, it can be put through more expeditiously. Thus, the problem should be made definite. Then, the reference librarian should place at the disposal of the enquirer his own more intimate knowledge of the scope, the idiosyncrasies, the defects, and the pitfalls of the reference books. Even more important than that, the reference librarian should know how the different sources supplement one another. Lack of familiarity with the last-mentioned feature of reference books is often responsible for the failure of even an experienced enquirer in helping himself. But the reference librarian should have acquired a good knowledge of it through experience. A few judicious questions should disclose the stage at which the enquirer took a wrong turn. Without any explicit remarks or any other open sign about the mistake of the enquirer, the reference librarian should take him over to the right track; and if he shows signs of exhaustion or despair, the reference librarian should lead him on further. This may have to be done occasionally, till the enquirer sights the information sought.

552 Hunter Enquiry

(*Case Study* 59)

A professor of economics generally used to help himself in ready reference matters. Once he came to the reference librarian. He asked for a brief biography of W W Hunter. At the same time, he expressed surprise at his not finding it in the *Dictionary of national biography*. The reference librarian took his statement to be correct. He, therefore, tried Buckland's *Dictionary of Indian biography*. It gave a very brief account of Hunter's life. It was inadequate for the professor.

Now it struck the reference librarian that the professor might have omitted to consult some of the supplements. So, he asked the professor if he had consulted the supplements. He replied that he had used the supplement of three volumes as well the next single volume bringing the work up to date. Here was the cause of trouble. The professor had not evidently seen volume 22. It formed the first supplement to the work. So, the reference librarian pulled out that volume, located the article, and gave it to the professor. He glanced at the article, glanced at the back, glanced at the reference librarian, said to himself "How is it!" and settled down to read.

553 Burnell Enquiry

(*Case Study* 60)

Another professor was seen walking confidently into the gangway containing periodicals in Indology. Fifteen minutes later, the reference librarian went to him and asked:

"Can I help you?"

"No, thanks. I remember having seen a picture of A C Burnell in one of these volumes."

"Do you want it to be located?"

"I have examined every volume. It is not there. I wonder where I could have seen it."

"Did you try the *Dictionary of national biography*?"

"Surely it doesn't give pictures."

"Nor did I say that it does."

"Then what's the good!"

"There is usually an iconographical note at the ends of articles."

"Is it so? There is a bibliographical note. Does it include pictures too?"

"Yes, try it."

He found the following passage:

"Another work undertaken jointly with Colonel Yule had been the occasional occupation of both for many years and Burnell's part in it was nearly completed. It appeared in 1886 (new edition 1903) as Hobson-Jobson, being a glossary of Anglo-Indian colloquial words and phrases. A portrait of Burnell is at p xiii". This note was found in v 3, p 385.

554 STROH-VIOLIN ENQUIRY
(*Case Study* 61)

C S Ayyar was a senior officer in the Financial Civil Service. He was a violinist by hobby. Some research work on violin technique was claimed to his credit. He dropped into the library.

"I had once seen a peculiar kind of violin in the hands of an expert in Germany. He called it 'Stroh-violin' or 'straw violin'. What can it be? I want the correct spelling."

"Will you try some of the books on violin?"

He had tried; but no light. He was asked to try dictionaries of music; still no light. He was asked to consult the linguistic dictionaries. He did so, spending much time.

"No, I don't find it anywhere. These reference books are all so incomplete."

"Did you try Webster? It is a mine of information."

"Yes, I did. Even that fails."

"Did you try the *New English dictionary*?"

"Yes. I looked up every possible place. But it is too old. My recollection is that this violin is a new invention."

"Then why don't you look up the Supplement?"

"Supplement! Supplement to what?"

"Supplement to the *New English dictionary*."

"Is there one?"

"Yes, it was published a few years ago. It contains all the new words that came into use during the last half-century."

"But where is it?"

"Here!"

"I took it to be one of the original volumes... Such a bulky supplement! How language grows!"

"Here is the definition: Stroh (=Straw).... Used attrib. to designate instruments of the violin class having a horn attachment for increasing the resonance."

"Thank you. I was about to go in disappointment. How easily one goes out-of-date in these matters!"

56 Final State

An important principle should be borne in mind in helping even newcomers. The final stage of actually locating the right information should be left in the hands of the enquirer himself. The reference librarian should invariably withdraw himself at that stage.

561 Joy of Self-Help

The enquirer should never be denied the joy of feeling that ultimately he had helped himself. This joy will help him enjoy the pursuit of facts by himself in future.

562 Abundant Caution

In any case, the enquirer should be made to read the information from the book with his own eyes. This will avoid the risk of his turning up later and complaining of having been *given* wrong information. Of course, there can be no question of legal responsibility. If he happens to connect any failure, loss, or discomfiture of his with such wrong information, he may be made to recall that the information was perused with his own eyes or copied with his own hand. Such cases may arise only occasionally. Yet it is better for the reference librarian to accustom himself to such a procedure by way of abundant caution.

57 Furnishing the Exact Information

In section 23 "Nature of Enquirers", mention was made of the different classes of visitors standing in need of being served with the exact information and not merely being shown the concerned reference books. First, there is the class termed "the absentee enquirer". He writes or phones for information. Then, we have the experienced customers, without time to help themselves. Lastly, there is the casual stranger. It is not worthwhile spending any time in showing him the way of helping himself. In a business library, the first group will be large (*vide* section 14). Public libraries will have experience of the other groups. In all these cases, the very circumstances indicate the furnishing of the exact information to be the only kind of service possible.

571 Service by Post

The enquirer may be absent. He may not be present even on the phone. The enquiry may come by post. Then the problem of getting him to enunciate his requirement in direct and exact terms becomes difficult. The reference librarian will not get the help of the enquirer. He will have to use his own unaided judgment. In some cases, an intermediate reference by post may become necessary. In extreme cases, even repeated correspondence may become necessary. But there is one compensating factor. His enquiry need not be attended to at the very moment. It can be taken up as pick-up work and gone into with calmness at leisure. But the reference librarian should remember to dispose it off before the next mail. The letter of request may be brought by a messenger. Then the matter must be attended to immediately. In case of enquiry by post or through messenger, alternative information may have to be given to meet the different interpretations admitted by the enquiry. It is desirable to keep a record of the sources of information and of the person, locating them. For, the enquirer is likely to write back for further elucidation.

572 Service By Phone

The enquiry may come by phone. In that case, the time problem becomes most acute. It is best to furnish the information immediately. This can be done if the question is a familiar definite one and does not involve anything more than looking up just one reference. From this point of view, the location of the telephone receiver in relation to the reference shelf should be carefully settled. It should be at the enquiry desk. And the reference shelf should be handy within a few feet. In addition, the oft-required ready reference books should be on the desk itself. Then, the reference librarian can look them up without leaving his seat. Experience will show the reference books to be so kept. They will vary with the library. Even in the same library, they will have to be reformed from time to time.

573 Deferred Service

The information sought through the phone may not be readily traceable. Then, after making sure of the exact enunciation of the information sought, the enquirer should be asked to ring up after a stated interval. This request may create queer situations if the person at the other end of the wire is a difficult customer.

574 Difficult Customer on the Phone

(*Case Study* 62)

"Your enquiry needs a reference to the stack-room. Kindly ring up half an hour hence."

"Never heard the like of it. You should know every book you have in stock. Put me through to someone that knows his business."

575 Tact on the Phone

Tact on the telephone is verily a rare virtue. We can only hope that a gradual dawning as to the working of a library will come in time to those darkened minds. And again, the antidote is not angry blustering. A quiet, reasonable but firm frankness is the correct means of handling a difficult customer.

576 Omnibus Information

Apart from such petulance, the phone may also bring an omnibus question. It may call for the furnishing of a set of statistical figures or long passages going even beyond a page. They are not easily transmitted by wire. In such cases it will be an advantage to both parties, to make a polite suggestion to the enquirer to call personally. Innocence and inexperience may be responsible for asking for such information by the phone. If so, the enquirer has only to be told and he would correct himself. But occasionally, a wilful person may excuse himself, pleading inconvenience to come all the way to the library. It shows utter lack of civic sense. In such cases, the reference librarian should know how to be firm without being incivil. Sometimes, a phlegmatic enquirer may make a fuss and lodge a one-sided complaint with the authorities. Usually they know how to treat it. If they don't, it is necessary to explain the difficulties of the situation as they may not have realised them. That a customer should think that the men at the phone on the enquiry desk are capable of answering any question is extraordinary enough; but that he should expect a whole page or chapter or a stream of figures on tap is the height of nonsense.

5761 "MYSTERY OF DEATH" ENQUIRY
(*Case Study* 63)

"Hallo! Who is the author of that beautiful poem on the *Mystery of death*?"

"Is that the exact title?"

"I am not sure. It is a well-known poem. It compares night and death."

"You don't know the author?"

"That is the rub. I think that this author has written only this one poem. It contains a line like 'If light can deceive us, why not life' ?"

"Just hold on .... Thank God! I have tumbled on it."

"How nice! How did you manage it?"

"I first tried 'Familiar quotations,' Brewer, Benham, etc. But at last the *Cyclopaedia of English literature* not only gave the clue but has reproduced the poem *in extenso*."

"How lucky! Will you please read out. I should like to make sure whether that is the right poem?"

A few lines are read.

"Yes....That is exactly what I want. Will you please begin again...a little more slowly? I am taking it down."

"Please excuse me. I have already been held up for fifteen minutes. Many readers are waiting for my help."

"Look here! I am frightfully busy."

"I am sorry; it won't take you more than ten minutes to come over to the library."

The telephone was disconnected. Again it began to ring. The same fellow! It is again disconnected. Ten minutes later the telephone rings again. Another reference librarian attends to it.

"Please bring the *Cyclopaedia of English literature*, V 2."

"I am ready. Here it is."

"Please turn to Blanco White."

"Yes! He is the author of *Night and death*."

"Exactly, how quick you are! Will you please read it out for me. ....You are too fast. I don't write short-hand."

The old scene repeats itself.

577 Service to Caller

The enquirer may appear at the library in person. And yet, he may expect the whole tracing to be done by the reference librarian. This will happen in a business library. His personal co-operation can be had without difficulty at least at the first stage of the exact enunciation of the problem. But it is not easy to keep him restful when the information is traced. There are irritating people demanding instant attention. They may claim to have been waiting for half an hour whereas they had only been in the library for half a minute. A possible remedy is to give some engagement to such flighty enquirers. They may be taken to the shelf of recent additions, if they are interested in books. In the case of some difficult enquirers, it is wise to leave them in charge of the chief librarian himself or some other senior who can keep them engaged! This should not be regarded as waste of official time. For is it not part of the official duty of the librarian to keep a customer in good humour till correct service could be rendered to him? If, however, the enquirer is considerate and would agree to call later for the information, the offer may be thankfully accepted. But there are some enquirers coming to a public library who couple their offer with the condition that the information may be sent by post. It is desirable to avoid taking up such an obligation as the correspondence of the library should not be multiplied by the ready reference desk.

CHAPTER 6

ASSIMILATION IN READY REFERENCE SERVICE

60 Need for Assimilation

Oliver Wendell Holmes has described the man who had an astounding knowledge of every subject under the sun if its name began with any letter from A to M, but showed an equally remarkable ignorance of every subject which came in the cyclopaedias anywhere between N and Z. Whether such a being ever existed or not, the findings of Jast's probing into his mind are significant. "His mind must resemble an ostrich's stomach, where, if my zoology is correct, everything swallowed, from a bully-beef to a Colt's revolver, is found in its original condition, mingled in an 'admired disorder' but not absorbed." [J2]. Similar will be the mental make up of the reference librarian of a busy library unless provision is made for rumination, digestion, and assimilation into the specific skill of reference service.

61 Inner Assimilation

Any skill improves by repetition. But the profoundness secured by practice for skill in reference service is remarkable. To a reference librarian, really enjoying his work, every contact with an enquirer and the pursuit of every new problem provide an additional opportunity for enrichment. It gives a delightful exercise to his flair. It invariably enhances his mastery over reference books. For, the pursuit of a new problem may disclose potentialities, unnoticed hitherto. How often does not a reference librarian hum to himself "Hallo, does this book contain this! I had missed it all these days." Sometimes while pursuing a problem, his eye casually falls upon some information, making him say to himself: "What a pity! That fat gentleman asked just for this the other day. But none of us could lay our fingers on it. I wonder if I can find out his address and inform him about it. How pleased he will be! I hope it will not be too late."

62 Nascent Awareness

A reference book cannot be read through. Hence, even a very

conscientious reference librarian can hardly know all its nooks and corners, by a formal study at the preparation stage. Absorption of its unusual features or the unexpected pieces of information scattered in it becomes far easier when a nascent awareness is stimulated and maintained at a high pitch by the thrill of grappling with a difficult problem in the presence of an expectant enquirer. A moment's experience or stay at this high level of energy can be far more productive in giving a masterful grasp of a reference book than hours or even days of a dull mechanical pouring over its pages. While in such a state, not only is the particular book on hand rendered transparent and illuminating, but it even discloses its integral relation to several other reference books and delightfully lands us at an eminence which gives a clear and lasting view of past reference experiences in almost a prophetic inter-relation with what awaits in future. It is impossible to describe this supreme type of experience in full detail as it is so essentially conditioned by its concreteness with all its infinite shades of context which go into our very being but get distorted by any attempt at generalisation or abstraction. Every reference librarian should strive, invoking the full weight of his will, to realise in his daily life this delightful stage of simultaneous and integrating contact with the readers and the books.

63 Sharing with Colleagues

Another phase of assimilation is sharing with the brother members of the staff one's new discovery either of reference books or of particular enquirers or even of human nature in general. This does not mean that it becomes a reference librarian to discuss the enquirers in a vein of waggishness. But, it is helpful to inform all the colleagues about what has been sensed about their temperament, range of interest, capacity for self-help and, what is particularly profitable, the reciprocal help which the staff could get by serving certain well informed enquirers. Information of this kind will be of much value in making the future contacts with the enquirers easy, pleasurable, and profitable to all concerned. Imagine the pleasant reaction which the enquirer will experience if, at his next call at the library, he is met by some other member of the staff with genuine familiarity and without once again being subjected to all the ordeal of a first contact. A library is a human institution and every such human touch tones up its functioning.

64 Economics of Sharing

Apart from this very desirable human side of the sharing of every experience with colleagues, there is also an economical side. The time and energy spent by one member of the reference staff in hunting up a difficult question should be made to yield a greater profit than that of merely serving that one new enquirer who prompted it. The finding should be made known to the other members if it is worth that. Further, all new discoveries incidentally made out of the reference books used should also be passed on to the colleagues so that they may also benefit by them.

65 Recording and Filing

Another mode of assimilation relates to elusive facts, disentangled from unexpected sources under the stimulus of the enquirer's presence. These may be easily forgotten. They may be requisitioned only occasionally. Virtually they belong to long-range reference service. But they may get spotted out by sheer chance in ready reference service. They need to be recorded in slips of standard size and filed in the reference cabinet. A reference cabinet built up in this way will become in the long run a veritable mine of information. Indeed it will become a locally compiled reference book in slips. For each fact included in it, there should be several slips—for the classified sequence and for the alphabetical sequence. Each slip should give the source of information. The routine for this is described in my *Library administration*.

66 Assimilation in Book Selection

Again in the actual process of service, gaps in the reference collection of the library come to notice. They must be noted for later attention. At moments of respite from direct service to readers, the bibliographical resources should be rummaged to select the correct books in order to fill up the gaps in the stock. These should be brought to the notice of the book selection section for further action.

67 Assimilation and Fugitive Material

In business and school libraries, the interest of the enquirers shifts from time to time. The early enquiries of the new type will be a warning to an alert reference staff about fugitive reference materials of a certain kind possibly soon coming to be in demand.

The best means of procuring them should be explored; and they should be got and brought to use expeditiously.

68 Clearing Meeting

Most of the modes of assimilation point to the need for frequent consultation among the reference staff and deliberation at the monthly meetings of the Staff Council. Such clearance meetings [R37] will keep a library ever resonating with the pulse of the patrons. Such a resonance will lead to the fulfilment of the Laws of Library Science. This fulfilment will justify the existence of the library.

Part G

Find Me Out

CHAPTER 1

INTRODUCTION

Reference librarians were first appointed in the Madras University Library in 1928. They were pioneers. They learnt their work by doing. Their monthly experiences in ready reference service were pooled in the monthly meetings of the Staff Council. It has been a good way of training. But it is a slow way. After the pioneering stage, formal training should take the place of informal training. This formal training should be backed by planned practical work. This accounts for this chapter.

For the benefit of beginners in reference service we conclude this part with two sets of questions.

The first set is an account of some of the reference questions that came up for attention in the Madras University Library in the course of one month. We hope that this set, which is taken from actual life and hence concrete, will acquaint all concerned with the reality of reference service.

The second set entitled "108 Facts to Find" will be a means to acquire familiarity, with the highways and byeways of reference books. Some may be ready reference questions, while others may turn out to be long range ones.

The systematic description of reference books, prescribed in the last chapter of Part H, should be practised side by side with the verification of the results in chapter 2 and the finding of the solutions to the questions in chapter 3 of this part.

CHAPTER 2

ENQUIRIES DURING ONE MONTH

(*Case Studies* 64-117)

Wherever possible, the nature of the enquirer, the chain of works consulted, and the time taken are indicated in brackets. The beginner should look up the reference book, and verify the results given under each reference problem.

1 Addresses of some prominent biochemists of India.

(A professor. In person. *Handbook of Indian universities*, 1938. *Year-book of the universities of the Empire*, 1939. *Official chemical appointments*, 1937. 5 minutes.)

2 The verses in *Kumarasambhava* describing the wedding of Parvathi.

(An artist. In person. Verses 71-91 of Chapter 7. 15 minutes).

3 Any material on the art of lettering.

(A lady. In person. The article on *Calligraphy in the Encyclopaedia Britannica*, ed14. *Reference catalogue of current literature*, 1938. Wade (Cecil): *Modern lettering from A-Z*, 1938. 15 minutes).

4 A description of the *Ekadasi* festival at Srirangam.

(Journalist. In person. . . .The three books in the library on Hindu festivals out on loan. Hence *Encyclopaedia of religion and ethics*. Not of help. *Imperial gazetteer of India*. Monier Williams: *Brahminism and Hinduism*; p 448-450. Not available in the library. Index to Indian antiquary. v i p 322. 15 minutes).

5 A picture of 'blunderbuss.'

(A newspaper office. By phone. *Encyclopaedia Britannica*. Funk and Wagnall's: *New standard dictionary*. 5 minutes).

6 The passage "Honour and shame from no condition rise", etc.

(An adult reader. In person. Bartlett's: *Familiar quotations*; p 319. 5 minutes).

7 A biographical account of Valmiki.

(An adult reader. In person. *Bharatiya caritambudhi*. Dowson: *Classical dictionary*. Insufficient. An article in *Austosh Mukherjee silver jubilee volume*, v 3, part I. No other biographical material. 30 minutes).

8 There was an advertisement in the *Hindu* of 23-11-39 calling for applications for the post of the secretary to the Mayor of the Madras Corporation. Experience in parliamentary practice is one of the qualifications. Any good book on the subject.

(An advocate. By phone. May's *Parliamentary practice*. Campion's *Procedure of the House of Commons*. Redlich's *Procedure of the House of Commons*. 5 minutes).

9 *Collection of treaties, engagements and other papers of importance relating to British Malabar* by W Logan, 1879.

(A government department. By phone. Book not available. But the second edition of the same material formed part 3 of Logan: *Malabar manual*, 1891. The 1879 edition was intended for use in the district offices only. Very few copies printed. 10 minutes).

10 Raymond's book on taxation.

(A government department. To be sent per bearer for reference and return. Not in the catalogue of the library. It turned out to be Green (*William Raymond*): *Theory and practice of modern taxation*. 15 minutes).

11 Some material on the Cochin harbour.

(A student. In person. *Madras states and Mysore directory*, 1937, p 661-664. *Maharaja's college magazine*, Ernakulam, December 1936, p 1-16. *Engineering* v 145, p 69. 30 minutes.)

12 Any reliable translation of the verse in *Bhagavadgita* in which Lord Krishna exhorts Arjuna to fight. The matter is urgently required as an article on the war is to be released for publication.

(A newspaper office. By phone. Dhan Gopal Mukerji: *The song of God*, chap 2, verses 2-3, p 13. 10 minutes).

13 Does the Royal Society of Arts publish any report or periodical or any other publication and also the address of the Society.

(A government department. By phone. *Official year-book of the scientific and learned societies of Great Britain and Ireland*, 1938. 5 minutes).

14 The subscription for *Manchester guardian weekly*, not the *Commercial*.

(A college. By phone. *Whitaker's almanac*, 1939. No. *Writers and artists year-book*, 1931 (only year available in library). No. *Newspaper press directory*, 1931. 10 minutes).

15 Any book containing figures of literacy statistics for different countries of the world in a tabulated form.

(Organisers of an exhibition. By phone. *Whitaker's almanac*, 1939. Under 'Illiteracy' in the index. Supplemented by *Encyclopaedia of social sciences* under 'Literacy'. 10 minutes).

16 The text of the Declaration of London.

(A newspaper office. By phone. Ascertained by a series of questions that this was the result of a naval conference at London held about the year 1908 or 1909. Asked to ring up half an hour later for information. Ready reference books did not yield the information readily. Books containing documents in international law examined. Whittuck (E A): *International documents*, 1909, p 254-274. 15 minutes).

17 Any book giving sterling equivalents to Indian currency and *vice versa*, which may be useful as a ready reckoner.

(A government department. By phone. Thacker's *Indian exchange calculator*. 5 minutes).

18 Any book by name *Seshadharma*.

(An aged reader. In person. *Catalogue of Sanskrit, Pali and Prakrit books in the British Museum*, 1876-92. 5 minutes).

19 The addresses of some journals published in different countries of the world, interested in the lives of saints and review books on them.

(A journalist. By post. *Who's who in occultism, new thought, psychism, and spiritualism*, 1929. 10 minutes).

20 Any material on "Constituent Assembly for India."

(A politician. In person. No satisfactory material at the time. Bimal Ghose: *Constituent assembly* contained in *Current thought*, v 1, n 4. 5 days).

21 Information about Asvatthopanayanam.

(A sanskrit pandit. In person. *Jayasimhakalpadruma*. 30 minutes).

22 How long do dogs live?

(A professor. In person. After examining many books in zoology and veterinary science, information was found in Chambers's *Encyclopaedia*. 30 minutes).

23 Any book giving the text or at least the substance of the Lytton Committee report.

(A lady member of the legislature. In person. Ascertained that the report was on Munchuko affairs. Report not in library. Takuchi (T): *War and diplomacy in the Japanese Empire*, p 393-398 containing summary. Supplemented by *International conciliation*, n 286, Jan 1933, p 58-87. 15 minutes).

24 The addresses of the publishers and annual subscriptions of the following (1) *Science abstracts*. Section A and B. (2) *Chemical abstracts*.

(A college. By phone. The records of the Periodicals Section. 5 minutes).

25 Ogden's *Alliterative poetry in middle English*.

(A professor. In person. Is it O-g-d-e-n? Yes. Not found. Bibliographical investigation led to Oakden (J P). 10 minutes).

26 Any book or article on beggar problem relating to India in particular.

(A local library. No book. Birendranath Ganguly: *Street beggars of Calcutta: a study of the problem and its solution* in the *Indian journal of economics*, v 8, 1927-28, p 373-386. 45 minutes).

27 Four latest parts of *Educational journal and teachers' world*.

(A government department. By messenger. Search revealed that *Journal of education* with which was incorporated *School world* was meant. 15 minutes).

28 The horoscope of Sri Rama.

(A retired district judge. In person. Swamikannu Pillai's *Indian ephemeris*, v 1, part I. *Samskrita bharati*, v 6. 15 minutes).

29 Some statistics of area under cultivation of tea and the quantity produced in India, preferably for each province.

(A student of the diploma course in Geography. In person. *Handbook of commercial information for India*, 1937. 5 minutes).

30 P 140 of Phillips: *Teaching of the Vedas* gives a quotation from the *Sacred poetry of early religions*. Who is the author of that book? You don't seem to have it here.

(A research student. In person. *Reference catalogue of current literature*, 1940 backwards up to 1913. No use. Subject index of the London Library, 1909. 30 minutes).

31 I am told that the words "Zamorin" and "Mappilla" are loan words from Persian or Arabic. The original of Zamorin is Tamuri and of Mapilla is Moufla. I shall be much obliged if you will let me know . . .whether there are any words in those languages exactly corresponding to them or resembling them. . . .

(A lecturer. By post. Yule's *Hobson-Jobson*. 10 minutes).

32 Please send Doulasce's *Eurymics*.

(A mofussil member. By post. Bibliographical investigation revealed that Dalcroze: *Eurhythmics* must be the one in view.

Reference catalogue of current literature. 1938. 15 minutes).

33 A portrait of Sir Michael O'Dwyer in any book.

(Several newspaper offices on the same day. By phone. *Times history of the war*, v 15, p 133. *Indian review*, 1915, p 488. Douie (J): *Punjab, North-west Frontier Province and Kashmir*, p 199. One hour).

34 Reserve for me Hamilton's *Psychic research*, to enable me to come and take it this evening.

(A member of the library. By phone. Not in the catalogue. Reported not available. But the member said he had seen it here. Hence asked to ring up half-an-hour later to enable investigation. Hamlin Garland: *Forty years of psychic research* happened to be the book in view. 20 minutes).

35 Any material throwing light on the problem of the "man in the iron mask".

(A member of the judiciary. In person. A busy hour in the library. Information sent next day by post as desired by him. Brewer: *Dictionary of phrase and fable*, (under 'Mask'). 10 minutes).

36 A translation of the saying: "Nihil sub sole novi."

(A teacher. By phone. Jones: *Dictionary of foreign phrases and classical quotations*. 10 minutes).

37 The statistics of average life of man in different countries of the world.

(An officer. In person. *Whitaker's almanac*, 1939, (under "Longevity"). *Statistical year-book of the League of Nations*, 1937-38, (under "Expectation of life"). 10 minutes).

38 The poem "*Allan waters*".

(A professor. In person. Ascertained that it was a ballad and the author was not known. Child (F J): *English and Scottish popular ballads*, v 4, p 184. 10 minutes).

39 An English translation of Ramanuja's *Vedarta sangraha*.

(An M A student. In person. No separate book in library. Translation of the work in *Brahmavadin*, v 1 and 2. Located with the help of *A supplementary catalogue of Sanskrit, Pali and Prakrit books in the Library of the British Museum*, 1892-1906. 10 minutes).

40 An archaeological map of India.

(An archaeological chemist. In person. *Imperial gazetteer of India*, v 26, atlas, plate 26. 10 minutes).

41 An up-to-date map of land and air routes.
(A student. In person. Rado (A): *Atlas of to-day and tomorrow*, 1938. Other atlases out of date. 10 minutes).

42 A book on Pakistan.
(A student. In person. Was told that it can be read only in newspapers and periodicals of the months as the problem was quite new. 1 minute).

43 A big portrait of the monastery at St. Edmundsbury.
(A teacher. In person. Dugdale's *Monasticon Anglicanum*, v 3, p 98. 15 minutes).

44 The address of the publisher and price of *Bhaktirasayana*.
(A member. By phone. *Catalogue of books relating to Sanskrit etc*, of Motilal Banarsi Dass. 15 minutes).

45 English scientific name of the herb called "Nerungal" in Malabar.
(A Malabar gentleman. In person. Nadkarni (K M): *Indian materia medica*. 5 minutes).

46 A brief account of the origin and history of the Maternity Hospital at Egmore.
(An advocate. In person. *Imperial gazetteer of India*, v 16, p 346-347. 5 minutes).

47 Information on Birknes theory.
(A student of geography. In person. Not found anywhere. Elicited by a series of questions that he is associated with 'Cyclones' and that his theory is otherwise called Polar Front theory. *Encyclopaedia Britannica* under *Meteorology* leading to many articles in the *Quarterly journal* of the Royal Meteorological Society, 1923 onwards. Birknes was found to be really Bjerknes. 15 minutes).

48 Description of Jog Falls.
(A tourist. In person. *Bombay gazetteer*, v 15, part 2, p 284-288. *Mysore gazetteer*; v 5. p 1325-1332. 10 minutes).

49 Is Sankara a crypto-Buddhist?
(A philosophy student. In person. Student also participated in the search. A series of articles by G V Budhekar entitled "*Is the Advaita of Sankara Buddhism in disguise*? in the *Quarterly journal* of the Mythic Society, v 24, 1933-1934. One hour).

50 Full name of the periodical, referred to as *Jbr. posen. landw. Berufsgenoss.*

(A research student. In person. *World list of scientific periodicals*, 1930-1933. 5 minutes).

51 Consumption of sugar in India per capita.

(A doctor. By phone. Gandhi (M P): *Indian sugar industry*, 1939. 10 minutes).

52 A comparison of the administration of the British empire with that of Roman empire.

(A student. In person. Allison (W H) etc.: *Guide to historical literature*. Led to (1) Cromer (E B): *Ancient and modern imperialism*; (2) Lucas (C P): *Greater Rome and greater Britain*; and (3) Bryce (J): *Ancient Roman empire and British empire in India* contained in his *Studies in history and jurisprudence*. 15 minutes).

53 Ancient Hindu system of medical jurisprudence.

(A lawyer. In person. Kautilya *Arthasastra*. Section on *Asumrita-pariksha*. 30 minutes).

54 Location of the original passage in Disraeli's works in support of the following statement of Dr Besant said to have been made in 1908: "Benjamin Disraeli, Lord Beaconsfield, who became premier of Great Britain, was a man Eastern in heart though he dominated a typical Western nation, a man revelling in the splendour of an Eastern imagination and with his mind ever steeped in the poetry and the glamour of the East. When he won for the British monarch, in the teeth of British prejudice and democratic feeling, the splendid title of Emperor of India, he argued for the adding of the Imperial to the Royal Crown, and he said that in the changes among nations Asia again might have her turn in Empire and that it might be that the centre of the Empire might shift from the unruly West to the loyal East, when the Monarch of the Empire might be enthroned in the great continent of India instead of the little Island of northern seas. . . ."

(An adult enquirer. By letter. Works of Disraeli. Biographies of Disraeli. Clarke (E): *Benjamin Disraeli: the romance of a great career*, 1804-1881, p 236. Disraeli: *Tancred*, 1847. "Let the Queen of the English. . . .transfer the seat of her empire from London to Delhi. . . ." 1 day).

CHAPTER 3

108 FACTS TO FIND

The beginner should locate the information sought in the following questions expeditiously and give exact reference to the source—call number, heading, title, page, and extent of information. It is also desirable to indicate in detail the entire route followed, the difficulties, disappointments, and helps met with.

1 Who are the awarding authorities for the Nobel Prize in Physics and Chemistry?

2 What are the terms of the Tata Scholarship?

3 On what day of the week was the Madras University opened?

4 What are the hill stations in India which are resorted to in summer and furnish information about each?

5 When was the Pamban Bridge opened?

6 Who got the Nobel Prize for Medicine in 1908?

7 What is the total number of divorces and annulments of marriages in England and Waies for the years 1924-1929?

8 What are the Imperial Wireless stations in India?

9 What is the date of foundation of the National Research Council of Japan?

10 Who publishes the *Journal of philosophical studies*? What is the subscription?

11 What are the terms of the endowment for the Gifford Lectureship? Can you produce the text of the will of Gifford relating to this endowment?

12 Why is Madras called Chennapattanam?

13 Who were the Jagad-Gurus of the Sringeri Muth in the 15th century? How long did each occupy the *Pitham*?

14 What are the symbols used in proof correction?

15 Who is Walter Gerlach? What are his works?

16 What is the subscription of the *Horological journal*? Who publishes it? What is its period?

17 "If the nose of Cleopatra had been shorter the whole face of the earth would have been changed." Who is the author of this saying? Where does it occur?

18 How many salutes are the following entitled to:

(1) Maharaja of Alwar,
(2) Nizam of Hyderabad,
(3) Maharaja of Bhavanagar,
(4) Maharaja of Travancore,
(5) Thakore Saheb of Rajkot.

19 Furnish the description of the Academic Robes in the Universities of Oxford and Cambridge?

20 Who is Fo-Hi or Fu-hee? Where can a short note about him be had?

21 When did M C T Muthia Chettiar die?

22 What are the works of Gamaliel Bradford?

23 What are the seven famous wonders of the World?

24 Who is "A E"?

25 Who is the ruler of Banganapalle?

26 What is the period of Isvar Chandra Vidyasagar? Furnish a short account of his career in English?

27 Where does the story of King Nala occur?

28 What is the story connected with Muharram festival?

29 Furnish a short biographical note on Sir T Muttusamy Aiyar.

30 What is the address of Emile Borel, the French mathematician?

31 What are the works of David Grayson?

32 When was Flora Annie Steel the Anglo-Indian novelist born?

33 Where can we get an abstract of Sir Isaac Newton's paper on the "New theory of light and colours"?

34 Name some important statues in the City of Madras?

35 What is the date of death of L T Hobhouse?

36 What are Sadras and Covelong noted for? Where are they situated?

37 What is Bara Wafat?

38 Why are the printed records of Parliamentary debates known as the "Hansard"?

39 What is Technocracy?

40 Where can be had a genealogical table of the kings of the Lunar Race in India?

41 Who are the diplomatic representatives of Persia in Great Britain and of Great Britain in Persia?

42 Select 5 or 6 dealers in perfumes in the City of Madras with their addresses?

43 In what part of Mahabarata does the Bhagavad-Gita occur?

44 Why is 'A1' synonymous with first rate?

45 Who are the present cabinet members in England?

46 What are serpentine verses? Give a line or two for illustration.

47 Furnish the address of any four Chinese Associations in London.

48 Furnish a plan of the City of Madras for the use of a foreigner who calls at the library.

49 Who uses the pseudonym "Alpha of the plough"?

50 Furnish a short biographical note on John Bruce Norton.

51 How many died of street accidents in London in the years 1928 to 1932?

52 Where can you have a short account of the Hindu ritual of Horse Sacrifice?

53 What is the address of George Bernard Shaw?

54 When were the following Royal Commissions instituted and what was the personnel?

(1) Royal Commission on Agriculture in India,

(2) Royal Commission on the Ancient and Historical Monuments in England,

(3) Royal Commission on Labour in India,

(4) Hilton Young Commission.

55 Where can be found a picture of (1) Srinivasa Ramanujan? (2) Andrew Carnegie?

56 What are the Indian Universities, which confer LT or BT Degree on submitting theses?

57 Who administers the Aden Government?

58 What is the address of the National Union of Teachers?

59 Give a list of a dozen biographies published in the year 1932.

60 Who were the Indian States' Representatives in the Second session of the Indian Round Table Conference?

61 Furnish a short account of the Academia Sinica.

62 Why is Sunday observed as a holiday?

63 Where was the 44th session of the Indian National Congress held? Who was the Chairman of the Reception Committee? Who was the President?

64 What is the Indian population in Egypt?

65 Furnish a short account of Tuskegee Institute.

66 Name some important official publications or some authoritative non official publications about the Argentine Republic.

67 What is the address of Wiley & Sons (booksellers) America?

68 Where can be had a short account of the Buckingham Canal?

69 What is the Tamil equivalent of Gendrussa Vuigaris?

70 When was Sir Thomas Munro Governor of Madras?

71 What is the address of the P E N Club with which Galsworthy is associated?

72 Furnish a short account of the King Institute, Guindy.

73 Where can you have a portrait of the Nizam of Hyderabad?

74 How many committed and how many attempted suicide in Great Britain in 1930?

75 Give the meanings of Abkari, Tahsil, Chaprasi, Pardanashin, Sangathan?

76 What is the date of foundation of the Geneva Institute of International Relations?

77 Give a brief account of the views of various nations about eclipses.

78 What is the value of the Hyderabad Rupee in terms of the British India Rupee?

79 Where can be had a map of India showing the principal economic minerals available therein?

80 What are the daily newspapers published in Delhi?

81 In the Japan year book 1934, it is stated on page 454, that the area cultivated with industrial crops in 1932 amounted to 232,513.19 ha. and the production was valued at §74,105,277. What is ha.? and what is §? What is the Indian value of each of these units?

82 What are the places in India where you have lighthouses?

83 What are the places in the Madras Presidency where graphite occurs? Name some publications which give an account of them.

84 What are the rules governing the exercise of casting votes by chairman?

85 Who is Steinach? When and where was he born?

86 Where can be had a list of articles contributed to foreign journals by Sir C V Raman?

87 What is the subject covered by the Nobel address of Max von Lane delivered in 1920? Has it been published? If so, when and by whom?

88 What books contain a picture or photograph of the Muttra Lion?

89 "When faith is lost, when honour dies, the man is dead!" Who said this and when?

90 What is the altitude of Kinchinjunga?

91 Furnish a map showing the possessions of the East India Company in India in the year 1792.

92 What are the conditions of registration and membership of the Royal Society of Teachers?

93 Furnish a map to illustrate the world distribution of water-power.

94 Name one or two persons who broke the record in the stratosphere flight in the year 1935. What was the height reached?

95 Who presided over the annual meeting of the British Association for the Advancement of Science in 1932? What was the subject of the address?

96 Who is Lady Murasaki? What is she noted for?

97 What is the English equivalent of the following coins? (1) Talari, (2) Drachma, (3) Dollar (St. Settlements), (4) Dollar (USA), (5) Schilling.

98 Where can you find a portrait of Jeremy Bentham?

99 Furnish a picture of the National Flag of Poland.

100 Who is the author of the drama *Poetasters of Ispahan*?

101 When and by whom was macadamising invented?

102 Can you furnish reference to *Tulabhara* (the ceremonial of weighing oneself against gold and giving it away as presents) as observed in India and elsewhere?

103 What is the significance of the Sikhs wearing the *Kirpan* (dagger)?

104 Who is the author of Existential Philosophy? Where can we get a short account of its principles?

105 What is "We Psychology"? Where is it expounded?

106 Where can the text of the address of Lord Linlithgow to the Central Advisory Board of Public Health be found?

107 Where can we find a biography of John Woolman?

108 What is the significance and the area of prevalence of the symbol of a coiled serpent?

Part H

Reference Book

CHAPTER 0

WHAT OF REFERENCE BOOK

01 Elusive Term

The term 'Reference Book' is second to none in library terminology in its elusiveness. This is responsible to a good deal of the haziness and inconsistency in the ground covered by books on reference book. We shall approach its definition along the following six lines [R3]:

1 Positive function of reference book;
2 Negative function of reference book;
3 Effect of terminology used in classification;
4 Enumerated form subdivisions in schedules of classification;
5 Enumerated common subdivisions in schedules of classification; and finally,
6 Internal characteristic of reference book.

02 Definition by Positive Function

An obvious definition is the functional one. According to it, a reference book is a book designed to be looked up for specific information. But one often looks up compendious treatises too for specific information. Mellor's many volumes on inorganic chemistry lend themselves admirably to be looked up for specific information. There are such treatises in many other subjects. Even ordinary text-books may have to be looked up occasionally for specific information. Sometimes, they may be the only source for information. An instance of this has been cited in section 44 of part K "Illustrative actualities" of this book. There, information has been sought on the Pamban Bridge. Volume 2 of the text-book *Indian empire* by Dudley Stamp proved to be the first source of information on the subject. This kind of use of text-books and treatises for specific information, in the absence of regular books of reference, has been responsible for the occasional inclusion of such text-books and treatises in some books on reference books.

03 Definition by Negative Function

There is another functional definition possible. A reference book may be defined as a book not lending itself to continuous reading. This definition brings in a personal factor of the reader. For, there are persons finding even dictionaries as fit forms of books for continuous reading. "Every morning, while shaving, I read through a few pages of the dictionary. I commend this practice to you as a method to gain proficiency in the use of the language," said Mr Brown, the Professor of Psychology of the University College in London in his lectures on "Methods of Study" to the freshmen of the College in October 1924. The medieval dictionaries of India were in reality so constructed as to admit of continuous reading and memorising. They used to be recited continuously. A professor in Madras once mentioned with pride his habit of sitting up till late in the night and 'reading from cover page to cover page' freshly received catalogues of second-hand books. In fact, the negative definition of this paragraph is charged with much of personal element. It is likely to lead one astray and in particular to inconsistency. We must look for a better definition.

04 Effect of the Terminology of Classification

In some of the books on reference books, there is some evidence of the influence of the schedules of library classification on the books included by them. About a century ago, schemes of classification began to include a schedule of 'form sub-divisions', at the head of the schedules of most of the main classes Some of these form sub-divisions were intended to represent and to take reference books. But some of the other form subdivisions were intended to represent and to take other kinds of books. But there is an inherent, superficial folk tendency to overlook such a difference among the isolates listed together in a single schedule. Later on, 'form sub-divisions' gave place to 'common sub-divisions'. Their schedules also showed a similar mixture. The inherent, superficial folk tendency persisted in respect of them also. This tendency has been perhaps responsible for some confusion in the listing of reference books. Some examples are given in the next two sections.

05 Effect of Form Sub-division

Some of the isolates included very early in the schedule of form sub-divisions were 'periodicals', 'yearbooks' and 'directories'. The two latter isolates truly denote reference books. The mention of 'periodicals' in the schedule as of co-ordinate status with 'yearbooks' and 'directories' had probably led to the inclusion of some 'periodicals' in some lists of reference books. However, this happened only in subjects poor in true reference books.

06 Effect of Common Sub-division

At a later stage in the evolution of the terminology of library classification, the term 'form sub-division' was replaced by the term 'common sub-division'. This term brought into its schedule common isolates such as 'biography'. The common isolate 'history' has been persisting through both stages. The mention of these isolates in the schedule as of co-ordinate status with 'yearbooks' and 'directories' had probably led to the inclusion of some biographies and historical books in some lists of reference books. However, this happened only in subjects poor in true reference books.

07 Definition by Internal Characteristic

Perhaps the best way of avoiding such involuntary lapses into inconsistencies of this kind is to define a 'reference book' by an inherent internal characteristic of it, instead of basing the definition either on function or on the practices of library classification. An ordinary book—that is, a book other than a reference book—has the following characteristic. It is made of continuous exposition. Sentences mount into a paragraph. Paragraphs mount into a chapter. Chapters get woven into a single swelling exposition, in the continuous pursuit of a single idea, simple or complex. A reference book does not have this internal characteristic. On the contrary, it is characterised internally by an ensemble of disjointed entries of short, though varying, lengths. The sequence of the entries is not determined, strictly by intimate thought-sequence. It is determined by the scheme of arrangement chosen. It is often alphabetical in the main. It is occasionally systematic. Even then, the connection between consecutive entries is not as compelling and continuous or as free from jerks as between the paragraphs in an ordinary book. Or, a reference book may consist mostly of formulae, statistics, diagrams, tables, maps, or lists including lists of documents with or without abstracts, annotations, and other features.

08 Varieties of Reference Books

The following varieties of reference books may be recognised.

The list is essentially based on the internal characteristic mentioned in section 07. For convenience of later reference, the list also takes into consideration some other characteristics such as the contents for further sub-division, in the case of some kinds of reference books.

- Atlas
  - Geographical
  - Other subjects
- Bibliography
  - Abstracting
  - Indexing
  - of bibliographies
  - of individual
    - 'by' kind
    - 'by and on' kind
    - 'on' kind
  - of subject
- Biographical reference book
  - Dictionary
  - Who's who
- Concordance
- Dictionary, Linguistic
  - General
  - Technical
- Encyclopaedia
  - General
  - of special subjects
- Formulae
  - Recipes
- Gazetteer
  - Guidebook
- Leading cases
- List
  - Alphabetical
  - Chronological
  - Systematic
- Statistics
- Tables
- Yearbook
  - Calendar
  - Directory

CHAPTER 1

EMERGENCE OF REFERENCE BOOK

11 Oral Age

Reference books of certain kinds appear to have been in existence in Sanskrit language from very early days. The *Niruktas* were virtually dictionaries of the vedic age. In that age, writing was not widely practised. Whole books were passed on from man to man and from generation to generation by word of mouth. It was an 'oral age'. The *Anukraminikas* too belonged to that age. They were indexes to the Vedas.

12 Manuscript Age

Amarakosa is reputed to be the earliest extant dictionary of classical Sanskrit. It is said to have been written in the fifth century. The *Puranas* are virtually encyclopaedias. Varahamihara's *Brihatsamhita* is a scientific encyclopaedia. These reference books belonged to the manuscript age. This practice naturally made the earlier reference books differ in several ways from the reference books of the modern printed age. Perhaps other classical languages too had their own reference books even in remote times.

13 Printed Book Age

131 Bibliography

In the modern age of printed books, the first variety of reference book to emerge was the Bibliography. Accrding to Besterman, the first bibliography to be printed was the *Libre de scriptoribus ecclesiasticis* (1494). It was compiled by Johann Trithaim, an abbot of the Monastery of Spanheim. The first attempt at a universal bibliography of printed books was made by Konrad Gesner of Zurich. His famous *Bibliotheca universalis* came out in 1545. Since then, the bibliography variety of reference book has been coming out regularly in several countries. To day, we have many hundreds of them published as periodical publications, in the form of national bibliographies, indexing periodicals, abstracting periodicals, and annual reviews of the progress of literature in several subjects. These will be described in a forthcoming book entitled *Enumerative bibliography*.

132 Dictionary and Encyclopaedia

The varieties of reference book brought into vogue even in the pre-printing age—namely, dictionary and encyclopaedia—came to be published only a couple of centuries after the invention of printing from moveable metal types. The first English dictionary was printed only in the eighteenth century. So it was with the first encyclopaedia.

14 Directory

The directory variety of reference book made its first appearance in the eighteenth century. The earliest known directories are J Brown's *Directory or list of principal trades in London* (1732); and Whitehead's *Newcastle directory* (1778). A directory is usually a book containing the names, addresses, occupations, etc., of the inhabitants of a town or a district, a list of the users of a telephone system, or of the members of a particular profession or trade, or a descriptive list of institutions, enterprises, or trades.

15 Year-Book

The year-book variety of reference book made its appearance only in the nineteenth century. Two of the earliest year-books were the *Year-book of facts in science and art* (1827) and the *Congregational year-book* (1846). They are now defunct. The now familiar *Statesman's year-book* was one of the earliest in the field. It was founded only in 1864. *Whitaker's almanac* made its appearance in 1861; and the *Year-book of the scientific and learned societies of Great Britain and Ireland*, in 1884. A year-book, it may be staetd, is an annual summary either of events throughout the world during the previous year or of general or local progress in some one department of administration, art, science, or industry. The International Institute of Intellectual Co-operation, which began as a dependent auxiliary of the League Of Nations in September 1921 and got itself established at Paris in November 1925, had a plan to edit a series of specialised year-books beginning with an international *Who's who*. Its successor Unesco is implementing its own plan in this matter.

16 Accelerated Growth

During the present century, there has been an accelerated growth in every variety of reference book. Several classes of knowledge of varying degrees of extension have begun to attract every variety of reference book. Here is the result of a rough count of such classes made in 1940.

Variety of Reference Book		*Number of Classes of Knowledge having it*
Atlas		81
Bibliography		
Abstracting and indexing	161	
of bibliographies	27	
of individual	188	
of subjects	520	
		896
Biographical reference book		42
Concordance		80
Dictionary, Linguistic		
General	336	
Technical	92	
		428
Encyclopaedia		164
Formulae book		21
Gazetteer		27
Guide book		52
List		21
Statistical reference book		17
Table		153
Yearbook and directory		148
Total		2,130

These are now being increased in number even at a greater rate than before. The newly awakened countries have begun to make their own additions to their number. Many experiments are being made in regard to them. On this basis, they are being continuously improved in several respects.

CHAPTER 2

SCOPE OF REFERENCE BOOK

21 Introduction

No two reference books of the same variety in the same subject are identical in scope. The fact that a new book is launched when another exists in the same subject may by itself lead one to infer that the newcomer should have a different scope. But the variation in scope may not be anything obvious. It requires intimate knowledge and familiarity to note the difference. Without a knowledge of such differences the reference books will not yield the best result. To size them up and to know their special features require persistence of application. This will be possible only for those specialising in them. Apart from offending the Second and the Third Laws of Library Science, there can be nothing more wasteful and even cruel than to have on the shelves volumes containing the exact information sought by an enquirer, and yet to let him to go uninformed, because the library has not got a person who with readiness and alertness can help in bringing the information to the notice of the enquirer.

211 Biographical Enquiries

(*Case Study* 118)

Almost every week in 1938 would bring into a busy library inexperienced enquirers that search the pages of the *Dictionary of national biography* for light on Lloyd George whose heterodox speech on the "Hitler-Chamberlain tangle" featured in the Daily of the previous night. Nor do we lack those who fidget with the leaves of the *Who's who* and throw it away in disgust because it does not inform them about Charles Darwin. Veteran readers may imagine this to be abnormal or unusual. And yet not a day passes without the reference librarian having to gently suggest the right books for adults in such predicaments.

22 Biographical Dictionary

Let us take the oft-used biographical variety of reference book. The geographical area covered is one characteristic causing difference in scope. The resulting groups are,

1 International; and
2 Regional or national.

The subject covered is a second characteristic causing difference in their scope. The resulting groups are,

1 General; and
2 Special.

The period covered is a third characteristic causing difference in their scope. The resulting groups are,

1 Retrospective, confined to the dead;
2 Contemporary, confined to the living; and
3 Mixture of the above two.

These three characteristics may be combined in every possible way. Then, twelve groups will arise. Nine of these groups are discussed and illustrated in the succeeding sections. The three groups not illustrated are,

1 International, special, and contemporary;
2 Regional, special, and retrospective; and
3 Regional, special, and retrospective as well as contemporary.

221 International, General, and Retrospective

Some of the so-called classical dictionaries are biographical reference books. They are international and general in scope. But they restrict themselves severely to the past, often to the distant past.

Example:

Smith (William). *Dictionary of Greek and Roman biography and mythology*. 3 v.

222 International, General, and Contemporary

1 *International who's who* has taken the place of the *Who's who* part of *Europa* mentioned in 2 below.

2 The *Who's who* part of *Europa*, was confined to living persons. But it covered all subjects and many countries.

3 The *World of learning* is another example.

223 International, General, and Contemporary as Well as Restrospective

1 Joseph Thomas's *Universal pronouncing dictionary of biography and mythology* is an example of the general and international type ranging over the past and the contemporary times. It includes the lives of men and women of many nations, living as well as dead.

It goes even a step further. For it has no objection to club with historic persons other beings ordinarily eschewed as mythological. Vyasa and Narasimha (names of the supernatural and the divine familiar to the Hindus), Gokhale and Naoroji (names of deceased Indian celebrities), and Tagore and Gandhi (names of then living Indian worthies) can all be found in its columns. As the scope is so wide, the information about each is naturally brief. A useful special feature which an ordinary reader may not know or remember is the pronunciation of names.

2 *Webster's biographical dictionary* gives names of noteworthy persons, with pronunciations and concise biographies.

224 International, Special, and Retrospective

M M Marie's *Histoire des sciences mathematiques et physiques* (12 t) is an example of a biographical reference book of a purely retrospective type, confined to a limited field of knowledge, but covering many countries.

225 International, Special, and Retrospective as well as Contemporary

Poggendorff's *Biographisch-literarisches Handworterbuch zur Geschichte der exacten Wissenschaften* is restricted only to the sciences. But in its restricted field, it is international, retrospective, and contemporary. Under each name are given a short biography, a full bibliography, and occasionally sources for fuller biography.

226 Regional, General, and Retrospective

1 *Dictionary of national biography* is an outstanding example of the category restricted regionally and temporally. But it covers all subjects. It gives long biographies of persons of the British Empire who had shed their mortal coil. It must be specially stated that Americans of the colonial period only are given space in its pages. The articles are by specialists. They furnish bibliographies both of the sources of the biography and of the works of the biographee. Iconographic information is another feature of this work.

2 *Dictionary of American biography* is similar in scope. But its region of interest is U S A. It includes also some Britishers of the colonial period. In recent years, its scope has been broadened to cover Canada and other pan-American areas and to include also persons of other areas of reference value in U S A.

3 Most nations have such national biographies. But India. . . .? As a partial substitute, we may mention *Bharatiya charitambudhi* or the *Dictionary of Indian classical characters*. It is in Hindi and gives biographies of the Hindu and the Muhammadan periods. It is not restricted in regard to the subject covered.

227 Regional, General, and Contemporary

1 *Who's who* is of the contemporary type restricted mainly to the British Empire. It covers all subjects. It is an annual giving under each name information about birth, parentage, education, marriage, family, profession, publications, accomplishments, hobbies, and present address. A special feature, usually overlooked, is the obituary list of the year inserted immediately after the list of abbreviations at the beginning.

2 *Who's who in America* is a biennial publication of the contemporary type restricted strictly in regional scope. It covers all subjects. Outstanding international personalities like Hitler, Mussolini and Stalin can be seen in the British *Who's who*, but not in *Who's who in America*. The Munroe doctrine appears to persist in its columns!

3 *Who's who in India, Burma and Ceylon* shows by its very title that it is contemporary and regional in scope. It covers all subjects. But there is one exception. For, it gives information about the members of the royal family of England and of the British cabinet. Of course, it fulfils the implication of its title by giving information about the viceroy and the governors of provinces of India, who's who among Indian chiefs, who's who in India, Burma and Ceylon and who's who in Indian industry and commerce.

Unlike in the other who's whos, there are as many alphabetical sequences in this book as the number of who's who sections. Consequently, it provides an alphabetical index covering all the sections. An enquirer has to be told about this unusual feature. Otherwise, he may be lost in its maze.

228 Regional, General, and Retrospective as well as Contemporary

C E Buckland's *Dictionary of Indian biography* is, regionally restricted. But it includes contemporary names as well as names going back to the middle of the eighteenth century. It covers all subjects.

229 Regional, Special, and Contemporary

The following are some examples of biographical reference books confined strictly to contemporaries in limited fields of knowledge:

1 *Who's who in library service:*
2 *Who's who in science;*
3 *Who's who in engineering;*
4 *Who's who in chemical and drug industries;*
5 *Who's who in occultism, new thought, psychism and spiritualism;*
6 *Who's who in art;*
7 *Who's who in literature;*
8 *Who's who among living authors of older nations;* and
9 *Who's who in finance, banking and insurance.*

23 Year-Book and Directory

Next we pass on to year-books and directories. These specialise in current information and statistics. Therefore, only the two area characteristics and the two subject characteristics can cause differences in their scope. These two pairs of characteristics can be combined in four ways. Therefore, the following four groups can arise in this variety of reference book.

1 International and general;
2 International and special;
3 Regional and general; and
4 Regional and special.

All these four groups are discussed and illustrated in the succeeding sections.

231 International and General

1 *Statesman's year-book* is a concise and thoroughly reliable manual of descriptive and statistical information on diverse subjects, about all countries of the world. For each country it gives the same pattern of information—its ruler, constitution and government, area, population, religion, instruction, justice and crime, pauperism, public finance, defence, production and industry, agriculture, commerce, shipping and navigation, communications, banking and credit, money, weights and measures, diplomatic representatives, etc. A distinguishing feature is a select bibliography at the end of the account of each country. Its chapters run as follows: Introduc-

tory tables giving world statistics of wheat, rye, barley, rice, sugar, petroleum, iron and steel, gold, life insurance, etc., comparative strength of navies, United Nations, etc., British Commonwealth, United States of America, and the other countries of the world in alphabetical sequence.

2 Whitaker's *Almanack* (complete edition) is another annual after the model of *Statesman's yearbook*. But it contains much more miscellaneous information. Its special features are: An elaborate dictionary of abbreviations, calendar of anniversaries, astronomical and meteorological information, historical events of the year, etc. One most important fact to be remembered by the reference librarian is its annual summary of the achievements of the year in the fields of science, literature, and art. Further, it has an elaborate index revealing every minute detail in the book. With a copy of Whitaker's *Almanack* on the table, the reference librarian can answer many ready reference questions.

232 International and Special

1 *International year-book of agricultural statistics* (Rome) is international in scope. But it specialises in agricultural matters. It is an authoritative compilation of statistics on distribution, acreage, yield, exports and imports, prices, farm animals, and so on. It has been changed as shown in 2 below.

2 *Year-book of food and agricultural statistics* is published by the FAO (Food and Agricultural Organization of the United Nations). It is in two parts: 1 Production; and 2 Trade. It is an authoritative compilation of statistics on land, population, crops (area, yield, and production), live-stock, means of production, prices, wages, and freight rates and trade.

3 *Year-book of education* (London) is international. But it is restricted to education. It gives a survey of education in Great Britain, the other countries in the Commonwealth, and many foreign countries. There are statistical data and many independent articles on current problems of education. Users are referred back here and there to previous volumes for further information. Thus, each volume of this set becomes a supplement to another. Therefore, it cannot be used as an educational directory.

4 *Educational year-book* of the International Institute of Teachers' College (Columbia University) is international in character, But, it is restricted to education like the *Year-book of education*.

(London). It presents another variation in the scope of its subject-matter. Each volume specialises in surveying a particular educational topic. Thus, the entire set is conceived as a whole. It has, therefore, to be used as such by the reference librarian. Periodically the same topic may come up for a resurvey in later years. The following is a sample of special topics:

1924	Method;	1932	Religious education;
1925	Elementary curriculum;	1933	Missionary education;
1926	Secondary curriculum;	1934	Higher education;
1927	Training of teachers;	1935	Teacher's organisations;
1928	Vocational education;	1935-36	General survey;
1929	Educational philosophy;	1938	Rural education; and
1930	Secondary education;	1939	The meaning of liberal education in the twentieth century.
1931	Colonial education;		

5 *Minerva Jahrbuch* and *Index generalis* are both international in character. But both are restricted to education. They present a still another variation in scope. They are not reviewing year-books as the two preceding ones. They do not contain long chapters or articles. They do not requisition the service of specialists. They are merely compilations of educational facts of an instructional, personal, and bibliographical nature, collected mostly from the calendars of the educational and research institutes and the learned societies of the world. They are, in fact, directories in the strict sense of the word.

233 Regional and General

1 *Europa* was restricted to Europe only. But its scope extended to many subjects. It consisted of three loose leaf books. These were kept up-to-date by the periodical addition of new leaves and the replacement of the old by new ones. The first volume was an encyclopaedia of Europe. The second was a European who's who. The third dealt with European archives. For every country, it gave a directory of political, industrial, financial, cultural, and scientific organisations. Its specialities were the valuable sections on the League of Nations, world politics and economics, international organisations, and non-Europeans in Europe. In arrangement, the international section occurred first and then followed the European countries in alphabetical sequence.

In 1938 the *Europa* developed a fourth part on the same model with the title *Orbis*. This was devoted to extra-European countries.

In 1960, the loose-leaf *Europa* and *Orbis* have been replaced by the *Europa year-book* in two volumes; 1 Europe; 2 Other continents. It is a compilation on religion, education, government, constitution, political parties, economic and statistical data, and legal system. Its directory part covers scientific, political, financial, industrial, and cultural organisations.

2 *Indian year-book* was regional. Its subject scope was not restricted. It was a "statistical and historical annual of the Indian Empire with an explanation of the principal topics of the day". After the independence of India, its name was changed to *India and Pakistan year-book*. Now its title is *Times of India directory and year-book*. It gives a historical account of the Indian Union and the constituent States. It also gives general information and statistical data of political, economic, and social interest. There are a directory and a who's who.

3 As examples of similar year-books may be mentioned *Asylum Press almanack and directory*, *Madras*, *China Year-book*, *Japan year-book*, and *Soviet Union year-book*. The first of these was begun in 1802; it was suspended in 1936; it was later revived and again suspended.

234 Regional and Special

1 *Constitutional year-book* is restricted both by region and subject. Its subject scope is chiefly political. It gives complete information for Great Britain relating to parliamentary constituencies, members, candidates and elections, election law and procedure, statistics bearing on elections, tables of statistics on many subjects essential for the study of current economic and industrial problems.

2 The following are some other examples of regional and specialised year-books and directories:

21 *Indian library directory*;
22 *Handbook to Indian universities*;
23 *Industry year-book and directory* (India).
24 *Indian financial year-book*.
25 *American art annual*.
26 *Labour year-book* (Great Britain).
27 *Cotton year-book* (Great Britain).

24 Statistical Year-book

Another class of ready reference books consists of the several statistical annuals published by the governments of various countries. Till recently the final assembling and featuring of statistics had been left in the hands of different departments of government without any co-ordinating agency. Hence readers meet with many difficulties. A whole volume of statistics may appear under the misleading title 'annual reports.' The headings in the volumes published by related departments may not be correlated. The period covered may vary from department to department and show irritating inconsistency even in the same department. Many countries have now begun to have a central Department of Statistics with the object of rendering their statistical annuals uniform and readily understandable by readers. In spite of it, they have not yet been made sufficiently fool-proof to make reference aid unnecessary. There continues to be subtle differences in the area covered by reference books of apparently similar scope. These evade the ordinary readers. The specially trained vigilance of the reference librarian is necessary to bring them home to the readers. Perhaps one example will do.

241 Agricultural Statistics
(*Case Study* 119)

The Ministry of Agriculture and the Empire Marketing Board of the United Kingdom do not deal with the same region. Their reports are perfectly clear. But readers do not always take notice of this difference. The Ministry of Agriculture Statistics refer only to England and Wales except in the summaries where they refer to Great Britain and the whole of Ireland, Irish Free State included. The Empire Marketing Board Statistics on the other hand refer to the present United Kingdom including the Isle of Man and the Channel Islands but excluding the Irish Free State. The two sets of figures are therefore not comparable.

25 Dictionary

Among reference books, dictionaries are used earliest and longest in one's life time; and yet they are not put to all the possible uses for which they are designed. In our every day experience, we come across readers leaving their seats and migrating to the stack-room and groping in the geography section to find out the location of a place or rummaging the books in the literature section to ascertain where a particular literary character occurs, thus wasting enormous time. This matter can, however, be often settled in no time from the dictionaries in the reference room itself. The dictionaries have not yet succeeded in impressing on the general readers—even on experts in different subjects—their full capacity for help and the vast extra-territories they have brought under their jurisdiction. Readers are yet to realise that some dictionaries combine in themselves both lexicographical and encyclopaedic features. Dictionaries contain not only the usual definitions of words but also antonyms, thousands of personal and place names. Some serve also the purpose of a gazetteer. Some others serve as a concise dictionary of biography. Initiation in their earlier visits to the library continues to be inadequate to habituate readers to their extended spheres. Almost on every occasion there is need for the reference librarian to make his appearance and lead the eyes of the readers to the appendices in dictionaries. Some illustrations are given in the succeeding sections.

251 New English Dictionary

Murray's *New English dictionary on historical principles* 10 v in 20 parts. This differs from all other dictionaries in its plan and purpose. Its purpose is to give the history of every word showing differences in meaning, spelling, pronunciation, usage, etc., from the middle of the twelfth century. The information given is supported by quotations from authors of different periods. It purports to include all words now in use and those that are known to have been in use since 1150 A D.

Within this chronological limit, this dictionary professes to include all common words of speech and literature. The limits are extended to science and philosophy, technical terms in general use, and dialectical words before 1500 and those of later date, if they continue the history of a word once in general use, or have literary currency.

Words are classified as main words, subordinate words, and combinations. Information about a main word is given under current modern spelling with cross-references from other forms. Information includes, identification, morphology, and signification. Illustrative quotations are arranged chronologically.

Though it is not its intention, it contains much encyclopaedic information. Further, it lists many colloquial and slang words, Americanisms, etc., not easily obtainable elsewhere.

A unique feature of this dictionary is the exhaustive semasiological help that it gives about every word.

2511 SUPPLEMENTARY VOLUME

Supplement to new English dictionary, 1933. The main work had taken nearly half a century for completion (1884-1928). During this period, many new words and expressions had come into currency. Corrections and amplifications of previous definitions had become necessary. Hence the supplement. It exhibits on the technical side a great enlargement of the terminology of the arts and sciences, *e g*, biochemistry, wireless, telegraphy, telephony, psychoanalysis, radio, cinema, etc. On the linguistic side, it includes many British, American, and colonial colloquialisms and slang. The supplement has gone beyond the limits of the original in having included a larger proportion of proper names.

252 WEBSTER

Webster's *New international dictionary* is noted for its encyclopaedic features. It contains, in one alphabetical sequence, the usual dictionary words, foreign phrases, proverbs, noted names of fiction, and all proper names except those relegated to the biographical and geographical lists given as appendix.

In the appendix, there is a dictionary of abbreviations, arbitrary signs and symbols, forms of address, pronouncing gazetteer, and pronouncing biographical dictionary. There are illustrations also.

253 FUNK AND WAGNALL

Funk and Wagnall's *New standard dictionary* is another dictionary with encyclopaedic-features. It is apparently on the lines of Webster. But it has subtle deviations. These will prove to be pitfalls to those habituated to Webster. Coloured illustrations form a special feature. The extra information, given in its appendix, includes disputed pronunciations, rules for simplified spelling, foreign words and phrases, statistics of population, and the history of the world day by day!

This dictionary subordinates the historical to the current information whereas the two preceding dictionaries follow the natural historical sequence. While Webster puts the dictionary of abbreviations in the appendix, Funk and Wagnall brings the whole list of abbreviations into the body of the dictionary under the word "abbreviations"—as a dictionary within a dictionary. While on every page of Webster there are two alphabetical sequences, one for major words and one for minor words, Funk and Wagnall puts everything in one alphabet.

254 SABDA-KALPA-DRUMA

Radhakantadeva: *Sabda-kalpa-druma*. This is an encyclopaedic Sanskrit dictionary. In articles of lexicographical character the author adopts the following arrangement: the word; its gender if noun; its grammatical character if not noun, definition, corresponding expression in Bengali and sometimes Persian also, then the list of synonyms in Sanskrit with their respective authorities.

On the encyclopaedic side it covers all *Puranas, Tantras, Mahatmyas*, the literatures of various religious sects, the sciences of mathematics, astronomy, and medicine, the Indian philosophical systems, *Kavya* and *Alankara*, fine and useful arts, law, grammar, etc. But it omits the *Vedas*.

255 BRIHAD-ABHIDHANAM

Taranatha Tarkavachaspati: *Brihad-abhidhanam*. This is another important encyclopaedic Sanskrit dictionary wider and deeper in scope than the preceding one. The features specially claimed for it are:

Panini on genders; suffixes; primitive and derivative words; derivations and different meanings with illustrations of all the words which are found in Wilson's *Sanskrit dictionary* and *Sabda-kalpa-druma* and words not found in them; derivations and meanings of words of the *Vedas* not found in the then published portions of Bohtlingk's *Sanskrit Worterbuch*; technical words and doctrines of the following systems of philosophy, Carvaka, Yogacara, Vaibhashika, Sautrantika, Arhata, Ramanuja, Pasupata Saiva, Pratyabhijna and the six Hindu systems; technical terms of the *Shrauta* and *Grihyasutras*; Hindu law; plan and scope of the *Puranas, Mahabharata*, and *Ramayana*. History of the kings of Ancient India as gathered from the *Puranas*; position and description of countries according to Hindu ancient geography; technical terms of the Hindu medical sciences, astronomy, *tantras*, poetics, rhetoric and prosody, music, military science, cookery, *siksha, kalpa, hatha yoga, vastu sastra*, and classification of the *Vedas*.

256 Abhidhana-Rajendra

Abhidhana-rajendra is another such dictionary but devoted to Prakrit language and to Jain culture. For Prakrit words explanation is given in Sanskrit.

257 Need for Reference Service

A comparative study of all the linguistic dictionaries in English and other languages will show how divided dictionaries are in their scope and arrangement. The idiosyncrasies are too many for a sympathetic reference librarian to leave the enquirer to his own resources.

Such variations in the scope and range covered by dictionaries, similar to all appearance, have a chance to be overlooked. Full satisfaction may not be obtained from them by an ordinary enquirer unless helped at the right moment by a sympathetic reference librarian whose daily use of them has resulted in a thorough exploration of their holdings.

258 Technical Dictionary

In addition to such general linguistic dictionaries, we have now quite a number of dictionaries confining their range to particular subjects. In such special dictionaries, the technical terms, belonging to their respective subjects, are thrown in helpful relief instead of as a heap of unwanted stranger words and phrases.

Here are some examples:

1 Henderson (Isabella Fotheringham) and Henderson (W D). *Dictionary of scientific terms in biology, botany, zoology, anatomy, cytology, embryology, physiology.*
2 Muller (Felix). *Mathematisches vocabularium, fran osisch-deutsch und deutsch-franzosisch.*
3 Weld (Le Roy D). *Glossary of physics.*
4 Manly (Harold Phillips). *Radio and electronic dictionary.*
5 Hackh (Ingo W D). *Chemical dictionary.*
6 Rogers (R J). *Dictionary of gems: precious and semiprecious stones.*
7 Stedman (Thomas Lathrop). *Practical medical dictionary.*
8 Warren (Howard C). *Dictionary of psychology.*
9 Weston (W G). *Pitman's dictionary of economic and banking terms.*

Many enquirers, who would love to have such specialised dictionaries in the subjects of their pursuit, do not know of their existence. Nor do they know where to look for them. Witnessing the relief which they get and the joy which they express when they are brought to their notice is a recompense for the labour of reference librarians.

26 Encyclopaedia

These are days of encyclopaedias. And still to many readers, encyclopaedia means only universal encyclopaedias. Strictly speaking, subject-characteristic alone causes differences in encyclopaedias. On this basis, we have two groups of encyclopaedias.

1 Special or Subject.; and
2 General or Universal.

Special or subject encyclopaedias do not admit of grouping on the basis of area-characteristic. But, general or universal encyclopaedias often devote a greater number of entries and larger space to their respective countries of origin. Their being universal in extension necessarily prevents them from going beyond a certain depth in intension. As usual, extension and intension are antagonistic as applied to scope of encyclopaedias.

261 Special or Subject Encyclopaedia

Today we have encyclopaedias at all levels of intension, with the degree of their extension moving in the inverse direction.

For example we have encyclopaedias for most of the main classes. Even several classes of the second order of intension, such as electrical engineering, organic chemistry, dairying, beekeeping, English literature, classical literature, banking; and the laws of different countries have encyclopaedias of their own.

In more recent years encyclopaedias are being produced even in subjects of still higher order of intension. For example, we have

Handbuch der Astrophysik;
Allen's *Commercial organic analysis*;
Mitzakis's *Oil encyclopaedia*;
Brett's *Rose encyclopaedia*;
Kirtiker and Basu's *Indian medicinal plants*;
Root's *ABC and XYZ of the bee culture*;
Dickens *Encyclopaedia*;
Encyclopaedia of Islam; and
Encyclopaedia of forms and precedents.

Many readers are not aware of the existence of encyclopaedias in subjects of such narrow extension. They have to be brought to their notice by the reference librarian.

262 UNIVERSAL ENCYCLOPAEDIA WITH GEOGRAPHICAL BIAS

The following encyclopaedias are all universal. But they show a bias towards the geographical areas indicated by their respective names.

Encyclopaedia Americana;
Encyclopaedia Italiana;
Hindi visvakosa;
Kalai kalanjiam (Tamil);
Maharashtra jnanakosa;
Andhra vignana sarvasva; and
Dairatul-maarif (Arabic).

The *Encyclopaedia Britannica* has a bias to Great Britain and the United States of America.

In all such cases, the reference librarian should warn the readers about the bias. Otherwise, it may not be fully realised and given due weightage by the users.

263 SCOPE VARIES WITH EDITION

In the *Encyclopaedia Britannica*, we find a tendency for a subtle variation in scope from edition to edition. Newer editions have necessarily to introduce new knowledge emerging in the interval between two editions. Perhaps to find room for them without undue enlargement of size, some older subjects have to be lopped out. Further, some other subjects have to be given a restricted treatment.

For example the article Aurora polaris (Borealis) runs to fifteen columns in the eleventh edition. But it has now shrunk to one column; and it has deprived itself of all the beautiful illustrations. Many of the articles in the ninth edition were elaborate monographs even now sought for their comprehensiveness, scholarly treatment, and charming style. They still retain the aroma of the personality of their authors. Few articles of the fourteenth edition belong to that standard. On the contrary, the earlier editions have naturally no value for a reader seeking information about new comers such as:

Atomic physics;
Jet engine;
Sputnik;
Space travel;
Electronic engineering;
Transistor;
Wireless;
Broadcasting;
Television;
Electronic computer;
Atomic engineering;
Biochemistry;
Cytology;
Pasteurisation;
Surrealism;
Bahaism;
Ahmadiya movement;
Humanism;
Psycho-analysis;
Dalton Plan;
Project method;
Contract technique;
Strato-sphere;
Pakistan;
Ghana;
East Germany;
United Nations;
F A O;
Bolshevism;
Nazism;
Fascism;
Planned economy;
Public utilities;
Private sector;
Public sector.

27 Gazetteer and Guide Book

271 Independent Gazetteer

Gazetteers are indispensable aids to ready reference service. Some of them are independent publications.

Examples:

1 *Chamber's world gazetteer and geographical dictionary*;

2 *Columbia Lippincott gazetteer of the world*;

3 *Nouveau dictionnaire universelle*;

4 *Imperial gazetteer of India*; and

5 Thornton (Edward). *Gazetteer of the territories under the government of the Viceroy of India.*

272 Gazetteer as Index to Atlas

Some gazetteers happen to be separately published as indexes to huge atlases.

Examples:

1 Index to Andrees' *Allgemeiner Hand-Atlas*; and

2 Index to the loose-leaf binding of the *Times atlas.*

273 Merged Gazetteer

And some have no separate existence. They are found only merged as part of dictionaries and atlases.

274 Scope of Gazetteer

In scope some are of international coverage; and some are

regionally restricted. In the range of information given, all possible varieties are discernible. At the one extreme we find in some gazetteers location, latitude, longitude and altitude only; and at the other extreme we have information which is almost encyclopaedic—name, pronunciation, other names by which the place was known, location, latitude, longitude, altitude, population figures, physical aspects, flora, fauna, local history, administration, finance, industries and institutions of the place, etc.

Examples:

1 *Imperial gazetteer of India*; and
2 *Nouveau dictionnaire de geographie universelle.*

2741 HORN OF PLENTY IN PRESENT-DAY INDIA

Especially for India with its history dating back to several milleniums with innumerable vicissitudes in her political fortunes, historical information about small localities and about persons or things associated with them has to be sought only in the national, state, and district gazetteers. In the absence of readily usable books on local history, reference questions of such local interest have to be answered largely with the aid of gazetteers. Readers do not know the possibilities of gazetteers. Again and again, they feel like drawing blank from the library while seeking local information; and yet on being helped by a reference librarian they find the gazetteers to be an '*Akshaya-patra*' (horn of plenty).

275 SCOPE OF GUIDE BOOK

Guide books are complementary to gazetteers. Though intended for travellers, they are very serviceable for ready reference. They contain much fuller information and more maps for smaller areas not obtainable anywhere else. Such maps include plans of cities, towns, and historical sites. Further, they contain information about museums, art collections, architectural and historical monuments, natural scenery, communications, distances from other surrounding cities, institutions, etc., relating to a given place.

Examples:

1 Murray's *Hand-book for travellers in India*, *Pakistan*, *Burma and Ceylon*;
2 Muirhead's *Great Britain* (*Blue guides*); and
3 Muirhead's *Switzerland* (*Blue guides*).

Old guide books are very valuable inasmuch as they contain

information discarded in later editions. Many streets are renamed; many small towns are absorbed or swallowed, as by an octopus, by industrial cities first begun as mere suburbs; and many places are wiped out of existence by the ravages of wars. In such contingencies, older guide books alone can give information about the state of affairs of the past.

276. STHALA-PURANA

The reference librarian in Indian libraries should not forget the encyclopaedic *Puranas*. They contain virtually many an old gazetteer scattered in their pages. The *Skanda-purana* is particularly rich in such gazetteer constituents. But as the *Puranas* have no index, it is almost impossible to use them as ready reference books for local history. Some however have been extracted and given independent existence as *Sthala-purana* (=local history). They have also been translated into the several modern languages and dialects of India. Most of these renderings were made, however, long before the present form of arrangement for gazetteers and guide books was arrived at. Hence they are neither alphabetical nor provided with suitable indexes. Most of them are in verse; and the requirement of prosody has kept out every possibility of gazetteer arrangement.

2761 MIXTURE OF FACT AND MYTHOLOGY

A responsibility of the reference librarian may have to make him a little careful into the sphere of critical interpreters in regard to the use of such *Sthala-puranas* by credulous as well as sceptically critical readers. On the surface such books appear as a mixture of facts and fables. An uncritical reader might take the entire information too literally unless a knowing reference librarian puts him on his guard.

2762 DELICATE PART TO BE PLAYED

At the same time it would be absurd to deface the passages not obviously factual in such books, in the way in which some censorial librarians would deal with betting news in the dailies displayed in the newspaper room. For the so-called mythical part of the *Sthala-puranas* are believed in Indian tradition to be oblique or even cipher versions of deep experiences and truths. It is true that neither the librarian nor the credulous reader possesses the key to their interpretation. But such keys are being handed down from generation to generation along some line of custodians. It is improper for the librarians to play the role of iconoclasts and do short work of the *Sthala-puranas* as a whole or the so-called mythical part of them, so as to over-reach themselves in their enthusiasm to hawk them about among those likely to be deluded by them. The reference librarian has a delicate part to play in respect of the *Sthala-puranas* as reference books.

28 Atlases

Atlases constitute another class of ready reference books. Most readers accustomed only to school atlases, are not aware of the variety of gigantic and specialised atlases. They vary not only in the subjects represented but also in the extent of the details given and the methods adopted to feature them.

281 Locational Atlas

For instance, some are predominantly locational in aim and scope; they include maps of the different countries of the world marking as many places as the size of the maps will allow. As a rule, they devote more space to the country of their origin and its colonies than to the other regions of the world.

Examples:

1 *Atlas universel de geographie*;
2 *Daily telegraph victory atlas of the world*;
3 *Encyclopaedia Britannica world atlas*;
4 Hammond's *New world loose leaf atlas*;
5 *National atlas of India*; and
6 *Times atlas of the world*, 5 v.

282 Atlas with Exposition and Pictures

Some atlases include also expository matter and pictures of scenery and people.

Examples:

1 Harmsworth's *Atlas of the world and pictorial gazetteer*; and
2 *New census atlas of the world.*

283 Systematic Atlas

Then come systematic atlases. They cover or relate to different topics of geography, such as solar system, geomorphology, hydrography, climate, vegetation, zoogeography, population and distribution of races, historical and political geography, economic products and commercial geography, for the world as a whole and for individual countries. Some outstanding examples are:

1 *Methodischer Atlas zur Landerkunde von Europa*;

2 Bartholomew (J G). *Atlas of zoogeography*;

3 *Atlante di geographia fiscia, politica ed economica*;

4 Bartholomew (J S). *Atlas of meteorology*;

5 *Atlas of ancient and classical geography*;

6 *Atlas international Larousse; political et economique*;

7 Horrabin (J F). *Atlas of current affairs*;

8 Rodo (Alexander). *Atlas of to-day and to-morrow*;

9 Associations of British Chambers of Commerce. *Chamber of Commerce atlas*; and

10 *Phillip's centenary mercantile marine atlas.*

284 Specialist Atlas

Yet other atlases specialise in various other fields of knowledge. *Examples*:

1 United States, Office of Farm Management. *Atlas of American agriculture*;

2 United States, Forest Service. *Forest atlas: geographical distribution of North American trees*;

3 Piney (A) and Wyard (Stonby). *Clinical atlas of blood diseases*;

4 Schmidt (P W). *Sprach-familien und Sprachenreise der Erde*;

5 Institute of Social and Religious Research. *World missionary atlas*; and

6 *Catholic world atlas.*

Few readers know or remember the existence of such specialised atlases. Many readers, therefore, go unserved in a library without reference librarians. The reference librarian too should keep himself informed of their utility. They should go forward eagerly to find users for such specialised atlases.

285 Peculiarities in Index

Atlases differ in the indexes provided in them. Large atlases usually publish their indexes as separate volumes. Atlases of smaller sizes carry their indexes in the same volume as the maps. Atlases differ also in their way of indicating location. Most of them indicate location by map number, latitude, and longitude. Some use locational squares improvised for location purposes. The *Times atlas* provides an independent transparent grid-frame. This should be placed on the map consulted for locating places. Such variations in location device in an atlas add their own case for the need for help to readers by a reference librarian.

CHAPTER 3

UP-TO-DATE-NESS

31 Difference in Up-to-date-ness

A reference book is sought for information. Information is of little value if it is not up-to-date. In any case, it is necessary to know the date upto which it has been brought. All reference books do not satisfy the test of up-to-date-ness to the same degree. Even in one and the same book, all pieces of information are not brought upto the same date. One should know their idiosyncrasies in this respect. Otherwise, one might go away with wrong information. The casual reader does not, however, get the chance to know their idiosyncrasies with sufficient intimacy. A reliable mastery of such details can be acquired only by the reference librarian handling and sifting them out, day after day and hour after hour. Readers can get reliable information out of the reference books only in a library providing the help of a reference librarian. From the point of view of up-to-date-ness, reference books fall into six groups. These are,

1 Regulars;
2 Those with no further edition;
3 Irregulars;
4 Those with annual supplements;
5 Those with correction slips; and
6 Those in loose-leaf form.

32 Regulars

At the one extreme, we have regulars such as the *Statesman's year book* and the *Who's who*. These bring out a new edition every year with the same kind of information brought up-to-date. They have developed an elaborate organisation and technique to bring the information up-to-date year after year. They have established contact with prompt correspondents in all spheres falling within their purview. With their help, they endeavour to be ever up-to-date. There are certain other ready reference books like the *Minerva Jahrbuch* and the *Who's who in America* bringing out new editions once in three or two years with equal regularity. In all these cases, it is necessary to know their period and evaluate accordingly the information contained in them.

33 No Second Edition

At the other extreme we have valuable ready reference books of vast magnitude, never being revised and brought up-to-date. These are defunct. Monroe's *Cyclopaedia of education* is an important book of its kind. No second edition has come out. The information contained in it is, therefore, half a century out of date. Similarly Hasting's *Encyclopaedia of religion and ethics* and Palgrave's *Dictionary of political economy* have not seen a later edition. Nearly half a century has passed by. An ordinary enquirer is liable to dress up his thought with unreliable facts overlooking that in some respects the information contained in them is out of date by half a century. In spite of their volumes showing their date prominently in the imprint of their title pages, a living voice is necessary to warn the reader about the period to which the information given by them belongs.

34 Irregulars

Between these two extremes, we have various possibilities. The *Encyclopaedia Britannica* illustrates in its history a certain evolution of attempts to keep such publications up-to-date. This well known ready reference book brings out its editions at fairly long intervals of fifteen or twenty years. The cost of production and consequently the price of a set are too prohibitive to attempt new editions at smaller intervals. At the same time the publishers are not oblivious of the march of events in the long interval. Hence about ten years after an edition, they used to issue a few supplementary volumes by way of bringing the information up-to-date. The basic volumes together with the supplementary volumes were taken to constitute a new edition. Sometimes more than one such improvised edition used to appear between two completely revised editions.

35 Annual Supplement

But even this was felt to be inadequate to meet the rapid changes of the modern days. Hence in 1938 the publishers launched a new venture known as the *Encyclopaedia Britannica book of the year*. In the words of the editor (p vii),

"The lapse in time between editions was necessarily lengthy

and the device employed to bridge the gap was that of supplementary volumes, ranging in number from three to seven, issued once, or rarely twice, in the intervals.

"This device, satisfactory in more leisurely days, seems to have outlived its usefulness in an age when scientific and technical knowledge expand in range and volume at a pace equalled only by that of commercial and political developments.

"The resources of the *Encyclopaedia Britannica* organisation have been marshalled to meet this situation by the issue, each spring, of a world-wide survey of the preceding year. The information. . .follows the plan of the *Encyclopaedia Britannica* itself, to which the book of the year is designed to serve as an annual supplement, thus keeping up-to-date the sets of the *Britannica* in the hands of subscribers."

What was arrived at with much hesitation and after several less satisfactory arrangements by the *Encyclopaedia Britannica* has been long ago hit upon and brought to familiar use by two other encyclopaedias of American origin. The *American annual* stands in the same relation to the *Encyclopaedia Americana* as the *Book of the year* does to the *Britannica.* Similarly the *New international encyclopaedia* has the *New international year-book* as its train-bearer. This procedure of annual supplements and cumulation at longer intervals has been in vogue also in other reference books like Halsbury's *Laws of England.*

351 Inherent Danger

But with increase in the number of annual supplements, an ordinary reader may fail to read them all together with the basic volumes, in the absence of help from a reference librarian. There is this inherent danger in the maintenance of up-to-dateness with annual supplements alone.

36 Correction Slips

In the case of many ready reference books the changes that have to be introduced from year to year, however essential and valuable qualitatively, are slight in quantity. Some numbers or names need alteration. Here and there a sentence or a paragraph needs recasting. Occasionally need arises for a few additional pages. The Law of Parsimony naturally raises the question: "Is it not possible to provide for all these changes without going through the whole hog of reprinting the entire book?" The clumsy method of the periodical issue of correction slips offers itself as a solution. These slips are expected to be cut out and pasted down at proper places. But human inertia makes these slips lie uncut in several libraries. In the case of the few active libraries, the original volume is bulged out; warped, and rendered uneven, uncouth, and repulsive. Therefore, it is unable to get users. As a result, humanity goes either wrongly informed or uninformed.

37 Loose Leaf

A recent attempt to meet the situation resulted in the invention of loose leaf books. A detailed history of the evolution of such loose leaf service culminating in the institution of a periodical whose issues are intended to replace sections of the basic volumes that have gone out of date will be found in an article of mine entitled *Regression in book production, the problem of loose leaf books* (R50). This economical mode of periodically bringing parts of a reference book up-to-date introduces an element of heterogeneity. At no time except in the year in which the basic volume is issued, are all the parts of such a reference book brought up to the same date. Different sections carry the information to different years. This is an unnatural feature. An ordinary reader cannot take this into account without a proper instruction and warning by a reference librarian. In his turn, a reference librarian should keep himself correctly posted with all the details of such loose leaf forms of reference books.

371 Publisher's Indication

The publishers of some loose leaf reference books indicate the details of the revision on the instalments of revised leaves. For example, the year of issue is printed on each leaf of Hammond's *New world loose leaf atlas*. So also, some mark is printed on the margin of each page or gathering of the *Europa year-book* to indicate revision. In each section of the loose leaf reference book *Pure cultural study of bacteria*, there is even a more elaborate indication of the year relating to its contents. For example, the sections dealing with the preparation of media and staining procedure, in the edition current in 1940, were those brought up to 1939. They were marked "Seventh edition". The sections dealing with the determination of pathogenecity and serological methods were those brought up to

1935 only. The other sections belonged to different intermediate years.

372 Necessary But not Sufficient

All such earnest attempts of the publishers to instruct the users often fail to achieve their ends. They are necessary. But they are not sufficient. Readers are not accustomed to such differential dating of the pages or the sections of a book. Therefore, they miss the instructions. A human agency in the form of a reference librarian has to invite their attention personally to such instructions. It has also to interpret the instructions to them.

CHAPTER 4

ARRANGEMENT

41 Kinds of Arrangement

The scope of ready reference books can be usefully compared only in the case of those relating to the same subject. But the variation in the arrangement of matter needs to be compared and studied in relation to all ready reference books irrespective of the subject matter. Broadly speaking we can recognise three types of arrangement.

42 Dictionary Arrangement

The most commonly occurring type is the dictionary arrangement. The entries are arranged alphabetically in this type. The linguistic dictionaries form the most familiar examples of this type of arrangement. Most of the biographical dictionaries and directories also follow the pure alphabetical arrangement. Some bibliographies also arrange their entries in the dictionary way. A classified index will increase their usefulness. The *Cyclopaedia of education* illustrates this.

43 Systematic Arrangement

At the other extreme, some reference books arrange their entries systematically by subjects. Systematic arrangement is coming into vogue particularly in bibliographies. This mode of arrangement is also adopted by several handbooks, recipes, and books of formulae. Systematic arrangement should be backed by an alphabetical index. Systematic arrangement with alphabetical index gives the best reference value.

Examples:

1 *Encyklopaedie der mathematischen Wissenschaften*;
2 *Handbuch der Physik*;
3 *Wiley engineering handbook series*;
4 Beilstein's *Handbuch der organischen Chemie*;
5 *Scientific American cyclopaedia of formulas*;
6 Allison (N H) and others. *Guide to historical literature*; and
7 Montgomery (R H). *Financial handbook*.

44 Hybrid Arrangement

These two clear types may not after all give much difficulty. A reader can soon familiarise himself with them. But the real trouble arises with the vast majority of ready reference books. The arrangement in them may lie anywhere between these two extremes. To all appearance, the arrangement will be alphabetical. But here and there will occur grouping of articles or entries based on similarity of subject matter. A formal conformity to alphabetical sequence will be improvised by devices such as inversion of words. In such a case the arrangement is virtually systematic. This may not be carried out uniformly in every possible case. We can find all degrees of fluctuation in this matter. This makes ready reference books rather treacherous. To pull the unwary reader through them, the service of a trained reference librarian becomes a necessity. No doubt an index may have been provided to aid in self-help. But how many have the knowledge of their existence and still less the habit or the patience to look them up! In spite of this, hybrid arrangement is found in many reference books.

CHAPTER 5

ALPHABETICAL ARRANGEMENT

50 Introduction

Of all the three types of arrangement, the alphabetical one may seem as simple as *a*, *b*, *c*; but it is not really so. There may be a branching of ways and difficulties at various stages of alphabetisation, *viz.*, choice of the entry word, its spelling particularities, and the sequence of the other essential words. In spite of the production of numerous ready reference books in the dictionary form and in spite of nearly the same public having to use all of them, no attempt has been made so far to arrive at an agreed common method of meeting all these problems. Individuality of treatment persists much in the alphabetical arrangement in the ready reference book. Therefore, an ordinary enquirer is almost thrown into despair, unless helped by a reference librarian with a knowledge of all possible vagaries of alphabetisation. We shall examine in the succeeding sections the sources for vagaries.

51 Conflict of Language

In Indian libraries an unusual major vagary in alphabetisation trips many an unwary reader off his feet. Some reference books in Orientalia use the Roman alphabet. The sequences of the alphabet in Sanskritic and Islamic languages are different from the one in Roman or Germanic languages. Some of these reference books follow the sequence of Roman letters. Others follow the sequence of their phonetic equivalents in the original languages. This difference in practice makes even highly educated enquirers often come to the reference librarian with the open pages of a book, imploring in despair for help in locating a particular piece of information in its alphabetical sequence.

511 Platt and Wilson

(*Case Study* 120)

Let us compare J T Platt's *Dictionary of Urdu, classical Hindi and English* and Wilson's *Glossary of judicial and revenue terms in Indian languages*. In both, the entry word is mostly Urdu. However, it is written in the Urdu script in the former and in the Roman script in the latter. The arrangement follows the respective scripts in the two books. The former adds immediately after the entry word in Urdu its transliteration in Roman alphabet. A person, not reading Urdu script, has naturally to guide himself by the Roman transliteration in both the books. His resulting confusion and irritation can be inferred from the following:

1 *Utar* and *Atarpal* occur on the consecutive pages, 14 and 15, of Platts. But Wilson inverts their seniority and puts *Atarpal* on page 37 and *Utar* on page 536.

2 Similarly the two words *Byora* (*Byaura*) and *Papar* occur as friendly neighbours in the consecutive pages 212 and 213 of Platts. But they encamp themselves as far away as possible from each other in pages 95 and 399 of Wilson.

Surely one must sympathise with the reader when he stands baffled by such apparent anomalies.

512 Bloomfield and Sorensen
(*Case Study* 121)

A comparison of Bloomfield's *Vedic concordance* and Sorensen's *Index to the names in the Mahabharata* furnishes another example. Both of them enter Sanskrit words in Roman script and profess to arrange the words alphabetically. But this apparent similarity will trip an unwary reader off his feet. Because Bloomfield is orthodox enough to arrange the words in the sequence of the Sanskrit alphabet; while Sorensen is thoroughly occidental and does not swerve from the sequence of the Roman alphabet. The discomfiture of the unwary reader can be realised if we remember the chaotic difference in arrangement. The two words 'Cura' and 'Daca' occur on the two neighbouring pages 221 and 223 of Sorensen. But, they get dispersed to pages 473 and 933 of Bloomfield with nearly 500 closely printed three-column-pages intervening.

In the face of such disagreement among reference books can anybody deny that ready reference service in a library is a necessity and not a mere luxury?

52 Conflict of Spelling

Apart from the conflict of languages, alphabetisation is rendered puzzling to the users on account of conflict of spelling. Entry word is prepptent in the dictionary arrangement of any ready reference book. Its prepotency is inseparable from its spelling. Therefore, many of the difficulties of enquirers are traceable to conflict of spelling and to the same word having variant spellings. Special mention should be made of the following conventions regarding spelling, elision, and the ignoring of honorific words in arranging words in the English language. These are conventions developed by one school of cataloguers.

1 Scottish names beginning with *Mac* and its abbreviated forms *Mc* and *M*: In arrangement the abbreviated forms are treated as if written in full;

2 Names beginning with *Saint* and its abbreviated forms *S St.* and *Ste*: Here the latter forms are treated as 'Saint'; and

3 Irish names with initial O' or other prefixes: Here prefixes are treated as if merged with the names.

4 German words spelt with *a, o* and *u* umlaut: Here the convention is to arrange them as if they were spelt *ae, oe*, and *ue*.

5 Sometimes the entire first word may have to be ignored, *e g*, when it is a definite article or an honorific like the 'Sri' in Indian usage. It must be remembered however, that titles like *Sribhashyam*, the well known philosophical classic, are exceptions.

6 The ordinal value of compound words may also be beset with the difficulties arising in spelling.

521 Scottish Name

(*Case Study* 122)

One illustration may be sufficient. It relates to possible violations of the aforesaid cataloguer's conventions about the equalization of *Mac, M'c, Mc* and *M'* at the beginning of names.

1 The index to the grand old *Encyclopaedia metropolitana* separates M'Culloch, M'Donald, M'Evoy, M'Intosh, etc. from their kith and kin who have not yet shed their 'ac'. The entries with M' begin on page 213. Those with Mac end as early as with page 202. There are 33 columns of stranger words ending with Mazzarino, Mazzuchetti, Mblakveh, Mborcbi, separating the two sets.

2 *Who's who in America* (1938-39) keeps up the tradition of the *Encyclopaedia metropolitana* and parts company with its English cousin *Who's who*. MacWhite, the last of the 'Mac's', is separated from McAdams, the first of 'Mc's', by nearly a thousand other names.

3 Monro's *Cyclopaedia of education* flouts convention in a more

irritating way. It clubs together all articles with entry words beginning with 'Mc'. It puts this entire group prior to the articles with entry words beginning with 'Mac.' As a result, McMurtrie and McPherson are given precedence over Macalister and Macdonald. One can understand the determination to be guided only by the apparent and the refusal to supply the elided 'a' mentally in fixing precedence. By what principle even loyalty to the apparent is sacrificed by putting 'Mc' before 'Mac', it is not easy to see. It is equally difficult to follow why a single 'Mac', *viz.*, MacVicar is taken away from the other 'Mac's' and put prior to all the 'Mc's.'

522 JUSTIFICATION FOR REFERENCE SERVICE

At any rate the confusion caused by such inconsistencies in reference books forms a sufficient justification for the readers asking for ready reference help.

523 ABSENCE OF UNIFORM STANDARD

For purposes of cataloguing, the library profession has gone into this question and arrived at standards and further invented what are known as *See* reference entries. But the profession of reference-book-production has not made any attempt to arrive at standardisation in such matters. As a result, the reference books do not yield to the enquirers their fullest help, without aid from a specially trained reference librarian.

53 Other Grammatical Factors

Not merely spelling; every problem in the grammar of the language of the ready reference book will similarly contribute to the dependence of the enquirer on the help of the reference librarian. Conflict of singular and plural, conflict between noun and adjective, conflict of synonymous words, conflict of alternative names, and conflict of popular and technical terms are some of the linguistic peculiarities that may render ready reference books difficult to use unless initiated and even helped at further stages by a reference librarian.

531 MOUSE AND MICE INSTANCE
(*Case Study* 123)

The *Encyclopaedia Britannica* has an article on 'mouse.' But Hunter's *Encyclopaedia of scientific agriculture* has an entry only under 'mice.' In fact even that is only a cross-reference in the form "mice *see* rats and mice." And there is no entry at all under mouse. On the other hand R P Wright's *Standard cyclopaedia of modern agriculture and rural economy* gives the substantive article under the singular form 'mouse'; but it also adds another article under "mice and moles—damage to woodlands."

532 Louse and Lice Instance
(*Case Study* 124)

The *Encyclopaedia Britannica* gives an article under 'Louse' but not under 'Lice.' The *British encyclopaedia of medical practice* gives a cross-reference under 'Lice' but no entry—either substantive or reference—under 'Louse.'

533 Woman and Women Instance
(*Case Study* 125)

The *Encyclopaedia Britannica* has no main entry or cross-reference entry under 'Woman.' It uses only the plural form 'Women.' But the *Encyclopaedia of social sciences* uses the singular for some articles and plural for others:

Woman, Position in society;
Woman, Suffrage;
Woman's christian temperance movement;
Women in industry;
Women's education;
Women's organisation.

534 Synonym Instances
(*Case Study* 126)

The *Encyclopaedia Britannica* has articles under 'Philanthropy'; 'Vaccination'; and 'Kindergarten.' But the *Encyclopaedia of social sciences* gives information on these subjects under the headings 'Charity'; 'Communicable diseases, control of'; and 'Pre-school education.'

535 Technical and Popular Term Instances
(*Case Study* 127)

The *Encyclopaedia Britannica* has an article on 'Biochemistry' but in the Chambers's *Encyclopaedia* the corresponding article is headed 'Animal chemistry.' The *Encyclopaedia Britannica* uses terms like 'Graphite,' 'Ground nut' and 'Brewing ' as headings of articles whereas Watt's *Dictionary of economic products in India* uses technical terms like 'Plumbago,' 'Arachis' and 'Malt liquors' respectively.

536 ALCOHOLISM INSTANCE
(*Case Study* 128)

The *Encyclopaedia Britannica* has an article on 'Drunkenness' which is linked by references to 'Alcohol, pathological effects of' and 'Liquor laws and temperance.' But the Chambers's *Encyclopaedia* uses 'Alcoholism' as the heading for the corresponding article. In the *Encyclopaedia of social sciences* 'Alcoholism' occurs only as a sub-division of the article on 'Alcohol.'

54 Homonym in Entry Words

Another factor complicating alphabetisation is the presence of several entries all having the same entry word. In some of the entries, the entry words may be the names of governments or governmental departments; in others, names of institutions; in still others, names of persons; while some may be names of subjects or localities. Further complications may arise by the entry word of one item consisting just of the first few letters of a much longer entry word of some other item. The following eighteen entries will illustrate the problem envisaged:

1 Madras.
2 Madras and Mysore.
3 Madras, High Court.
4 Madras, History.
5 Madras, Bibliography.
6 Madras, City.
7 Madras, (Pseud).
8 Madras (Saint).
9 Madras (Henry).
10 Madras (Henry), Smith (John).
11 Madras (Henry), Biography.
12 Madras (Henry), *Ed.*
13 Madras (Henry), (1800-1900).
14 Madras Christian College.
15 Madras Educational Series.

16 Madras Terrace.
17 Madras-Eye.
18 Madraspatam.

541 Gestalt Alphabetisation

Hardly two ready reference books agree entirely in the sequence of these eighteen entries. As a matter of fact, even library catalogues, have not yet found a fool-proof technique to arrive at a unique arrangement in such cases, in spite of their greater progress in systematisation. The first attempt to lay bare the difficulties at great depths in this matter was made in 1938. [R63]. Then was shown the desirability for separating the 'legislative' from the 'executive' phase of the problem. Such a distinction led to the discovery of the difficulties really transcending the capacity of the mere ordinal values of the alphabet. A possible line of solution involved the invention of the *Gestalt value*—that is, value depending upon the pattern presented by the entry. The *Gestalt value* has to recognise not only the letters of the alphabet but also punctuation marks, other symbols like brackets, spaces between words, such as word-spaces, comma-spaces, sentence-spaces, and paragraph-spaces. Further it has also to vary the value of combinations of letters and of words according to the style of writing and perhaps also according to the way of their combination with or without brackets. Having attempted a model solution of this problem of alphabetisation with an improvised scale of *Gestalt values* an appeal was made to the library profession and to those engaged in the production of ready reference books to pursue the matter further along those or similar lines on an international basis so that the alphabetisation of reference books may be brought to some uniform system. This suggestion was taken up by the Indian Standards Institution in 1957. Its Documentation Committee is investigating it. [K1].

5411 HELP TO REFERENCE LIBRARIAN

The help of a reference librarian will be necessary as much when a uniform principle is followed in all reference books as when the present chaos obtains. To-day the reference librarian is wanted to pull the enquirers through the mutually conflicting varieties of alphabetisation in different ready reference books. But when a uniform standard is evolved and adopted, the system would be too complicated for the ordinary enquirer to understand and master.

Whether based on the proposed *Gestalt value* or on any other equivalent principle the rule of alphabetisation would have to be artificial. It could not be naturally thought of. Hence the services of the reference librarian will always be in requisition. If there is need for help in either case, it may be asked what is the gain in adopting a complicated technique to secure uniformity in alphabetisation. The advantage here is for the reference librarian himself. He need not carry in his head the load of the vagaries of reference books. He need not fumble about in the presence of the enquirer. He can lay his hands on the required piece of information with assurance and confidence. This will have a tremendous effect on the enquirer's mind. Apart from this psychological advantage, a good deal of time will be saved for the reference librarian. Every minute of staff-time saved can be diverted to the direct and immediate service of readers to a better satisfaction of the Fourth Law.

542 Nothing Before Something

All this is on the assumption of reference books having already adopted alphabetisation based on *Gestalt value*. But the very theory is new. It has not yet received the approval either of the library profession or of those engaged in the production of reference books. But a principle in alphabetisation usually called "nothing before something" rule has been playing hide and seek for nearly a century. It is really a 'gestalt' rule in an incipient stage. An enquirer seldom knows whether this rule is or is not in favour with a particular reference book. It is worse. He does not know this principle either by name or by appearance; with the result, he is rightly bewildered when he looks up two different reference books for a comparative study of some subject. An example will make this clear. We have put down in the next section in parallel columns the titles of the articles beginning with the word 'Land' in two popular encyclopaedias.

542 'Land' Entries Instance
(*Case Study* 129)

Seligman's *Encyclopaedia of social sciences*	*Encyclopaedia Britannica*
Land Bank schemes	Land
Land Grant colleges *See* Agricultural Edn. Universities and colleges.	Landau
	Landaulet

Seligman's *Encyclopaedia of social sciences*

Land Grants
Land Mortgage credit
Land Nationalisation *See* Socialization; Single tax
Land Reforms *See* Socialization; unearned increment; single tax
Land Registration *See* Land transfer
Land Settlement
Land Speculation
Land Taxation
Land Tenure
Land Transfer
Land Utilization
Land Valuation
Landauer (Gustav)
Landed Estate
Landlord and Tenant

Encyclcpaedia Britannica

Land chainage *See* Drainage of land
Landeck
Land Economics *See* Agricultural Economics
Landen, John
Landen, Battle of—July 29, 1693 *See* Neerwinden battle of
Lander, Richard Lemon
Landes
Landeshut
Land-grant colleges and Universities
Land groove
Land laws *See* Real property and conveyancing
Landler
Landlord and tenant
Land naturalization
Landon, Letitia Elizabeth
Landor, Walter Savage
Landour
Landouska, Wanda
Land reclamation
Land registration *See* Land, title to
Landsberg An lech
Landsberg—An-der-Warthe
Landsberg Bei Halle
Landscape Architecture
Landscape painting
Landseer, Sir Edwin Henry
Land's end
Land shut
Lands-Knecht
Lands-Krona
Land-slip
Land-strum
Land-taxe
Land Tenure: Economic and Agricultural aspects
Land Tenure; primitive
Land Tenure Title
Landuman
Landwehr.

These two columns show the effect of observing and not observing the 'nothing before something' rule. 'Landlord and tenant' comes early in the *Britannica*; while it comes last in Seligman. A busy reader hard up for time may miss the article in either the one or the other. No doubt, one may ask why should he not know all this difference; but we are only concerned with the fact that many do not know. This difference comes into their experience at such long intervals that they are not able to carry it over in their minds. We frequently come across enquirers who casually remark in resignation that it is unfortunate that an otherwise good and up-to-date cyclopaedia like Seligman's has no article on 'Landed estates.' This impression is due to the article in question occurring as late as page 140 whereas the first article on 'land' occurs on the page 29. Surely it is the business of the reference librarian, who experiences them almost every day, to help the enquirer with his knowledge and not allow him to go away without the information.

55 Choice of Entry Word

Apart from such vagaries in alphabetisation, ready reference books vary also in the very choice of entry word in the case of an item denoted by a word-group instead of a single word. An obvious example is a name-of-person. To individualise a name-of-person, it has now become the practice in all communities to use two or more words in the construction of a name-of-person. To have the fullest benefit of multiworded names-of-persons, ready reference books find it necessary to expand the initials and write all the constituent words in full. Now, the incidence of prepotence is not the same on all the constituent words. In making entries for alphabetical arrangement the prepotent word should be brought first. This is required by the Canon of Prepotence [R8].

551 Western Name

In modern European names this principle has been fully adopted; and the practice of writing the surname first and the forenames thereafter has become universal. In spite of the practice being universal, there is no denying that there is an element of artificiality about it. Not to take the constituent words in the sequence in which they occur in usage but to invert them in a peculiar way will not occur naturally to those not told about it. The consequence is that freshmen easily mislead themselves. The case of the literature honours men who looked for 'Bernard Shaw' under 'Bernard' has already been mentioned in section C3511. Thus even in the case of

European names which are definitely standardised, freshmen find the help of the reference librarian necessary.

552 Indian Name

But when we come to Indian names we find that no uniform standard has yet been evolved regarding the sequence in which the constituent words should be written in alphabetical reference books. There is so much local variation that there is confusion in regard to their entry. Is it Rabindranath Tagore or Tagore (Rabindranath)? Is it Krishnaswami Aiyangar (S) or Aiyangar (S K)? They seem to be still moot points. The confusion now prevailing in the reference books of India has been brought out by Puranik and Phadnis[P7].

553 South Indian Name

5531 Buckland Instance

(*Case Study* 130)

South Indian names first, as they form the last straw to break the camel's back. In the absence of an Indian-made National Biography, the only reference book to be pressed into service, when enquirers come for the lives of South Indian worthies of the last century, is C E Buckland's *Dictionary of Indian biography* (1906). T Gopal Rao, Sir T Muthuswami Aiyar and C V Ranganatha Sastri are three well known names frequently looked up. When Buckland is put in the hands of the enquirers nine out of ten return it with the remark of disappointment, "It is no use." Because they naturally look under the prepotent words 'Gopal,' 'Muthuswamy' and 'Ranganatha' whereas they are entered under the impotent words 'Rao', 'Aiyar' and 'Sastri.'

Except for those who are ultra-resourceful and who still maintain their curiosity at a child's level, all the others would go away unhelped if the living voice of the reference librarian does not put them on the right track.

5532 Who's Who Instance

(*Case Study* 131)

Buckland has at least the virtue of consistency. But when we come to contemporary reference books inconsistency forms a further source of trial for the enquirer.

Here are three names:

1 Rao Bahadur Sir C V Ananthakrishna Ayyar;

2 Sir C P Ramaswami Aiyar; and
3 Sir P S Sivaswami Aiyer.

The *Who's who*, 1939, enters the last name under the impotent word 'Aiyer' and the first two under the proper prepotent words 'Anantakrishna' and 'Ramaswami' respectively. What is worse, in the earlier editions of the same *Who's who* Sir C P Ramaswami Aiyar appears under 'Aiyar.' Probably this accounts also for a still another inconsistency in the current edition: 'Ramaswami Aiyer' is given a cross reference under 'Aiyar' while 'Ananthakrishna Ayyar' is denied it.

Such internal inconsistency is responsible for many an awkward discomfiture among enquirers, if an obliging reference librarian does not lend a helping hand.

554 North Indian Names

North Indian names too add their own quota of pitfalls. Here the trouble is often inconsistency between one reference book and another.

5541 RAM MOHAN ROY INSTANCE
(*Case Study* 132)

'Raja Ram Mohan Roy' will not become visible in the *Encyclopaedia of social sciences* unless one looks up 'Roy'. But the *Encyclopaedia of religion and ethics* and the *Encyclopaedia Britannica* present him under the entry word 'Ram'.

5542 DAYANANDA SARASVATI INSTANCE
(*Case Study* 133)

'Swami Dayananda Sarasvati' is another well known name which divides encyclopaedias into different camps. Seligman enters him under 'Sarasvati'. But the other two encyclopaedias plump for 'Dayananda' in addition to tripping the enquirer off his feet by denying the name an entry in the text and hiding it in the index.

555 Function *vs* Position

The *Classified catalogue code* has evolved a technique for rendering a name-of-person [R10]. But it has not yet been universally adopted. An historical account of the struggle of the library profession in this matter is given in a paper entitled *Rendering of Hindu names in*

library catalogues, function vs position by S R Ranganathan and K M Sivaraman. [R 67]. The reference towards the end of that paper to the unfortunate way in which the rule of the *Classified catalogue code* has been reworded in the revised rule of the *Anglo-American code* [A6] proves how difficult the problem is even for librarians. How much more tantalising would it not be for the ordinary reader! Surely he would be glad to have the help of a reference librarian in looking up Indian names.

556 Arabic Name

Need for help of reference librarian will be even more imperative in looking up Muslim names. They have often half a dozen constituent words. Even the library profession is at sea in dealing with these names. Some systematisation has been attempted in the *Classified catalogue code* (R11). The choice of the entry word has been rendered as mechanical as possible; but it cannot be claimed that it clarifies the situation absolutely. Even in the case of librarians—we may say even in the case of Muslim librarians — the head begins to swim when faced by an Islamic reference book. The illustrations are taken from T W Beale's *Oriental biographical dictionary* and the *Encyclopaedia of Islam.*

5561 AL BERUNI INSTANCE
(*Case Study* 134)

The former enters 'Al Beruni' as 'Abu-Raihan al-Biruni' — that is under 'Abu' an impotent epithet. The latter, however, puts the name under the correct prepotent word 'Biruni'. But even here the leech-like adhesion of the article 'al' to the front of 'Biruni', though ignored in alphabetisation, is likely to mislead an unwary reader.

5562 AL MUSTAASIM INSTANCE
(*Case Study* 135)

The confusion of the enquirer gets worse confounded when this ignorable article 'al' is raised to the dignity of entry word by Beale who expects the enquirer to look for 'Al Mustaasim Billah' under 'Al.' Supposing the information given by Beale is inadequate, the exasperation of the enquirer becomes even more unbearable when he turns to the *Encyclopaedia of Islam* for further light. For he won't find this name under 'Al.' For that encyclopaedia enters it in the correct style as 'Musta' Sim Bi-Allah, Abu Ahamad ab Allah B 'al Mustan Sir.'

But how is an innocent reader to find his way among such conflicting renderings in books equally reputed to be authoritative. Surely ready reference service is a necessity and not a mere luxury.

557 Rational Approach

A rational approach to the choice of entry word in a name-of-person is a statistical approach. This will satisfy the Canon of Prepotence [R8]. This was first suggested and worked out in 1953 in a report to Unesco [R51]. The Unesco has not yet published it. It has therefore been brought out again in a published paper [R54]. Choice of entry word on the basis of such a rational approach will bring consistency in all reference books. This consistency will be of immense help ot the reference librarian. But all the same, most readers will still need the help of a reference librarian. For they are accustomed to the occurrence of the words in a name-of-person in the sequence given to them by popular usage in mentioning it in public as well as in private. Popular usage is brought about by folk-pressure. And folk-pressure on language—and particularly in respect of name-of-person—is seldom rational. Nor has it produced uniform results in all cultural groups. At any rate, the sequence of the words in a name-of-person, as it is current in popular usage, is contrary to the indication of the Canon of Prepotence applied by statistical methods for purposes of alphabetical arrangement.

558 Corporate Name

Similarly the names of institutions add their own quota to the difficulties of ready reference books. Here also, the choice of entry word gives difficulty. Are the institutions to be entered under their specific names like the 'Presidency College,' 'Loyola College,' and 'Lady Willingdon Training College'? Or are they all to be brought together under the generic label entry 'College'? Whether 'College' is improvised as an additional label entry word or it is brought to the first position by inversion, it makes no difference. The deplorable way in which the Canon of Consistency [R56] is often thrown to the winds even in one and the same alphabetical list is easily illustrated in telephone directories.

5581 TELEPHONE DIRECTORY INSTANCE
(*Case Study* 136)

In the *Madras telephone directory* (1939), 'Loyola College' occurs under 'Loyola'; and 'Lady Willingdon Training College' occurs under 'College'; while 'Presidency College' occurs twice, once under 'College' and again under 'Presidency'.

No wonder that haunted by vagaries of this kind most enquirers feel relieved when a ready reference librarian anticipates their trouble and offers help.

CHAPTER 6

CLASSIFIED ARRANGEMENT

61 Use of a Standard Scheme

When even the apparently simple alphabetical arrangement bristles with so many difficulties, one should expect something worse in a classified arrangement. For such an arrangement implies the faithful adoption of a scheme of classification. Trouble may arise either because the faithfulness is not kept up thoroughly or because the arrangement has to bear all the burden due to the difficulties and the faults in the scheme of classification adopted. Classification of subjects is now a major branch of library science and professional librarians have to go through a considerable grind to master it. The library profession is slowly realising the futility of deluding itself that a relative index can atone for all the ills of a scheme of classification [B6]. Hence it is surely unreasonable to expect that an ordinary enquirer can help himself with reference books of a classified nature, unaided by the reference librarian.

62 Use of Improvised Scheme

But even librarians, who have acquired a familiarity with standard schemes of classification, do not find it quite easy to look up classified reference books as each such book uses a scheme of its own — often a scheme improvised by specialists not in classification but only in the subject matter of the reference books, often without regard to the Canons of Classification. This makes the aid of the reference librarian even more imperative.

621 Allison's 'Guide' Instance
(*Case Study* 137)

Let us consider the *Guide to historical literature* ed by William Henry Allison etc (1931). It is a classified bibliography and is in frequent use as a reference book. The contents pages give the lay-out of the scheme of classification. Here the major subjects are represented by the capital letters of the Roman alphabet. Except for A which stands for "History and auxiliary sciences", all the other letters constitute an inexpansive scheme of geographical divisions. H, I, and J amount however to chronological divisions in addition. Index I, though entitled 'Scheme of classification and numeration,' is a peculiar hotch-potch of classes. They include

1 Form-divisions such as

I—20 Bibliography

2I—40 Encyclopaedias and works of reference

701—900 Biography

921—940 Academy, university and society publications

941—1000 Periodicals;

2 Quite a number of 'Points of view' divisions; and the

3 Apex of hotch-potch—

201—600 Histories of special periods, regions or topics—which throw all canons of classification overboard.

The canons are violated still further in the details worked out at the beginning of each section.

The scheme given at the beginning of 'Section U Asia, including India, China and Japan' will furnish proof of all kinds of such violations. It would take us too far if we attempt a detailed criticism of the classification used in this book.

Even the reference librarian experiences some difficulty in tracing out references in it. The readers will leave the book severely alone or at best fail to get the maximum benefit out of it if an experienced reference librarian does not help him.

622 Cyclopaedia of Formulas Instance

(*Case Study* 138)

The *Scientific American cyclopaedia of formulas*, 1932, ed by Albert A Hopkins, adopts a peculiar alphabetico-classed arrangement of its own. But it gives a plain warning in the last paragraph of its introduction in p 31 in the following terms:

"The reader is strongly urged to never look up a subject without a perusal of the Index, which has been made with special care and is the key to the whole work. The arrangement under the various chapters is a common sense subject-grouping which has been evolved after an experience of twenty years. . . . Still, the book may be used without undue reference to this classification by a proper use of the index."

Even to invite the attention of the enquirer to this warning a reference librarian is necessary. In practice, it is found that he has to do much more to make the enquirer help himself with the maximum information possible in this useful work of reference.

623 Beilstein Instance
(*Case Study* 139)

Another well-known work of reference which has worked out a scheme of classification all its own is Beilstein's *Handbuch der organischen Chemie*. In this "the general scheme of arrangement is according to classes of compounds, as hydrocarbons, ketones, and other main classes." [M6]. The entire host of organic compounds are classified elaborately by their structure into 4877 systems.

"Under each class the general information concerning the compounds is arranged as follows: nomenclature, properties, behaviour, analytical methods and derivatives. Following the statement of the general proportion of the class, individual compounds themselves are next considered, starting with the simplest member of the class. The arrangement of the material for each compound is according to the following outline:

Structure, configuration, historical, bibliographical.

Occurrence, formation, preparation.

Properties (color, crystallography, physico-chemical compounds).

Chemical transformations (including effect of light, electricity, etc.)

Physiological behaviour.

Uses.

Analytical data (detection, examination, estimation). Derivatives." [M6]

It is seldom that all the users of this work learn these 'system numbers' or the arrangement of details under each number while at college. The task of initiating them into their meaning and helping them to locate references until they become adepts falls mostly to the share of the reference staff of the library.

63 Sanskrit Reference Books

Ancient Sanskrit reference books, now being brought to print, are mostly of the classified type. They were composed in the pre-printing days and some even in the pre-writing days. At that time even reference books had to be transmitted and preserved by oral tradition. One can imagine what a load this should have meant to memory. But the ancient Indians had discovered that this load on memory could be considerably reduced by a classified arrangement; for it required the use of rational memory instead of bare rote memory. Whatever their origin, we are now concerned only with the fact that we do have reference books of the classified type and their exploitation by ordinary readers cannot be easy or thorough unless ready reference help is provided by librarians.

Examples:

1 Varahamihira. *Brihatsamhita.* Fifth century AD
2 Somesvara. *Abhilasitartha cintamani.* 1131 AD
3 Basavaraja. *Sivatattva ratnakara.* 1709 AD

CHAPTER 7

MIXED ARRANGEMENT

71 Encyclopaedias

The majority of encyclopaedias adopt a mixed arrangement.

711 Example 1

Glazebrook's *Dictionary of applied physics* arranges the major headings in a classified sequence. But the articles in any ultimate class are arranged alphabetically.

712 Example 2

The *Encyclopaedia of social sciences* welds into one organic whole articles which should, for a purely alphabetical encyclopaedia, be scattered under different letters of the alphabet. There is no doubt that this kind of systematic grouping is more helpful. But it is by no means easy to be sure which topics had been subjected to alphabetical scattering and which have been channelised and concentrated about particular foci.

713 Example 3

The *Encyclopaedia Britannica* also shares these features. No doubt these two cyclopaedias are provided with an alphabetical index; but few enquirers know of their existence or remember to use them. Further in spite of special devices like the use of antique type the reference under most of the terms in the index are so many that most of the readers get tired out in looking up these references one by one until they reach the one which would give them the information they seek. This tiring out process is greatly accelerated by the fact that some of the references are so flimsy that when the page is turned up one finds nothing more illuminating than the occurrence of the word in question with very little light shed upon it by the context.

7131 Illustrations

1 Matter: *see* Kinetic Theory of Matter; Atom; Nucleus; *see also* 1—348*c*; 17—880*b*; 8—958*a*; 5—62*a*.

2 Nitrogen: 16—468*a*; 5—361*a*; 7—721*c*; 8—347*d* fol.; 18—968*a*.

3 Parliament (Brit.): 17—313*c*; 8—9*a*; 6—314*c* fol.; 19—45*c*; 10—562*c*.

72 Progressive Change in Mixing

The degree of mixedness between alphabetical and systematic arrangement changes progressively from edition to edition of the *Encyclopaedia Britannica*. The earlier editions with huge monographic articles recall to mind the *Encyclopaedia metropolitana* which was much in vogue in the early nineteenth century. Let us illustrate with one subject.

721 Algebra Articles Instance
(*Case Study* 140)

The article on algebra occupies 108 quarto pages of double column of the *Metropolitana* (v I. p 524-631). This is equivalent to a crown octavo of about 300 pages—the normal size of a systematic text book on algebra.

In the ninth edition of the *Britannica* we see the beginnings of the attempt to escape from such systematic arrangement and lengthy articles. In it algebra occupies only—but still—52 pages of double column (v I. p 511-562).

A further deviation from systematic arrangement is attempted in the eleventh edition. It reduces the article on 'algebra' to 21 pages (v I. p 599-562). Much of the contents of the ninth edition and still more of the *Encyclopaedia metropolitana* have been scattered with due deference to alphabetical arrangement. However, respect to the memory of the deserted systematic arrangement is shown at the end with the suggestion *See* Mathematics—references. This respect is really more than what it seems on the surface. For when we return to the 'M' volume and look up the reference at the end of the article on mathematics, we find a plethora of them overflowing a page. If we bravely dive into them and gather together those that have to do with algebra, we get quite a handful: algebraic forms; arithmetic; combinatory analysis; determinants; equations; fractions, continued; interpolation; logarithms; magic square; probability.

When we reach the fourteenth edition, we find algebra shrunk to five pages (v I. p 663-667). The array of references at the end has, however become formidable. Here it is: aggregates; analysis; analytic method; barycentric calculus; binomial formula; differential calculus, absolute; calculus of differences; combinatory analysis; complex numbers; determinants; equations; differential forms; algebraic forms; graphical methods; groups; limit; linear algebra; logarithms; mathematics, foundations of; maxima and minima; number; number sequences; numbers, theory of; polynomial; probability and error; quaternions and ausdehnungslehre; series, statistics; trigonometry.

73 Young Leading the Old

This seems to be a case of the young leading the old; for the ideal towards which the hoary *Britannica* seems to be moving has been set by the junior Chambers's *Encyclopaedia* and Brockhaus' *Konversations-Lexikon*. From their very inception, these encyclopaedias split and atomised the subjects and provided articles only on ultimate specific topics as they are bound to commonly occur to our minds. This non-conformity among encyclopaedias and among successive editions of the same one is enough to make it impossible for an enquirer to get the full value out of them if timely assistance is not forthcoming from the reference staff.

74 Incomplete Alphabetisation

The latest edition of the *Encyclopaedia Britannica* has not however arrived at the same degree of nearness to the ideal of alphabetical scattering in respect of all subjects; for, side by side with short articles, monographs still persist in many subjects. Consequently an enquirer may not readily get his topic under its name; it may lie submerged in a monographic article on a subject of far greater extension. The salvaging of it often requires the skilled assistance of the reference librarian.

75 Submerging in Alien Subject

(*Case Study* 141)

Salvaging without external help is sometimes rendered more difficult by an article lying submerged in the alien subjects (alien according to current ideas) with which they went in the last century.

For example an enquirer will not find a straight article on 'atomic theory' in the 'A' volume. The reference librarian will have to put him on to the article 'Chemistry' to find it out. Similarly 'graphic statics' will be found camouflaged under 'diagrams.' The exasperation of the enquirer will really reach breaking point if he seeks general information on the grafting of plants. In the 'G' volume he will find only two entries:

1 Grafting of animals—a regular article; and
2 a cross-reference: Graft hybrids *See* Chimaera.

There is every chance of his overlooking this instruction and not looking up 'Chimaera' as this word may be unfamiliar. If he has enough fortitude he may then turn to the index volume. It has a laconic entry 'Graft (Bot). 5,502 d; 11,775 b.' The eleventh volume simply mentions the word. If impatience has not yet overcome him, he will find what he wanted in the fifth volume.

No! It is unfair to try the enquirer in that way. He must be provided a human guide. The idiosyncrasies of cyclopaedias are too many to the wit of an ordinary enquirer. Reference staff is a necessity and not a luxury.

CHAPTER 8

STRUCTURE AND CONTENTS OF A REFERENCE BOOK

81 Scheme of Study

A beginner should gradually acquaint himself with the structure and contents of each of the important reference books in frequent use. He should make a comparative study of the coverage of reference books in respect of:

1 Subject field;
2 Kind of information given;
3 Geographical area;
4 Period of time; and
5 Method of maintaining up-to-date-ness.

In each subject field, the student should make a comparative study of two or more reference books giving the same kind of information. This he should do for reference books on every kind of information. The comparative study should be in respect of:

1 Minor difference in the subject field;
2 Arrangement of the information; and
3 Distinguishing and out-of-the-way features found in any one of them but not in others.

Section 82 gives a skeleton as an aid to the systematic study of reference books. The student should have a note-book for such a systematic study of reference books. In it, he should set apart a page or two for each reference book. It is desirable to have the note book in loose-leaf form. This will enable the maintenance of the leaves on the reference books in a classified sequence and the interpolation of leaves for new reference books in the proper place in the classified sequence. He should also keep an alphabetical index of the titles of the reference books in a separate note book with its cut edges showing the letters of the alphabet.

82 Skeleton for Description

The following skeleton gives a sample of the headings under which the student should look for and record information about each reference book.

1 **Aid to location**
11 Call number
12 Heading
13 Title section
141 Edition
142 Year

2 **Collation**
21 Format
22 Pages
23 Nature of binding

3 **Imprint**
31 Name of publisher
32 Name of place of publication

4 **Contents**
41 Subject field
42 Kind of information
43 Period covered
44 Geographical area covered

5 **Medium of exposition**
511 Language
512 Illustrations
513 Diagrams
514 Maps
52 Arrangement, such as
Alphabetical
Broad subject-groups and then alphabetical
Classified pockets
Classified, with the name of the scheme
53 Peculiarities in the arrangement
54 Alphabetical index
Ordinary, or
Relative, or
Expressive

6 **Up-to-date-ness**
61 Closed or open
62 If open,
621 Year of commencement
622 Periodicity
623 Supplement, or
Correction slip, or
Correction leaf, or
New edition, or
Cumulated edition at intervals

7 **Special feature,**
not normally expected,
nor implied in the title,
nor found in other similar publications
71 Special feature in particular issues
72 Bibliography given or not and of its nature, such as brief, select, etc.

8 **Range of stock in library**

Part J

Long Range Reference Service

CHAPTER

WHAT OF LONG RANGE REFERENCE SERVICE

10 Introduction

Long-range reference service will not be totally absent in any type of library. However, it is a special feature of a research library such as that of a learned body, university, and a business enterprise. The boundary line between ready reference service and long-range reference service may be indefinite and elusive. But it is not difficult to recognise their distinguishing features, at their respective phases sufficiently far from their point of transition from one to the other. The two types of reference service differ in the time involved, the materials used, and the nature of the information sought.

11 Time Test

As implied in its very name, there can be no question of giving immediate satisfaction in long-range reference service. No doubt, information collected for one reader by prolonged investigation may be recorded for future use and served to later enquirers at a moment's notice. But then it has ceased to be long-range reference service. (*See* examples in section 23 of part F). In the library of a business enterprise, even long-range reference service may have to be rushed through. For, time is an important economic factor with a business enterprise. But even there, compared with its time-standard for ready reference service, long-range service is allowed an appreciably longer time. It may be difficult to answer the question "What is the minimum duration of search to make reference service long-range?" At any rate, a sharp answer is not possible. Most ready reference questions are solved in a few minutes, while some take a longer time but seldom more than half-an-hour. Similarly, few long-range reference questions take less than half-an-hour, while some take a whole day and even weeks. This is the only nebulous answer possible.

12 Source Test

We get better light on the what of long-range reference service by looking at it from the angle of the sources used. In ready reference service, the field for search is usually confined to ready reference books—dictionaries, directories, encyclopaedias, year-books, calendars, who's who, and the like. But, in long-range reference service, the search does not end with them. It only gets started with them. It has to be continued beyond them into ordinary books, pamphlets, and periodicals.

121 Use of Outside Sources

The search may have to be carried beyond the walls of the library into the resources of other local libraries. Even this may not give satisfaction. Then libraries in the other parts of the country and, in extreme cases, even libraries in the other parts of the world may have to be pressed into service. (*See* chapters 2 and 3 of Part K). The search may have to extend also into the archives,—local, national, or international—and as far as available consultation even of the current files of offices and business houses. In extreme cases, long-range reference service may take us even beyond all recorded sources. It may make a search into the brains of living persons a necessity.

122 Aurobindo's Enquiry (*Case Study* 142)

A call came from an international spiritual centre. Sri Aurobindo wanted the exact location of the passage "Brahma satyam jagan-mithya." The *advaitic* (monistic) ring in the passage made us think of Sankara. But Sankara's works occupy twenty volumes. Surely this is a problem to be solved with a reference apparatus. The catalogue and classification cannot be of any help. But no collected edition of Sankara's works had been provided with an index. There was no independent concordance either. But how could the reference librarian dare to turn down this inquiry? For, the answer was surely somewhere on the shelves of the library. Will not the curse of the Second Law (Every Reader His Book) and of the Third Law (Every Book Its Reader) fall on the head of the reference librarian? We were in a tight corner. We were cursing the reference apparatus that would not come into existence. Fortunately at that moment, there stepped into the library a walking concordance to Indological literature—Sri T Sundarachariar of Shiyali. He picked out the passage in a moment. It occurred as the first quarter of the twentieth and last substantive verse of the minor lyric *Brahma-*

jnanavalimala. The honour of the library was redeemed; and a most creative reader was served. Thus what would have been a ready reference service, if the production of reference books had reached proper standards, turned out to be a long range reference service, calling for a search into the brains of a living person! [S5].

123 Bardan Enquiry

(*Case Study* 143)

A member of the research staff got stuck up at the term 'Bardan' carriers. No dictionary or any other kind of reference book was of any avail. According to the enquirer, the term occurred in relation to labour in the State of Bombay. This made the library start local inquiry in the Bombay area. One of the librarians, working in that state, furnished information as follows: Bardan was an English-Marathi jargon for burden. The term "Bardan-carrier" had become the specific name for labour in the cotton trade of Bombay. Thus long range reference service had to go beyond books and land itself in a local inquiry.

124 Dance Enquiry

(*Case Study* 144)

Here is a third example. *Bhagavata mela nataka* is a School of Dance developed in the courts of the kings of Tanjore. The recent revival in Indian dance has stimulated a large volume of inquiry for dance literature. But the *Bhagavata mela nataka* School has not yet been recorded in print. There were only just a few manuscripts in the possession of some private individuals. Therefore, the most satisfactory form of long-range reference service in this respect was to establish contact between the enquirer and the individual custodians of tradition, found scattered in the neighbourhood of Tanjore and, in particular, in the villages of Melattur, Sulamangalam, and Uttukkadu. Bharatam Nallur Narayanaswami Ayyar was the outstanding living exponent of the art. His name was also given in the *Journal* of the Indian Society of Oriental Art (5; 1937; 168).

125 New Developments in Organisation

In modern libraries of all kinds, the Third Law "Every Reader His Book" even takes the form "Every Reader His Information". It reigns supreme. The library world has not yet completed refitting itself to meet this new demand of the Third Law. But the reorganisation is making rapid progress. Some of the new apparatuses and concepts that are being forged are Depth Classification based on Facet Analysis [R46] and Zone Analysis [R47]; machinery for search, abstracting, and translation; documentation work and service [R19]; union catalogue; regional library system; National Central Library; International Library Centre; and so on.

13 Kind of Information

Any given piece of information will fall in the category of ready reference service or that of long-range reference service according to its having been incorporated in a reference book or not. If it is, it can be readily located. Otherwise, prolonged search will become necessary.

131 Indian Information

Indiana is very poor in reference books. Hence, many kinds of problems figuring as ready reference questions elsewhere have to be dealt with in India as long-range ones. Let us illustrate: In India we have few comprehensive biographical dictionaries, or encyclopaedias, or indexes to periodicals. America and many European countries have many reference books of these kinds. Japan and South Africa are also making headway in this matter. Ready reference books of these kinds have been discussed in part H. Index to national periodicals will be studied in the forthcoming book *Documentation and its facets*. The following examples will show the great strain put on the reference librarians in Indian libraries by the absence of ready reference books. What should normally be ready reference service has to be pursued as an involved and elongated long range investigation.

1311 APPAYYA DIKSHITA ENQUIRY
(*Case Study* 145)

Appayya Dikshita was a versatile and profuse Indian writer. He was a contemporary of Edmund Spencer. But there is no reference book giving any information about his life. For information about him, the only course is to examine every modern edition of his numerous works and commentaries for the off-chance of finding a biographical introduction or remark in any of them. Here are a few editions offering such help:

1 *Vedanta Desika Yadavabhyudaya with a commentary* by Appaya

Dikshita, v 2, (Vani Vilas Sanskrit series, 4), contains a biography of Appaya Dikshita by A V Gopalachari in p i-xxxii of the introduction.

2 Appaya Dikshita's *Sivadwaita nirnaya*, ed by S S Suryanarayana Sastri, gives about eight pages of biographical information and eight more pages of bibliography. This book leads to item 1 given above and to the following sources:

3 *Appaya Dikshita's age* by Y Mahalinga Sastri (in the *Journal of oriental research*; 2; 225-237;

4 *Age and life of Appaya Dikshita* by Y Mahalinga Sastri (in the *Journal of oriental research*; 3; 140-160; and

5 *Appaya Dikshita* (in the *Siddanta dipika*; 4; 261).

By long-range reference service alone such sources could be spotted out and the needed information unearthed from them.

1312 JOURNALISM IN INDIA ENQUIRY
(*Case Study* 146)

To illustrate the difficulties caused by the absence of an Indian encyclopaedia or national bibliography, let us consider how the reference librarian had to meet a demand for information on "Journalism in India". In the process of acquainting themselves with the wave-front of knowledge as laid down in section 433 of this part, he had noted a piece of information found in part 2 of the *Annals* of the American Academy of Political and Social Sciences (Philadelphia), for 1929. It contained a symposium on India. A perusal of this volume disclosed two articles on journalism: Ramananda Chatterjee's *Origin and growth of journalism among Indians* (p 161-168) and A H Watson's *Origin and growth of journalism among Europeans* (p 169-174).

Another unexpected source was located after prolonged search. It was K Subba Rao's *Revived memories* (1933) and an article by K P Visvanatha Ayyar in the *Madras tercentenary volume*. One of the readers helped with these materials brought to the notice of the library, on a later date, the book *History of Indian journalism* by S P Tyagarajan. This book could not be easily known as there was no national bibliography for India at that time.

All this is so chancy. Journalism in America or Europe could be successfully and readily dealt with as a ready reference question with the aid of the encyclopaedias of the appropriate countries.

132 Nascent Thought

The volumes of *Essay index* and similar national or linguistic bibliographies bring to the category of ready reference service, information on the nascent thought in different nations. But the absence of any similar bibliographical aid in India swells the category of long-range reference service.

1321 WOMEN POETS OF INDIA ENQUIRY
(*Case Study* 147)

A reader sought to know about recent writings on the women poets of India. Several hours of search were necessary to locate the following information:

1 Krishnamachariar (M): *History of classical sanskrit literature*; 1937; p 391-397: *Poetesses*;

2 Haranchandra Chakladar: *Early Indian poetesses* (in *Sir Asutosh memorial volume*; 1926-28; part 2; p 65-74);

3 Raghavan (V): *Sanskrit and Prakrit poetesses* (in the *Quarterly journal* of the Mythic Society; 25; 49-74; 26; 137-138; and 27; 279-290).

4 Swaminatha Ayyar (U V): *Sangattamizhum pirkalatamizhum*; 1929; p 79-88; and

5 Raghavacharyulu (K): *Some South Indian poetesses* in the *Quarterly journal* of the Mythic Society; 26; 41-48.

133 Opinion and Point of View

Apart from this, long-range reference service brings within its purview many types of information. These cannot form fit subjects for ready reference service. Roughly speaking, the range of ready reference service is confined to the finding of facts. But the range of long-range reference service includes not only facts not readily found; but it covers also other categories of information. Exposition of a subject or a problem from a particular point of view may be sought. Obviously there can be few ready reference books to help us in its location. Search into ordinary books is the only way of getting at it. Or opinion of a particular shade may be sought. Search into ordinary books is the only means of getting at this also.

1331 SAFETY FIRST ENQUIRY
(*Case Study* 148)

Information on the problem of 'Safety first' from the point of view of education was sought. There was no article on the subject in the *Encyclopaedia Britannica*. The *Cyclopaedia of education* too did not mention the subject. The *Encyclopaedia of social sciences* had an article entitled "Safety movement." But it dealt with hazard to workers, factory legislation, insurance laws, etc.—all from the industrial point of view. But the enquirer was pursuing the subject from the educational point of view. Therefore, these were of little use to him. The only recourse left to the reference librarian was to examine the books in the class 'Education.' After some laborious search, he located a fairly full account of the subject in chapter 18 of *Introduction to education and teaching process* (1931) of Jessie E Adams and William S Taylor. The bibliography at the end of the chapter led him to the *Twenty-fifth year book* (1926) of the National Society for the Study of Education. It turned out to be a fairly exhaustive symposium on safety education. The odds would have been very much against the reader locating this symposium if left unaided by the reference librarian.

1332 LANGUAGE-NATIONALISM ENQUIRY
(*Case Study* 149)

Another example was in connection with finding reading materials on opinions in favour of "Language as a factor in nationalism." No ready reference book was of any help. Only a prolonged search disclosed the following books containing opinions of the kind sought.

1 Shenton (H N): *Cosmopolitan conversation: Language problems of international conferences*; 1933;

2 Jespersen (Otto): *Mankind, nation, and individual from a linguistic point of view*; 1925;

3 Marvin (F S): *Western races and the world*; 1922; (chapter 2: Language as a link by J A Smith);

4 Ruyssen (Theodore): *What is nationality* (International conciliation; March 1917); and

5 Boaz (Franz): *Race and nationality* (International conciliation; January 1915).

1333 REASON *vs* RELIGION ENQUIRY
(*Case Study* 150)

The imagined or real conflict between reason and religious experience and between science and religion is a topic creating a perennial demand for opinions of different shades. And yet, such opinions could not get recorded in ready reference books. Modernism has to be ever modern. Every advancement in science demands a re-examination of the problem. New shades of opinion arise therefrom. Hence this topic falls pre-eminently in the sphere of long-range reference service. It is the business of the reference librarian to turn his thoughts to this problem during the hours of shelf-study. He should build up and maintain a balanced bibliography to serve the enquirers. Here is such an illustrative select bibliography:

1 Macmurray (John): *Reason and emotion*; 1936; p 171-212 "Science and religion";

2 Brown (William Adams): *Life of prayer in a world of science*; 1931;

3 Inge (W R): *Science and ultimate truth*; 1926;

4 Whitehead (A N): *Science and the modern world*; 1926;

5 Macfie (Ronald Campbell): *Science rediscovers God or the theodicy of science*; 1931;

6 Streeter (B H): *Reality: a new correlation of science and religion*; 1926;

7 Cross (F Lestre): *Religion and the reign of science*; 1930;

8 Boodin (John Elof): *God and creation: God, a cosmic philosophy of religion*; 1934;

9 Barnes (Ernest William): *Scientific theory and religion, the world described by science and its spiritual interpretation*; 1933;

10 Price (George McCready): *Modern discoveries which help us to believe*; 1934;

11 Eagle (Albert): *The philosophy of religion versus the philosophy of science*; 1935; and

12 Simpson (James Young): *Garment of the living God: Studies in the relations of science and religion*; 1934.

134 Too Recent or Too Out of the Way

In a research library, information about developments and discoveries, too recent for inclusion in reference books, may have to be located. This will involve a prolonged and systematic search through files of periodicals. Or again, the information sought may be of too specialised a nature and too little in demand for makers of ready reference books finding it worth while to have it explored and incorporated in their publications. It may be hidden all the same in some periodicals on the shelves of the library. It is the business of long-range reference service to bring it to light.

1341 STRATOSPHERE ENQUIRY
(*Case Study* 151)

Stratosphere flight was then a topic of recent origin. The *Encyclopaedia Britannica* had no article on it. Its index made reference only to a passing mention of the topic in the articles on *Atmosphere* and *Teisserenc de Bost* (*Leon Philippe*). Chamber's *Encyclopaedia* made no mention of the word. The *Encyclopaedia book of the year* (1938) gave two columns to the subject and made mention of Adam breaking the record in June 1937. Whitaker's *Almanack* for 1939 devoted six columns to the subject. But they were purely historical. But the enquirer wanted only a descriptive account. Therefore, the probable books and periodicals had to be searched.

First (Dorothy): *Exploring the upper atmosphere* (1934) was the only book on the subject available in the library. But it did not give full satisfaction to the reader. Hence periodicals had to be searched. With the aid of the *Index* to the *National geographic magazine*, the following sumptuous articles were located. They gave satisfaction to the enquirer.

1 *Ballooning in the stratosphere: Two balloon ascents to ten-mile altitudes presage new mode of aerial travel* by Auguste Piccard (In v 63; p 353-384);

2 *Exploring the earth's stratosphere: The holder of the American altitude record describes his experiences in reaching the "ceiling" of his plane at an elevation of nearly eight miles* by Lieut John A Macready (In v 50; 1926, p 755-756);

3 *Exploring the stratosphere* by Capt Albert W Stevens (In v 66; 1934; p 397-434);

4 *Man's farthest aloft rising to* 13.71 *miles, the National Geographic Society — US Army stratosphere expedition gathers scientific data at record altitude* by Capt A W Stevens (In v 69; 1936; p 59-94); and

5 *Scientific results of the world record stratosphere flight* by Capt A W Stevens. (In v 69; 1936; p 693-712).

1342 GLASS FIBRE ENQUIRY
(*Case Study* 152)

Glass fibre was another topic of recent origin. The first enquiry came from an orthopaedic surgeon. The *Encyclopaedia Britannica* gave only a short article of ten lines under the heading *Glass cloth* without any bibliography. The *Encyclopaedia Britannica book of the year* (1938) disposed of the subject by adding six lines towards the end of the article on *Clothing industry* without any attempt at bibliography. The 1939 volume of the same work of reference just gave a small paragraph under *Applied chemistry*. It also gave reference to two general books on chemistry. But, unfortunately, these books were not available in the library. Obviously, the topic was then too recent for any adequate treatment in standard reference books. It was too recent also to be found generally in all standard treatises. Pursuit of this subject involved a rapid search into each of the recent volumes of the *Industrial and engineering chemistry*. These volumes were then too recent to be covered by the published cumulative indexes. Volume 30 belonging to 1938 had an informing article of four pages. It was entitled *Fibre glass: Mechanical development*. This long-range reference service started the enquirer on his line of pursuit.

1343 HYDROPONICS ENQUIRY
(*Case Study* 153)

The term 'Hydroponics' baffied the reader and the reference librarian alike. Dictionaries gave but little clue. What could it mean? The enquirer had heard the word casually; and even its spelling was not definite. A short article in the *Encyclopaedia book of the year* (1939) mentioned it as a recent technique in crop production, first conceived in 1927, and applied to floral production in 1934 and to vegetable production in 1935. But this article did not give details. However these three references started the enquirer as well as the reference librarian on an adventure of further exploration. The following references were got:

1 *American journal of botany*; 16; 1929; 682; gave *Agriculture — means of crop production*.

2 *Science*; 85; 1937; 177-178; gave *Hydroponics—crop-production in liquid culture media*.

3 *Science*; 88; 1938; 568-569; gave *What is soil?*

4 *Nature*; 141; 1938; 536-540; gave *Crop production without soil*.

1344 MITOGENETIC RADIATION ENQUIRY
(*Case Study* 154)

Mitogenetic radiation was then a recent biological development.

It had not yet found a place in any reference book. The etymological make-up of the term was itself an evidence of its recency. This problem had to be pursued as one of long-range reference at the instance of the classifier himself. The following books caused this enquiry:

1 Guruwitsch (A): *Mitogenetişche Strahlung*; 1932; and

2 Hollander (A) and Clans (W D): *Experimental study of the problem of mitogenetic radiation*; 1937. (Bulletin of the National Research Council (U S A), 100).

This new subject had to be provided with a new class number co-extensive with the subject in all its facts. The analystico-synthetical nature of the Colon Classification in use implied an assurance of the practicability of constructing co-extensive class numbers. But it demanded as a pre-requisite a fairly accurate knowledge of the subject in terms of fundamental concepts. For this, the reference librarian had to feed the classifier with as much literature on the subject as could be found in the library. This meant a most arduous, though interesting, search of a long range nature. A start was made with the *Biological abstracts*. The references under 'mitogenetic rays' ultimately led the classifier to arrive at the most appropriate placing of the books in question by synthesising the correct class number for the topic.

1345 MOLECULAR RAY ENQUIRY
(*Case Study* 155)

Molecular ray was another topic of recent origin. Here too, the classifier himself had to initiate long-range reference service. The term described a curious state of matter. Its concept had originated with the brilliant pioneer work of Dunoyer published in *Radium* in 1911. Details of the pursuit of this then recent subject by the classifier are given elsewhere [R43].

135 GONE OUT OF VOGUE

Sometimes certain types of information go entirely out of vogue. Therefore, they may not find a place in current reference books. Even the reference cabinet may have been cleared of all traces of them. So also, they might have been wiped out of the memory of the reference librarian. Therefore, they may be lying unheeded in long forgotton reference books of past years or in the dusty tomes of books and periodicals closely packed in the tertiary sequence [R35]. These old out-moded volumes might even have been sent away to the distant dormitory collection. However, an occasional demand for them may come from a research worker. Then, they should be exhumed. This would involve a prolonged search. Thus ready reference service of one period may become long-range reference service of a later period.

1351 REGIOMONTANUS ENQUIRY
(*Case Study* 156)

An enquirer asked for information about Regiomontanus, a German astronomer of the fifteenth century. It looked like a problem in ready reference service. The current edition of the *Encyclopaedia* gave only half a column of information. This was too meagre for the enquirer. The reference librarian had to go far beyond all recent reference books. Ultimately, he had to bring out from the tertiary sequence the *English cyclopaedia* of 1857 and the *Penny cyclopaedia* of 1841.

136 Too Many Facets

Another form of long-range reference service is that of assembling together parts of an information, lying scattered in several books. These books themselves may have been scattered in diverse classes. No doubt, information requiring such an assemblage of parts will be a complex one. Indeed, complexity of the information sought is another factor distinguishing long-range reference service from ready reference service. Invariably the latter is concerned only with the location of simple information. But the information sought may have several facets. All of which should be located and brought together. Then only, the enquirer will get a complete and reliable picture of the information sought by him. This search for all the facets leads to long range reference service.

1361 PRE-COLUMBIAN AMERICA ENQUIRY
(*Case Study* 157)

An enquiry about pre-Columbian America involved search for materials in several classes according to the many facets presented by the subject. Worthwhile materials were ultimately traced for the enquirer among the books belonging to the classes: astronomy, smithy, carpentry, fine arts in general, architecture, engraving, pottery, music, linguistics, Buddhism, geography, travels, world history, American history, archaeology, inscriptions, and anthropology.

137 Linguistic Hurdle

Long-range reference service may assume a still another form. It is helping the enquirer to get his facts or information from books and periodicals in a language unknown to him. The inclusion of this kind of translation service in the obligations of library staff may appear far-fetched. But in libraries maintained by industrial and commercial enterprises, it is certainly not foreign to the purpose of their establishment and maintenance. Even in libraries of research institutes, like the Indian Institute of Science in Bangalore, this function of the library staff has been for long considered prepotent. Indeed while recruiting their librarian some years ago, the authorities of that Institute preferred proficiency in a multitude of foreign languages to a knowledge of Library Science. This did not, of course, receive the approval of the library profession. Even in other types of libraries, neither serving research nor having a flavour of quasi-private ownership, the provision of help for the readers to cross the linguistic hurdle is slowly being recognised as a proper step. This is done, however, with some hesitation. This is evidenced by the tendency to make a small charge for this extreme form of reference service.

1371 Translation Service in Chemistry

Some regarded this as merely a speculation, some twenty years ago. But we were greatly reassured by an occurrence one morning (21-11-39). I reached the library after wording the above paragraph for the first edition. The foreign mail, considerably delayed by the menace of the German submarine, brought the usual bag of scientific periodicals. The first periodical picked up happened to be the issue of *Science* of 6 October. On opening its contents-page, the title *Literature service for chemists* [G2] attracted my attention. It is fully extracted in support of the aspect of long-range reference service under consideration. (Italics are mine).

"Beginning in October 1 the Hooker Scientific Library, Fayette, Missouri, inaugurated a new literature service for chemists. Dr Julian F Smith is leaving the du Pont Company, where he has been doing chemical literature work, to become associate director of the 'Friends of the Hooker Scientific Library,' of which Dr Neil E Gordon is director.

"Through Dr Smith the library will offer translations and literature searches, backed by facilities for providing filmstat or photostat copies of any matter in the more than twenty thousand volumes comprising the collection. To his chemical education (B S, Illinois 1916; M S California 1920; Ph D, Chicago 1922) and his long experience in chemical literature work Dr Smith adds linguistic skill acquired by years of practice in translating from German, French, Spanish, Italian, Portuguese, Dutch, Scandinavian, Polish and Russian.

"The combination of a specialist in technical literature and one of the most comprehensive chemical libraries ever assembled is unique in chemical *reference service*. It offers an unprecedented opportunity to all chemists to have technical literature or patents clearly and accurately translated by a chemist, and *to have the literature on any problem skilfully combed by an experienced searcher who is not hampered by language barriers*.

"The Hooker Scientific Library will render these services at cost (on a self-supporting but not a profit basis) to members of the 'Friends of the Hooker Scientific Library.' The minimum fee for an individual life membership is \$10; for a permanent corporation or institutional membership, \$100. All who are interested are invited to write to Dr Neil E Gordon, Central College, Fayette, Missouri."

1372 INSDOC TRANSLATION SERVICE

Fifteen years later, a similar offer came to be made in India. This is being given as part of documentation. Since 1948, I had been striving for the establishment of a Documentation Centre in India. It gained the support of the Government of India only in 1950. The Insdoc was finally established in 1952. Its full name is Indian National Scientific Documentation Centre. One of its functions was accepted to be the furnishing of translations of learned documents on demand. A nominal fee is charged. This is only to keep out frivolous and irresponsible requests. The demand for translation service has not yet become large enough to have translation service in State Centres and still less in individual libraries. Even the Insdoc does not get sufficient requests to maintain a full quota of permanent translators for several languages. It, therefore, works through a panel of part-timed translators on the basis of piece-work contract. To make each library or each National Laboratory to make its own translations is to ignore the managerial concern for economic viability. To make the research worker himself to do it is worse. It is a criminal waste of the research-potential of the nation.

CHAPTER 2

WHY OF LONG RANGE REFERENCE SERVICE

20 Introduction

In the last chapter we examined the wide field covered by long-range reference service. Obviously, such a variety of service should imply reference librarians with high qualifications. Indeed, long-range reference service requires a twofold qualification. A reference librarian should necessarily be proficient in library science. This goes without saying. But he should also have done some research work. Then only he can help specialists with sympathy and understanding. All this should mean a high salary level. Is it necessary to spend so much on long-range reference service? All the Laws of Library Science unanimously and emphatically say 'yes'. There is first the simple advocacy of the Fourth Law, based on its slogan "Save the Time of the Reader." The Second Law is no less insistent on grounds of its own. It would plead that "How to Use a Library" is by no means a simple matter. In an involved question to be tackled, the difficulty sometimes becomes so acute that the search is given up by the enquirer in despair. Even an experienced research worker betrays his inability to think of the sources to be looked up. Or, a reference needing hours on his part is found in a few minutes by a reference librarian. The enquirer is then ever so grateful. His feeling of helplessness is reflected in his general attitude. He makes up his mind that libraries are mysterious institutions, making him feel like a baby in a wood of dusty tomes and dismal shelving. He wanders down gangways appalled by the thousands of books. Moreover, occasionally, a kind of fear possesses him. He makes a few more fevered attempts to hunt down his quarry, fails, and leaves the library in despair. Further, the elucidation of the various types of long-range reference service given in the last chapter contains in an implicit form several other answers to the why of long-range reference service. We shall now seek to make them explicit.

21 Time Factor

Some enquirer may think that he can, if he had the time, find out and elicit from the mute books the secrets kept hidden by them under a camouflage of similar and inexpressive faces. But he too should be glad to have his time saved by a competent reference librarian. This dependence on reference librarian, on grounds of inadequacy of time to help oneself, is not always a pretension. It may be genuine in the case of an enquirer engaged in serious study. In the case of a person, engaged in the extension of the boundaries of knowledge, the reference librarian ought to share the work with him. He should release for the research worker the time to be spent by him, otherwise, in the necessary literature-search for the furtherance of his work. Unfortunately the past has bequeathed to us a misleading tradition, in the relation of such an enquirer with the library staff. It militates against the rapid and healthy development of an economic sharing of labour. The research worker has a tendency to equate his helper in the library with the laboratory attender. He is at best taken to be a subnormal, far beneath himself in intellectual equipment, general ability, and social status. His business is believed by him to be simply to fetch the book he is asked to bring. Just the ability to read the backs of books is taken to be a sufficient qualification in a helper in the library. A classified arrangement of books is resisted by a research worker. For, he thinks that in that case he himself will have to go to the stack-room and pick out his books. The implication of this is obvious. The helper in the library —rather the library attender according to the designation given by the research worker—cannot know the inside and the mutual relation of books. The research worker does not realise the amount of his valuable time to be saved positively, by leaving literature-search in the hands of a capable reference librarian with ability to understand the intricacies of his subject and, by constant practice and specialisation, even better than himself. A vast quantity of information germane to his investigations appear in rapid succession in diverse periodicals. The research worker should realise the saving of his own valuable time by leaving to a reference librarian the searching, the sifting, and the digesting of all the information so as to suit his specific point of view. Then he will realise the advantage of a reference librarian having a learning of his own. Without all this realisation, the research worker either wastes his own time in doing it or goes without the benefit of such a digest. The human resources of a community are to be put to the most economic use. To secure this, there should be a definite division of labour at this point. This has been discovered after a long experience of trial and error. Every research organisation and every business enterprise are known to become more efficient if the research staff and the top management are made to share their work with a competent reference staff of equal status. Status has to be insisted upon for the sake of the research-worker himself. Otherwise, he will not accept the help of the reference librarian profitably or heartily. Provision of a learned and well-paid reference librarian adds to the genuine research time of an organisation to a remarkable degree.

211 Research Library

Here is a confirmation of this sentiment:

"In future the functions of 'searcher' and 'researcher' will become more distinct. The qualifications demanded of them are also in many respects distinct; accuracy is, of course, vital to both, but the 'searcher' need not possess the very high scientific ability that is required in a first-class research man; and in view of the overloading of learning, the latter needs to be relieved of the burden of acquiring foreign tongues and spending on spade-work time that he could much more profitably devote to his researches." [R68]

212 Business Library

No one, closely in touch with the development of industrial research by the state and private enterprise, will fail to realise the importance of providing for ample long range reference service. Bringing the recorded knowledge to proper use is of equal, if not temporarily greater, practical importance than the extension of knowledge itself. Here is a realisation of this by a business enterprise.

2121 Titanium Business

I was in New York in 1950. The Librarian of the Nickel Company of New Jersey came to me for help. The company was making research in the utilisation of titanium. Most of the literature on the subject consisted of its own House Reports. Still it could not be ploughed back efficiently into the research team. That was the difficulty of the librarian. Much money was being wasted as a result of this. That was the difficulty of the management. The librarian learnt Colon Classification, its facet analysis, and its analytico-synthetic approach to the organisation of documents. Within a few months, the management got a better return from its investment on research staff. To cut the story short, at the time of my leaving USA a few months later, the management expressed their appreciation of the better reference service received as a result of my technique. The appreciation took even the material form of a large titanium diamond.

213 Public Library

The same is true even in a public library. The general public will become more efficient in their varied occupations including the necessary occupation of keeping the home by their time being saved by a reference librarian, capable of keeping them continuously better informed in their respective fields of interest by long-range reference service. The public libraries in industrial towns, such as Sheffield, Manchester, and Birmingham, already give such intensive long range reference service. Surely each community and each major industry should have at least one long-range referenece centre in common. It should be the clearing house of information. It should save the time of the community by the offer of adequate long-range reference service.

22 Document Flow

221 Overwhelming Quantity of Books

Two hundred years ago Dr Johnson wrote "It is indeed culpable to load libraries with superfluous books." Since then at least ten million separate works have been added to the world's collection; and it will not take fifty years to make another ten millions; for, the present annual rate of book production in the world is about 250,000. One may wonder what Dr Johnson would say if he were asked to indicate the superfluous books. Probably he would not have difficulty in deciding on the destruction of a good deal of modern fiction. But when it came to works purporting to contain useful information, even Dr Johnson might have doubted as to his own judgment.

221 Potentially Great Plenty

We must make up our minds that the volume of recorded knowledge will continue to swell at an overwhelming rate and address ourselves more eagerly than the past to put them to better use. Yes. We are suffering from a terrific accumulation of the materials and instruments of knowledge. No savant however eminent can now afford to say "What I don't know is not knowledge." Long-range reference service is necessary to make the vast stores of information available to those who need them and can put them to active use. Otherwise our potentially great plenty will be nothing but a mockery.

222 Overwhelming Quantity of Periodicals

The need for reference service is made even more pressing by periodical literature. Excluding patent specifications, between a million and a million and a half scientific and technical papers are published each year. They get published in about 20,000 scientific periodicals. The periodical is the most dreadful and insidious form of print ever invented. If we are induced to subscribe for one year we feel we must go on. An incomplete or broken set is revolting to all the best feelings of the true librarian. The reason for the increase of periodicals is the enormous increase in the number of research workers all over the world. At present every one of them feels, if he wishes to get on in life, that he must publish at least one paper a year. Enthusiastic heads of departments feel that they must grind out papers corresponding in number to the size of the department. Most of them in conformity with university regulations publish the students' exercises, gaining research degrees. Some publish almost all of their notebooks!

2221 Necessity to Peruse

Of course the periodicals may not be much read. Particular papers may be simply noted for possible future use. One or two only may be read. But they cannot be ignored. Even to know that there is nothing worth knowing in a particular issue of a periodical it has to be perused and sized up. Yes. For the expert or the research worker, this is the age of periodicals.

2222 Necessity for World Coverage

He can no longer depend merely on the facts, data, news, and views being put forward in his own country. Information is essentially a world-wide product. And he is required to know, not merely what is said and done in his country, but what is done and said throughout the world. This makes the quantity of materials falling within the purview of any worker quite enormous. For example there are perhaps a million volumes which can properly take their place in an agricultural library either as basic material or as necessary material on allied sciences. The two largest agricultural libraries in the world—that in the Department of Agriculture in the United States with about 200,000 volumes and of the International Institute of Agriculture at Rome with about 320,000 volumes—contain only a small fraction of what exists in print. Thus the literature is so overwhelming in quantity that any expert is in need of sharing the work of literature search for information with an expert long-range reference librarian.

23 Telescoping of Information

Again the various branches of sciences and technology on the one hand and the social sciences and the humanities on the other are becoming more and more dependent upon one another. Development in one field has immediate repurcussions in others which formerly pursued a distinct path. Witness for example the intimate relation between development in acoustics, electricity, and optics in connection with recent technical applications such as broadcasting, wireless, talkies, etc. The radio has affected even the dramatist. The radio play-wright is obliged to invent new techniques as his audience is denied ocular aids. He has to produce all the necessary effect through the aural sense alone. Such interdependence of the sciences and other fields of knowledge gives rise to increased difficulties in tracing information in printed materials. The contents of many of which may be of considerable interest if not of importance to more than one field of thought.

231 Ramifications of Rubber Industry

Let us take an example from another place. Let us consider the rubber industry. How many are the sciences involved! In the cultivation of the rubber tree, the botanists and the mycologists are perhaps of great importance. The subsequent stages of manufacture demand the specialist knowledge of the chemist, the physicist, and the engineer. In addition, the business side calls for expert statisticians, accountants, production engineers, personnel officers, public relations men, and management specialists. Needless to say many countries are interested in this great industry and information is printed in most of the principal languages of the world.

232 Weather Report and Cotton Crop

Let us take another example. The weather reports were used by a bank to determine the basis on which a loan to a firm in one of the Southern States of America could be granted. The firm's ability to pay depended upon the cotton crop. The cotton crop depended upon the boll-weevil. It was known that the boll-weevil propagates under certain weather conditions. Therefore, the study of weather reports can help in fixing the limit to loan to a firm.

How true are the words of Francis Thompson [T3]

All things by immortal power
Near or far
Hiddenly
To each other linked are,
That thou canst not stir a flower
Without troubling of a star.

And so the bank was obliged to get information from weather reports through the reference librarian.

233 Future of Reference Service

It is not yet widely realised that the reference librarians can do much for the advancement of science, industry, and learning. For it is not yet fully realised how they may do their share to help original thinking. Till recent times, library service to readers had been largely passive. Organised reference service of an active type is still only in its infancy. Only latterly have librarians learned that their duties do not end merely in storing and cataloguing information and literature and their most important successes are to be achieved by an active policy of bringing their information and literature to the notice of those in need of them. With sufficient effort exerted by the profession and the public, long-range reference service should develop greatly in the next few years. The present-day prejudice will disappear. Scientists and authors will begin to realise that the man in the library can be of great service to them. The advanced workers will no longer look down on their colleague working in the library. They will realise how much relevant information can be revealed in a remarkably short time by a man spending his life amidst books and on books. As this realisation matures, long-range reference service will form the most vital and the most considerable part of the work in all important libraries. The future of reference service will be assured.

24 Abstracting Periodicals

241 Their Inadequacy in Coverage

There is yet another reason for long-range reference service. The volume of scientific and research literature published throughout the world at the present time is very large. It is obviously impossible for any individual worker to read all the publications, relating even to his own particular branch of activity much less to keep abreast of general progress by direct reading. Scientific abstracting has been invented to overcome this difficulty as far as possible. The abstracting periodical itself publishes no original work. It only abstracts the articles in other periodicals and sometimes even books. The total number of such abstracting periodicals now current is about 500. They contain about 1,500,000 abstracts. If duplicates are ignored they refer only to about 380,000 different papers; and it has been estimated that only a third of the scientific papers are now being covered by the abstracting periodicals. The other two-thirds are missed altogether.

242 Haphazard Variation

This is not the only trouble. The abstracting periodicals leave much to be desired from a variety of other points of view. Unfortunately, there is little co-ordination in their undertakings to-day. The systems of classification adopted by them vary far too much. It is impossible either to amalgamate the various entries into a single index or switch on from one abstracting periodical to another. The variation from one periodical to another is very haphazard. Many a worker fails to get full use. To get full use, he should be helped on every occasion by a specialist reference librarian.

243 Vagaries of the Alphabetical Index

The entry elements of many subject entries in the alphabetical index are often multi-worded. No standard is followed in respect of their permutation. Therefore, there is no consistency in the choice of the entry word. Hence the arrangement of the index part of the abstracting periodicals presents all the possible vagaries in even a more pronounced degree. Owing to the mass of synonyms available, articles of essentially similar contents lie hopelessly scattered under a series of headings. Even an elaborate system of cross references can hardly correlate them. A living man—a reference librarian—specialising in understanding their vagaries should help the enquirer.

25 Linguistic Reasons

Before World War I, practically all the important learned bodies published their periodical publications in English, French, German or Italian. Anyone, able to read these languages, could follow most of the progress in the several sciences. But, to-day, the wave of nationalism is introducing a linguistic hurdle. For example, formerly Russia used to produce only a few, though good, papers. Now, it publishes more voluminously than any other country. It should be remembered that to-day Russia publishes 709 learned periodicals of high standing. They are distributed as shown below:

Library science	20
Natural sciences and their applications	190
Fine arts	13
Education	18
Social sciences	193
Total in Russian	434
In other languages	275
Total	709

251 Renascence in Asia and Africa

If this were all, it would simply add one more language to the list. But it is not all. Among the nations set free after the last war are some very gifted persons. Their investigations cannot be ignored by an expert concerned with their particular subjects. But with the liberation of the nations came also the liberation of their languages. Even the most ruthless oppressors never succeeded in stamping out their languages. The use of their language is for the people of the new nations a pious duty. Naturally they seek to perform it most passionately and devotedly. Research workers in these newly liberated nations now publish in their own languages, and not as before the war, in one of the four imperialistic ones. The ancient countries of Asia and Africa have also begun to emerge from their lethargy.

They have nearly completed their probation of expressing their discoveries in foreign media. For some years, Japan and China were experimenting with bilingualism. Now they have taken the next step of shedding the alien language except for brief summaries. The adults of India too have begun to talk of the mother tongue. But the youth of the country have gone a step further. They have, already, taken the school and college magazines to the bilingual stage. In all probability, on their reaching adulthood, the mother tongue will gain full status. The research output of India cannot be ignored by anybody in the world, on account of its quantity as well as quality. This would add, not one, but a dozen new languages to the list. So an expert, having obtained access to a paper wanted by him may have the mortification of finding it to be in a language not even identifiable by him.

252 Rehabilitation of Languages

Some of these languages had never in the past been used for science or indeed for any high intellectual activity. They contained no scientific terms. Sometimes they did not have the word to express even so simple a notion as a 'percentage.' Quite undeterred by this difficulty, the scientific workers have proceeded to coin new words to express new scientific conceptions. We should not blame them. During the long years of repression, the chief tie keeping them together was their language. Children learnt it from their mothers, sometimes under difficulties and even threats of dire penalty. By a true instinct, they knew that, so long as they kept their language, they had the key which would one day loosen their fetters. And now that they have their liberty, they are remaining faithful to the old mother tongue.

253 Translation Service

What light does all this throw on the why of long-range reference service in research libraries, business libraries, university libraries, national and state central libraries, and at least to some extent, even in big public libraries? The small Madras University Library, with only a hundred thousand volumes on its shelves and taking only a little over a thousand periodicals thirty years ago, had to handle thirty languages. This happens in all the libraries of the world. Are the materials to smoulder on the shelves and become a diet for worms? Or is the library to break through the linguistic crust, pick out the meat inside, dress it in a palatable form, and serve it to the readers with an appetite for them? The Laws of Library Science have no hesitation in saying "yes" to the latter question. Libraries must arrange for translation service.

CHAPTER 3

HOW OF LONG RANGE REFERENCE SERVICE

31 Introduction

As stated in the preliminary paragraphs of the last chapter, long-range reference service needs a staff with high qualifications —persons not only proficient in library science but also with experience of research work. Even such a highly qualified staff should make arduous preparation to fulfil the demands of long-range reference service in an efficient way. They should have a high sense of duty. Their own conscience should prompt them to do their best. Hardly any genuine enquirer knows the extent of help to be drawn from the reference librarian. Therefore, in most cases, long-range reference service implies voluntary offer of service.

32 Stimulation by Service

A conscientious reference librarian is stimulated by the very act of service—actual, active service—to rise to his highest level. Indeed the greater the demand from enquirers, the richer becomes his experience and the more profound become his resources. The after-effect of an exasperating search for some refractory piece of knowledge, in co-operation with an advanced research worker hungering for it, is most exhilarating to a reference librarian. Indeed the process of assimilation after long-range reference service is even more elevating and pleasurable than after ready reference service.

33 Three Processes

In section 302 of part F, the how of ready reference service was said to consist of three processes. It is so in long-range reference service also. They are preparation, service, and assimilation. These three processes are but phases of one continuous experience. They are not temporally exclusive of one another. They really co-exist for every reference librarian giving himself away absolutely to his noble work. They are less separable in long-range reference service than in ready reference service. For, there is this difference between them. More than the latter, the former is a persistent type of work. By its very nature, the idea pursued has to be ever kept alive. It must be allowed to simmer continuously in the mind.

34 Yoked with the Idea

The ideal reference librarian eats, drinks, sleeps, and talks his long range reference problems throughout the twenty-four hours, the week, the month, and the year. His physical whereabouts at any one time is immaterial. He carries his problem with him home. He brings it back with him in the evening and in the morning to the library. He is, in effect, as much engaged with it outside the library as inside it. He cannot shake off his problem at any time. He is very much like the person with the mind in Yoga (yoked with a pursuit). Whatever his apparent action, he is not in it but in Yoga with his problem. As the Lord puts it:

"When he sees, hears, tastes, smells, eats, moves, sleeps, breathes, speaks, takes, ejects, opens his eyes or closes them, he holds that it is only the senses acting upon the objects of the senses." [B4].

CHAPTER 4

PREPARATION

41 Skeletal Knowledge of Subject

In long-range reference service, the problem of discovery is an active one. Before undertaking to discover the information in a written form available and suitable to a particular enquirer, it is necessary to make certain preliminary investigations and survey. The subjects of interest to the library clientele in general are first to be correctly understood. The next step is to get a working knowledge of the subjects involved. This requires a careful reading of a few authoritative publications and a rapid survey of the literature of the subject as a whole. The goal of such a survey is to obtain a broad skeletal knowledge of the subject, its parts, and phases. It is also to discover the relationship of the parts among themselves and to other fields of knowledge. It is again to acquire a wide vocabulary of the subjects.

411 Emphasis within a Subject

Again the emphasis within a subject will depend upon the nature of the library in the case of special libraries and the nature of the enquirer in the case of general libraries. The clientele of a business library, for example, and the industrial and commercial enquirers of a general library more often need current information than historical information. The detailed description of practices and methods are more often wanted than of theory and opinion. Reference books—that is, books, handbooks, annuals, directories —and transactions and proceedings of associations, articles, surveys, etc, have to be more often pressed into service than ordinary books. Detailed and technical treatments are necessary. Elementary and general or popular book or article is seldom of value. On the other hand, an antiquarian enquirer or one interested in anthropological work will make the reference librarian dive into materials of just the opposite kind.

42 Source

421 Three Kinds

The preparation in long-range reference service usually involves search for specialised materials. This requires the use of three different groups of bibliographical sources:

1 Bibliographies in the particular subject field, especially abstracting and indexing periodicals, annual reviews, and periodicals containing reviews;

2 Similar bibliographies, not limited to the particular subject field, but of broader ones including it along with others; and

3 Comprehensive bibliographies covering all subject fields, but limited to a particular kind of publications such as periodicals, articles, theses, etc, and limited chronologically or geographically.

422 Collateral Sources

Examination of the third group of materials often yields a rich harvest, valuable in a particular field, though originated outside that field. They are often missed by the bibliographies prepared specially for that particular field. Discovery and recognition of the value of the occasional publication prepared for one use, but valuable in an entirely different field, is an important service expected from a reference librarian. To do this service, he should, of course, know the special subject. In addition, he should also know the important bibliographical sources in related or collateral subjects. Many of the sources may not have arranged their entries according to subjects. Or if they are classified, the classification may not correspond with, but represent, a cross-section of, the subjects of interest to the problem pursued. It is therefore necessary in many cases to check through entirely. A knowledge of such sources and of the methods of checking them through has to be built up gradually by each reference librarian. The number of abstracting and indexing periodicals is now in several hundreds. The reference librarian should scan the relevant ones systematically.

423 Unprinted Sources

Long-range reference service in special fields frequently need information not yet brought to print. The reference librarian should therefore keep himself informed of the research in progress on the frontiers of the subject of specialisation. The research work may be conducted in academic institutions or co-operatively in learned associations, or in individual business corporations, or in research foundations or in national laboratories. A pre-requisite for the discovery of such nascent activities is to secure for the library membership in the learned bodies and other organisations carrying on research. The announcement, membership bulletin, and annual reports, often give information proving to be effective starting points. The research activities of government bureaux are generally indicated in their annual reports. Through them, the reference librarian can discover research projects, in advance of their publication. A number of universities issue lists of theses in preparation. A few publish their doctoral dissertations as annuals. Others have them published in periodicals such as the *American economic review* and the *Political science quarterly*. Some other periodicals often mention investigations under way, informally or as news notes. Examples of this sort are

Domestic commerce issued by the United States Bureau of Foreign and Domestic Commerce; and

Personnel journal issued by the Personnel Research Foundations.

424 Newspaper as Source

Sometimes research studies and investigations are reported in the newspapers at their inception. Sometimes newspapers have feature articles on important conclusions brought to light. It is extremely worthwhile for a reference librarian to record such investigations by their subjects, either in the catalogue or in the reference cabinet, so as to file with the materials on the same subject. This must be done in the first announcement of a project. Thereafter, it is often possible to obtain some desired information, even during the progress of the investigation. Reports to be published may often get advance mention in the daily press. This makes it possible to secure them sooner than in the case of dependence on the post-facto trade lists alone. To do all this, requires rather close scanning of both newspapers and periodicals. Such a scanning is really necessary for useful, intelligent long-range reference service.

425 Social Sciences

Abstracting and indexing periodicials are beginning to appear rather late in the social sciences. To add to this, newspapers often form the media for first communication in the field of political and economic affairs. It may take long for them to reach the stage of inclusion in regular periodicals and books. Some of them may not reach that stage at all. And yet, communications—particularly those made by government' organisations and by leaders—are of great current value. Newspapers are rich in such communications. Generally, newspapers are not covered by abstracting and indexing periodicals. Therefore, the reference librarian should scan newspapers and note down information about useful items.

426 Newspaper Cutting

This work is now being organised properly. In a specialised library, relevant cuttings from newspapers are filed. They are also classified and listed. A classified indexing circular is brought out periodically. For example, P N Kaula started a monthly list of this kind for the field of Personnel Management. As librarian of the Library of the Ministry of Employment and Labour of the Government of India, he has been issuing such circulars on a monthly basis. He got the inspiration for such a preparation for long-range reference service from the account of the Newspaper Cuttings Service seen by me in the Chatham House, London, and in the Bibliographical Institute in Copenhagen, and the scheme furnished by me for adoption by the headquarters office of the Indian National Congress at Delhi (R40).

43 Gathering

Next to scanning the sources comes the gathering of information. The information may have to be gathered either on demand or in anticipation. The variety of questions actually brought up by enquirers and of the questions anticipated on the basis of local knowledge and contemporary happenings should get interlaced in the mind of the reference librarian. With the back of his mind filled with such an amalgam of problems, he should explore the resources of the library and gather information in a systematic way. From this point of view, we may recognise three distinct fields for search: The old stock of the library, the recent additions, and the current issues of the periodicals taken by the library.

431 Shelf-Study

Of these three fields for search, the old stock of the library forms the most formidable one. The books already in stock need to be re-read frequently. Their potentiality is seldom exhausted. They act like a kaleidoscope. Every change in the angle of approach yields a new pattern. What the old stock can yield depends upon what we take to it in our apperception. As the enquirers, actual and anticipated, grow, our apperception grows too. Books or passages in books, without any meaning in the past, splash out a new message when pursued—perhaps a hundredth time it may be—with a newly enriched apperception. This repeated skipping through the old books we shall call shelf-study. Shelf-study forms one of the corner stones in the preparation for long-range reference service. A reference librarian should steal every possible minute for this important mode of gathering information.

4311 RESPONSIBILITY OF THE LIBRARY AUTHORITY

The library authorities should realise that the library can render its greatest possible good to the community only if it provides in the time-table of the staff sufficient free time for such a preparatory shelf-study by the reference librarian. They should also realise that this would ultimately mean increase in reference staff. Quite unaccustomed to the benefits of the right kind of long-range reference service and perhaps being fortuitously so placed in life that they had got on gloriously without such intimate service, many a man in power is quite blind to the need for shelf-study. He imagines, under the pressure of nineteenth century tradition which alone he knows, that work in a library is a mechanical one and a soft one. He laughs at the suggestion that the reference librarian has to read most of the books and re-read them from time to time. He even quotes a Victorian saw out of its context and strives to score against the librarian, amidst the laughter of an admiring but ignorant pack of lookers-on, with the epigram "A librarian who reads is lost"! Perhaps if he is of a generous nature, he may put down such a reading of books merely to the credit of an unusual type of individual librarian who happens to love reading.

4312 HOPE FOR THE FUTURE

But we hope that this state of affairs will change very soon. The excellent results already achieved, often in spite of reference sections being seriously understaffed and working under adverse conditions, show that the wholesale development of long-range reference service, adequately staffed and financed would have the most momentous results on national and international progress. Such a development is sure to come as soon as the present generation of youth, now being accustomed to long-range reference service, grow into adulthood and come to occupy positions of power. This hope is already beginning to be realised though it was expressed in the first edition in 1940 only.

432 Record of Result

To make the discoveries made during shelf-study available for ready use on all future occasions, the long-range reference librarian should adopt one of two methods:

Either he must suggest to the Technical Section the preparation of additional analytical or cross reference entries; or if the matter does not admit of them, he should himself prepare the necessary slips and file them in the reference cabinet.

433 Wave-Front of Knowledge

Unlike the old stock in the library, the current issues of the periodicals provide opportunities for the reference librarian to keep himself abreast of the world's progress in knowledge. Indeed, he should in that way "keep ahead of the game." The periodicals give the very wave-front in the advance of knowledge. Frequently a short note in a periodical reveals the existence of an important paper emanating from an obscure source but exactly answering the needs of an enquirer. An experienced reference librarian assisted by an intelligent junior can at one and the same time survey the periodical publications, not only for the purpose of gathering information, but also for helping the Book Selection Section. He could spot out much literature which, but for his efforts, might remain out of sight for months after publication. The reference librarian knows the needs of the clientele far better than any other section.

> "The toad beneath the harrow knows
> Exactly where each pin point goes."

says the poet. Similarly the reference librarian knows exactly for what topics it is vain to send a reader to the stack-room, and, by inference, in what subjects his library is weak.

434 Secondary Wave-Front

The recent additions of books give the secondary wave-front in the advance of knowledge. The books are no doubt behind the periodicals in point of time. But, they have the advantage of giving a more comprehensive exposition of the new discoveries and in particular give their correct orientation in relation to existing knowledge. The new arrivals in the library should be perused rapidly by the reference librarian. If they form a considerable number, a careful distribution of the universe of knowledge among the different reference librarians will suggest itself obviously. This work of perusing the new arrivals is best done during the period of their display in the show case before being released for loan—a week or a fortnight according to the practice of the library. If a minute system of classification is used in the library, the work of the Technical Section—the class number and the analytical entries—would minimise the time to be spent by the reference librarian on this preliminary perusal. The reference librarian knows more intimately than the Technical Section the topics engaging the attention of the clientele most. Therefore, it is his duty to advise that section about worthwhile analytical entries.

44 Recruitment of Reference Librarian

441 Subject Specialisation

This calls for a principle to be followed in the recruitment of reference librarians in a large library. The reference posts should be distributed among several subject-fields so as to cover the entire universe of knowledge. This should be similar to the distribution of teaching posts in an educational institution among several subjects. The shelf-study of the old stock and the scanning of the new books, periodicals, and newspapers will then be done more systematically, intensively, and effectively than otherwise.

442 High Level of Recruitment

A real 'live' reference service can only be created by a personnel with a special flair for locating, as if by a sense of scent, useful information in the most unexpected quarters and for disseminating it in the most useful way. A large amount of work is necessarily routine. But it must not be allowed to become too much so. In long-range reference service, initiative is of high importance. It is thought in some quarters that it can be built up and worked by the use of card indexes operated by dull creatures and even by semi-literate office boys. It is wrongly believed that the apical position in a library is that of a dignified official whose main job is the unwinding of red tape and hob-nobbing with the executive of the main body of which the library forms a part, and who believes it to be beneath his dignity either to read books or to find out the needs of the clientele in a personal way. Reference service cannot and never will succeed in offering consistently the required exact information on specific subjects, if the policy of the top-management encourages or even tolerates such an attitude in librarians of any grade. Only a negligible proportion of long-range reference service can be performed to maximum efficiency by cheap labour driven by indolent officers. Experience indicates that money 'saved' by the employment of low salaried staff is rather 'wasted', owing to the resultant loss of time and energy on the part of the senior staff and the troubles arising from inaccurate work done by those whose training does not render them sufficiently appreciative of the importance of the considerations involved, frequently in matters of detail. The situation becomes deplorable when work in a library is taken to be wholly clerical and raw hands are thrown in on every pretext; and it becomes a real heart-break when even these raw hands are taken away frivolously to other departments as soon as they pick up a few weeks' experience and another brand new hand is thrust in.

443 New Danger

A new danger is taking shape to-day. The number of library schools has increased like mushroom. They are mostly run by overworked part-timed teachers or by full-timed indolent misfits. There is hardly any grind in classification and cataloguing. No trouble is taken to widen the basic knowledge of students or even to familiarise them with the basic reference books and treatises. No practice is given in doing or even observing reference service being done or in constructing bibliographies or in literature search. What is worse, no discrimination is made between elementary and advanced courses in Library Science. The employer is made to expect anybody with elementary training to do reference service. It is like expecting a draftsman to design a monumental building or a holder of a school-final certificate to conduct college classes.

45 Contact with Specialists

To create a real 'live' reference service the reference librarian should have not only intimate acquaintance with printed matter and manuscripts but also with men steeped in information. In some cases the enquiry may have to be circulated to a number of specialists so that the greatest possible measure of knowledge and experience can be brought into play. This applies to enquiries about items of knowledge too recent or too unsettled to be answered merely by reference to literature. For its efficient operation, such work demands, not merely knowledge of the technicalities of the subject, but also a wide knowledge of scientific and technical personnel all over the world.

451 Research Consultant

The system of honorary or part-timed research consultants in the Congressional Library of the United States shows the direction in which national libraries should move to make the reference service of the country as unerring and complete as possible.

452 Community Potential to be Tapped

Even local libraries should adopt the same principle to exploit local talents effectively. The local library should have a list of the specialists residing within its area—particularly of the ripe old retired specialists who are too old to take regular service but whose mature experience and accumulated knowledge should not be allowed to run to waste. In most cases such experienced scholars will be very glad to place their knowledge at the service of the local library if they are approached in the proper way; for such congenial work will relieve them of their tedium. The community potential for reference service should be diligently tapped. It can be seen from this that the reference librarian has but little to do as a mere curator of books. He must be a man capable of making contacts and of maintaining good relation with scholars of eminence.

46 Contact with Documentation Centres

During recent years it has been realised in most countries that this process of consulting specialists should be better organised. It has been found to be an advantage to entrust the work to a body designed to act as liaison between the different libraries and the world of scholars. The correct thing, it has been realised, is to pool the resources on a regional, national, and even international basis. There should be a hierarchy of pooling organisations. The reference librarian should keep himself informed of all such bodies. These are now-a-days called Documentation Centres. In some countries, directories of such documentation centres exist. But India is yet to have one. There are also directories devoted to documentation in special fields of science. The reference librarian should be thoroughly familiar with them. He should know where to apply for reliable information when the capacity of the collection in his library and of the specialists in his area proves inadequate.

Such documentation centres fall into four classes if classified by the geographical and subject characteristics. We may label them as:

1 National (special) Centre;
2 National (general) Centre;
3 International (special) Centre; and
4 International (general) Centre.

Some examples are given in the succeeding sections.

461 National (Special) Centre

4611 Agriculture

One example is given by way of illustration. Thanks to the strong line taken by the Imperial Agricultural Conference at Westminster in 1927, there are now established in the United Kingdom eight agricultural bureaux. The function of each of them is to supply information on subjects coming within its purview to any agricultural expert within the Commonwealth. The prescribed channel of communication is through the official correspondent. But in practice a very liberal interpretation is put on this; and information is freely given to any *bona fide* enquirer. Certainly any enquiry from a librarian would receive full attention. The following is the list of the bureaux established as a result of the Conference, with a list of the subjects handled by them:

1 Commonwealth Bureau of Soil Science, Rothamsted Experimental Station, Herpendon. Soils, fertilisers, crop-production.

2 Commonwealth Bureau of Plant Genetics, Agricultural Buildings, Alexandra Road, Aberystwyth. Grass and forage crops.

3 Commonwealth Bureau of Fruit production, East Malling Research Station, Kent. Fruit-growing and transport.

4 Commonwealth Bureau of Plant Genetics, School of Agriculture, Cambridge. Plant breeding, especially cereals.

5 Commonwealth Bureau of Animal Health, Veterinary Laboratory, New Haw, Waybridge, Surrey.

6 Commonwealth Bureau of Agricultural Pathology, Winches Farm, Hatfield Road, St. Albans. Parasites of animals.

7 Commonwealth Bureau of Animal Nutrition, Reid Library, Rowett Institute, Bucksburn, Aberdeen. Animal nutrition.

8 Commonwealth Bureau of Animal Genetics, King's Buildings, Edinburgh University. Breeding of Animals.

4612 OTHER SUBJECTS

Some national bodies publish periodical bulletins containing abstracts of the latest contributions to the subjects in which they specialise. The reference librarian should be thoroughly familiar with those in the subjects in which he specialises. Here are some examples:

1 British Cast Iron Research Association: *Quarterly bulletin* (1923). The last section contains abstracts from foundry literature, including abstracts of patent specifications.

2 British Non-ferrous Metals Research Association: *Bulletin.* The section "Advances in non-ferrous metals industry" contains a series of notes on the most important publications.

3 The Royal Institute of International Affairs, founded in 1920 for the scientific study of international questions, political, economic, and legal, has an information department. It deals with enquiries on international affairs. It also publishes a *Bulletin of international news.* This gives notes of forthcoming international meetings and references to texts of agreements or official correspondence appearing in periodicals. The Information Department is prepared to assist in any serious enquiry concerning international affairs. Where research is involved which cannot be dealt with by the permanent staff in the time available, arrangements can be made for the employment, on payment, of a skilled research worker at whose disposal the resources of the Department are placed.

462 National (General) Centres

Here are some examples of national documentation centres which handle a variety of subjects:

1 India: Indian National Scientific Documentation Centre, denoted by the term Insdoc. It covers the Natural Sciences. There

is a demand to have another National Centre for the Social Sciences [R66].

2 Great Britain: Association of Special Libraries and Information Bureaux, denoted by the term Aslib. It publishes the *Aslib directory*. This is a guide to sources of information in the United Kingdom. The ed of 1957 is in two volumes. It mentions 3,307 libraries.

3 United States: Special Libraries Association. This body published its *Special libraries directory of the United States and Canada* extending to 253 pages in 1935. In 1957, it brought out ed 5 of the *Handbook of commercial, financial, and information services* by Walter Hausdorfer.

4 Russia: The following is a useful publication of the Indiana University: Horecky (P L). *Libraries and bibliographic centres in the Soviet Union*; 1959. Viriti is the national centre.

5 Germany, Sweden, Denmark, and Switzerland have all similar general national centres. Deutscher Verband Technisch-Wissenschaftlicher Verein (German Central Technical Information Service) was created as an Agency for Information on Sources of Scientific and Engineering Literature as an independent and neutral clearing house in such a way that it could co-operate with the existing information departments without interfering with their independence or individual development. Enquiries received by the Agency are forwarded to the sectional information departments best qualified to deal with them; and the latter could communicate with the enquirer direct. By such a decentralisation, large expenses are avoided, while prompt and satisfactory action is ensured. The sphere of action of the Agency is in no way restricted. All enquiries whether from home or abroad are handled in the same way. Thus this new agency represented merely an organisational measure for the systematic co-ordination of the existing individual information departments.

463 International (Special) Centres

The following publications list the chief international documentation centres, specialising, in particular subjects before World War II:

1 *Repertoire international des centres de documentation chimique*. Paris. Office International de Chimie; 1935; 115.

2 *Guide mondial pour les bibliotheques et centres de documentation agricoles, a Rome*. Institute International d'Agriculture; 1938.

3 *Repertoire des centres nationaux de documentation peagogiqued.* Institute International de Co-operation Intellectuelle. (Paris). 1934; French and English; 87

4 *Institutions pour l'etude scientifique des relations internationales.* Paris. French and English. 87 pp.

5 *Repertoire international de centres de documentation politique*; Paris. French, English and German; 177 pp.

International documentation centres for specific subjects are rendered unstable and impermanent due to political factions.

464 INTERNATIONAL FEDERATION FOR DOCUMENTATION

The aim of the International Federation for Documentation is to see that the products of intellectual work are rendered as accessible as possible to mankind and serve the original purpose of their authors. It is usually denoted by the term FID.

465 DIRECTORIES

The following are the directories published by international organisations on documentation centres which deal with a wide range of subjects:

1 The League of Nations published a *Handbook of international organisations* in which organisations are classified according to subjects. The first issue came out in 1921. The latest which was published in 1938, extends to 491 pages. It must be remembered that this handbook excludes bodies set up by the League of Nations itself.

2 The Institute International de la Co-operation Intellectuelle published a periodical known as *Bulletin de la co-operation intellectuelle.* A special number of this *Bulletin* came out in 1937 with the title *Numero special sur la documentation.* This number occupies pages 177 to 240 of the volume for the year. It describes the documentation centres of Europe and particularly the national unions of documentary organisations. Directories of a similar nature are being promoted by FID and Unesco.

466 MERCHANT OF LIGHT

Long-range reference service has to send its tentacles far outside the library, into such national as well as international documentation centres of general as well as specialist varieties. In this respect their function is similar to what "One of the Fathers of Solomon's House" described in the following terms:

"For the several employments and offices of our fellows; we have twelve that sail into foreign countries; who bring us the books and abstracts, and patterns of experiments of all other parts. These we call Merchants of Light." [B1]. Yes the reference librarian should function as a "Merchant of Light."

CHAPTER 5

SERVICE IN LONG RANGE REFERENCE SERVICE

51 Introduction

We shall next examine the core of long-range reference service. This is the service to the seeker of a specific piece of knowledge. There are three stages in service:

1 Precise enunciation of the item of knowledge sought;
2 Search for the documents; and
3 Giving the documents to the seeker.

The clientele in long range reference service may range from the generalist seeker at the one end to a specialist seeker of the severest kind at the other. Viewed from another angle, the seeker may be an active one himself coming forward and asking for help or a passive one needing nearly aggressive offer of help. The nature of the documents to be brought into service will vary with the characteristics of the seeker. The mode of service also will vary with the seeker.

52 Generalist Seeker

A generalist will need documents giving a simple, but up-to-date, exposition of the A B C of a subject of fairly large extension. He will need, ordinarily, a macro document—that is a whole book—in preference to a micro document—that is,—an article in a learned periodical. The first step in serving him is to find out his intellectual attainment, the subject of his interest at the moment, and his standard of knowledge in that subject. These will have to be found out in a genial and often casual or oblique way. Blunt questions may not elicit answers. They may make the reader withdraw within himself. They may even be taken to be offensive. Having formed reliable impressions on these points, the reference librarian should show the seeker an assortment of general books on the subject, written up for general consumption. The assortment should contain seminal books written by master minds in non-technical language, books written with flair, and orientation books. An illustration of books with such intangible qualities has been already given in chapter 7 of part D of this book. Viewed from this angle, a specialist in one subject may become a generalist seeker in another subject.

53 Joint Selection

The reference librarian and the seeker should then jointly evaluate the books. This joint work should be done by the reference librarian with great patience and at low speed. I generally take for a model the salesman pulling out one *saree* (the main apparel of an Indian lady) after another, replacing them all, and again pulling them out at request for re-examination, and helping the customer in the delicate comparison of the colours of the *sarees* and of the treatment of their borders. Thus, by trial and error the right books should be found. The Second Law of Library Science wants this to be done even to the point of offence to the Fourth Law. Sometimes, a book may be too large a document for the seeker. He may require something short to be studied quickly. A good micro document may suit him better. The issues of the *Readers digest* may contain something suitable to him. In general, the *Essay index* will be a suitable bibliography for the use of the reference librarian in such a case.

54 Specialist Seeker

A specialist will need highly technical documents giving precise, advanced, up-to-the-minute account of a subject of narrow extension. Macro documents may seldom be sufficient in his case, even though hot from the press. He will need micro documents. He will need nascent micro documents appearing as articles in the current issues of learned periodicals. Usually a micro subject sought by a specialist will have many facets. They will have many rounds of facets. In each round, there may be many levels of facets. The isolate of the subject sought, inside a personality or a matter facet, may be a superimposed isolate [R17]. It may even be an environmented isolate [R7].

Examples:

1 "Alpha brass below 4.2 K. degrees," as studied in the article *Heat capacity of alpha brasses below 4.2 K°* by J A Rayne. (Physical review; 108; 1957; 22-25).

2 "Cold-adapted rat," as studied in the article *Regulation of heat production in cold-adapted rats* by W H Cottle and L D Carlson. (Proceedings, Society of Experimental Biology and Medicine; 92; 1956; 845-849).

3 Para-social group, as studied in the article *Mass communication and para-social interaction* by D Horton and R R Wohl. (Psychiatry; 19; 1956; 215-229).

55 Facet Analysis of the Subject Sought

The first step in serving an actively participating specialist is to get the subject brought up by him enunciated precisely. This is best done by judicious questions based on facet analysis [R38]. All the facets of the subject should be ascertained. The precise isolate in each facet should also be ascertained. The procedure is similar to the facet analysis of the subject of a document based on postulational approach. [R22; R42]. This facet analysis should be done in a genial way. There should be no trace of pretentiousness. The difficulties in this step in service are illustrated in the actual cases described in part K of this book. This requires both knowledge and tact. A sincere and well-meaning approach will generally secure free co-operation from the specialist seeker.

56 Search for Documents

The second step to be taken by the reference librarian is to construct mentally the class number of the subject sought by the specialist. Armed with the class number, he should look up the library catalogue, the bibliographies, the abstracting and indexing periodicals, and the documentation list prepared locally or at the national documentation centre to make a temporary coverage of the latest micro documents, not yet covered by the bibliographies and even by the abstracting and indexing periodicals. Even at this stage, the seeker should be consulted at intervals to eliminate out-of-focus entries.

57 Supply of Documents

The third step is to supply the documents to the seeker for study. Having narrowed down the number of entries as much as possible in the second step, the reference librarian should collect and place before the seeker the documents described in the surviving entries. The document needed may not be in the library. Then comes the fourth step. That is the prompt making of arrangements to get the document on interlibrary loan. The knowledge of the reference librarian about the documentation centres, referred to in section 46 of this part, will help him in this step. The document needed by the seeker may be in a language not understood by the seeker. Then, the reference librarian should promptly make arrangements for the translation of the document. The seeker may wish to have a copy of the document for his file. Or, the library having the document may not be able to lend it. Then the reference librarian should promptly make arrangements for the making and supply of a photostat or micro-film copy of the document. No published document answering the needs of the seeker may exist. Then the reference librarian may have to establish contact between the seeker and an appropriate research consultant or some other scholar.

58 Passive Clientele

In a business or industrial library attached to a particular institution, the passive clientele may be served by information circulars and bulletins issued periodically. To make this system successful, the reference librarian should have a sound knowledge of the specific needs of his clientele. It may be acquired in various ways: directly by conversation or enquiry, or indirectly by watching the kind of literature asked by the enquirers now and then, and in other ways. In a large organisation, the maintenance of a record of the special interests of individual enquirers provides a valuable tool. The tradition of cloistered aloofness should go even from university libraries. The reference librarian should go out and 'sell his wares' so to speak. With this class, the problem is in part a psychological one — that of arousing the interest or of lulling the suspicions.

581 Ultra Violet Ray Incident
(*Case Study* 158)

The following letter, sent by me to the professor of physics of a constituent college is typical of the kind of long-range reference service due to a passive clientele.

University Library,
9-12-39

My dear friend,

I remember your telling me about a year ago about a correspondence, originated by the Surgeon-General during your predecessor's time about the ultra-violet energy content of the solar radiation in our city. You said that the Surgeon-General sought your co-operation in estimating it.

At that time I could only lay my hands on some scrappy materials in the *Journal of research* of the American Bureau of Standards, the *Journal* of the American Institute of Electrical Engineers and the *Public health bulletin*.

I wonder if you are still interested in the subject. If you are, I have come across something which may be of real use to you.

This morning the foreign mail brought the October issue of the *Journal* of the Franklin Institute. It contains an article entitled *A four-year record of the ultra-violet energy in daylight*, by Mathew Luckiesh and others of the Lighting Research Laboratory of the General Electric Company.

The bibliography at the end of the article mentions the following five titles:

1 Luckiesh (M). *Ultra-violet energy in daylight—a two-year record*. (*Journal* of Franklin Institute; 223; 1937).

2 Juller (L R) etc. *Cadmium—magnesium alloy photo-tube*. (*Journal* of the Optical Society of America; 25; 1935).

3 Luckiesh (M) etc. *Erythemal and tanning effectiveness of ultra-violet energy*. (*General electric review*; 42; 1939).

4 Luckiesh (M) etc. *Production of erythema and tan by ultra-violet energy*. (*Journal* of the American Medical Association; 112; 1939).

5 Luckiesh (M) etc. *Nomenclature and standards for biologically effective radiation*. (JOSA; 21; 1931).

The first of the above articles gives a detailed description of the necessary apparatus. It may be of great interest to you. There are twelve further references. These too may be of interest to the Surgeon-General.

Perhaps you may call at the library for these references. I have assembled all of them in my room to save your time. You may call at any time between 9 AM and 6 PM.

I am sure it will be very nice if your laboratory can build up data for our city.

Yours sincerely,

_____

Librarian.

CHAPTER 6

ASSIMILATION IN LONG RANGE REFERENCE SERVICE

61 Introduction

Assimilation in long-range reference service is similar to that in ready reference service, described in chapter 6 of part F. The inner assimilation process is similar; only reference books of other kinds give place to bibliographies and normal books. The effect of nascent awareness in the presence of the seeker is similar; only, grasp of reference books gives place to fuller acquaintance with the happenings in the wave front of the development in the universe of knowledge. The sharing of experience with colleagues is similar. The use of the meetings of the Staff Council [R37] as a clearing house is similar. There are also some additional forms of assimilation.

62 Deepening of the Knowledge of Bibliography

To a reference librarian, every occasion to serve a generalist reader, seeking readable, reliable books on a subject, provides an opportunity to get a deeper understanding of the bibliographies and especially of the popular reading lists in the field. It also makes him seek out the books in the library collection, rich in the intangible qualities needed by a generalist reader. It also enables him to become sensitive to the different shades of the various intangible qualities. This sense cannot be acquired either from reading or from hearing about such qualities. As in the case of physical taste, this delicate sensitiveness can only be acquired by actual experience. The reference librarian has an immense opportunity to have that experience in the company of readers of diverse tastes and attainments. This is a valuable kind of assimilation following long range reference service to a generalist reader. Again, every nook and corner in an abstracting or indexing periodical does not catch the eye in an ordinary perusal, all by oneself, at the stage of preparation. Even if it does, it does not get properly assimilated in the apperceptive mass in one's mind. But the chances for it are much greater in the purposeful diving into bibliographical tools to help a particular specialist reader.

63 Familiarity with the Wave-Front of Knowledge

It is not easy to keep track of the details of the development in the wave-front of knowledge by the mere perusal of the periodicals. But a grasp of it becomes natural and lasting in the joint pursuit of diverse problems along with a specialist in his own subject-field. His reaction to the entries in a bibliography, his appraisal of articles, his involuntary remarks on them, his preference as between them, and the exchange of questions and answers with him—all these give an insight into the new trends in the subject-field. The assimilation of them becomes effortless and lasting. Such experiences with specialists in diverse subject-fields, coming closely one over another, helps the sensing and the assimilation of a panoramic view of the happenings in the wave front of knowledge. No profession other than that of the reference librarian has the chance to get such a joyful view of the universe of knowledge.

64 Recording and Filing

Long-range reference service to each specialist will be a long drawn out process. The time required for it is not realised. It is desirable to keep a record of each search. It is good to maintain a day book. It may mention items such as the following:

1 The time of commencement and end of each pursuit in long range reference service;

2 The name and other details of the seeker, such as subject of specialisation, occupation and office held, and remarks about participativeness and other intangible but useful items;

3 The specific item of knowledge sought;

4 The route followed in the pursuit—that is, the bibliographies, the cumulative indexes, the periodicals, the handbooks, the books, etc used in succession and the help received from each of them;

5 The help or suggestion received from the seeker himself at the different stages in the route;

6 The documents found to be finally useful; and

7 The resulting information found and its source.

Periodically, say once in a week, the entries in the day book should be digested. All items found worthy should be assimilated in the reference cabinet mentioned in section 65 of part F.

65 Assimilation in the Library Catalogue

Occasionally, the pursuit of a particular item of knowledge may suggest the desirability of incorporating certain subject analytical entries in the library catalogue. Some additional species of subject analytical entries also may suggest themselves. These should be brought to the notice of the Technical Section. The Reference Section is the only tentacle of the Technical Section transmitting to it the feel of the requirements of the users of the library. Therefore the two sections should work in close collaboration. They should discuss together in a friendly way the problem of subject analytical entries. These form a necessary tool for the fulfilment of all the Laws of Library Science.

66 Assimilation with Acquisition Work

Occasionally, the pursuit of a particular item of knowledge may disclose gaps in the library's holdings of bibliographies, cumulative indexes to periodicals, abstracting and indexing periodicals, annual reviews, basic handbooks, and treatises. These should be brought to the notice of the Periodical Publications Section and Book Section respectively. Here again, the Reference Section forms an important tentacle of the library to be fully used by the Book Selection Section.

67 Assimilation with the National Documentation Centre

Occasionally, the pursuit of a particular item of knowledge may suggest desirable changes or improvements in the national documentation list brought out periodically as an aid to research workers. That list is usually restricted to topics being actively pursued in the country. These will change from time to time. In particular new topics will be taken up here, there, and everywhere. The National Documentation Centre should be informed about them. The reference librarians of each service library have to be used by the Centre as its tentacles to feel the appearance of new topics needing inclusion in its documentation list. If a specialist reader suggests new periodicals to be taken, the coverage of those periodicals also in the national documentation list should be suggested by the reference librarian to the National Documentation Centre.

68 Assimilation with International Abstracting Service

Another sphere needing the help of the actual field-experience of the reference librarian is that of international abstracting and indexing periodicals. Reference librarians form an important and enlightened class of consumers of these bibliographical tools. The producers can improve these tools only with the aid of their consumers. The reference librarians form the most competent among the consumers to make suggestions in respect of

1 Coverage of literature;

2 Classification and featuring;

3 Adequacy of index entries—both subject and author and title;

4 Scheme of alphabetisation used in the index;

5 Avoidable duplication of international effort; and

6 Fallow regions of knowledge to be provided for.

The FID (International Federation for Documentation) and the Unesco are coming forward to act as co-ordinating agencies. They cannot have direct experience of the faults in the existing international abstracting and indexing service. They can only pool together the experiences of those directly using them and helping the use of them by specialist readers. To make their work realistic, they have to use the reference librarians in the diverse service-libraries of the world as their tentacles. Therefore, an important international function of a reference librarian is to note the findings come across during long-range reference service and to pass them on to the international agencies for collation and assimilation.

CHAPTER 7

STRUCTURE AND CONTENTS OF A BIBLIOGRAPHY

71 Scheme of Study

A beginner should gradually acquaint himself with the structure and contents of each of the important bibliographies in frequent use. He should also build up his knowledge of special bibliographies in different subject fields, on different authors, and on different countries, regions, or other geographical areas. In due course, he should also extend his search for bibliographies found in other publications. In particular, he should gather information about the periodical publications giving special sections for lists of documents, or reviews or abstracts of documents. The student should have a note-book for such a systematic study of bibliographies, similar to the one described in chap 8 of part H for reference books.

72 Skeleton for Description

The skeleton for the headings for description may be similar to the one given in section 82 of part H for reference books, with the following modification of 5 and its subdivisions.

5 **Nature and Range**
51 Annotated, or
Bare list, or
with Abstracts, or
Review type
52 Lists
Books alone, or
Articles alone, or
Both books and articles, or
Special kinds of documents such as
Periodicals,
Biographies,
Reference books,
Any other forms
53 If Author bibliography,
On, or By, or On and By type
54 If Area Bibliography,
On, or In, or On and In type
55 By Agency of creation, whether
551 Printer's catalogue
552 Binder's bibliography
553 Copyright list
5531 National bibliography
5532 On, or In, or On and In, or By the Nationals Type
5541 Publisher's catalogue
5542 Book-seller's catalogue
5543 Second-hand bookseller's Catalogue
5544 Bibliophile's catalogue
5551 Aid to book selection
5562 Library catalogue
5571 Author's bibliography
5572 Reading list
5573 Documentation Agency's publication,
Regional, national, or international
561 Exhaustive
562 Select, with indication of criterion for selection
571 Primary
572 Secondary

Part K

Illustrative Actualities

CHAPTER 1

GENERAL OBSERVATION

10 Introduction

We have seen in the last three chapters the involved ramifications of long-range reference service. We shall first summarise them here. We shall then illustrate them by giving a detailed description of some long range reference service done in the Madras University Library before the publication of edition 1 of this book.

11 Enunciation of the Problem

The exact enunciation of the problem is often difficult of achievement. The enquirer himself has often only vague notions about it. The first few questions elicit only a very general statement of his wants. It is, usually, far wide of his actual needs. Several solutions have to be brought up to him. To one after another, he says "Not this, not this." In this way, the reference librarian has to narrow down the field for search step by step. The difficulties of the enquirer in giving an accurate straight statement of his needs are often due to genuine and unavoidable causes. He might have come across the problem in a casual conversation or in listening to a lecture or during the study of a book, not giving the reference correctly. Title of the document sought by him might have been reconstructed by him or by others for him, out of some terms occurring on the title page or in the text. Sometimes the enquirer might be interested in a particular aspect of a book; and he might give it a title of his own just representing that aspect; with the result, he really asks the reference librarian for a book that does not exist at all. Even in such cases, it is not proper to turn him away. A few minutes of discussion with him will disclose his actual needs.

12 Routeing

After arriving at the exact enunciation of the question, routeing the investigation may often prove exhausting. No general rule can be given regarding it. Nothing can be definitely stated even about the starting point. An encyclopaedia, a gazetteer, a directory, a periodical publication, or even a text-book may provide the starting point. At the earlier stages, the range of investigation may be far too wide both in the period to be covered and in the material to be examined. Every step in the routeing should aim at narrowing down these two factors. The upper limit and the lower limit of the period should be brought closer and closer. While this itself would eliminate a good deal of materials, every other possible means should be used to bring their range to a manageable size. Even within such a restricted range of materials, the method of random sampling should be adopted with great skill. Sometimes the ultimate source of information may be the newspaper file of a bygone year. A dive into its pages is very exhausting. No reference librarian would enter that stage of investigation before utilising other sources to reduce the number of issues of the newspaper to be rummaged. Again he should exhaust all the resources most sincerely before passing the question on to external agencies for further investigation. This is but proper.

13 Close Touch with the Enquirer

During the routeing of the problem, the reference librarian should keep himself in close touch with the enquirer, either by personal conversation or by correspondence. He should keep the enquirer informed of the progress made, the difficulties met with, and the sudden turns encountered. Such reports often enable the enquirer either to re-enunciate his problem or to recollect and communicate further clues for investigation. Without such contact with the enquirer, the reference librarian is likely to go astray far too much from the actual needs.

14 Record of the Sources

The final information arrived at must be promptly communicated to the enquirer. He may then probably ask or write back for further elucidation; the information furnished may raise further issues in his mind. Intelligent enquirers are often impressed by the success of the reference librarian. It makes them eager to share with him the pleasure of retracing the whole route. Experienced enquirers find a delight in this process. They also expect or wish to know the details of the process adopted by the reference librarian in arriving at the information. For their sake, a full record of the sources used should be kept. Such people set more value on "becoming" rather than "being." Enquirers with such a participative attitude give the greatest delight to the reference librarian.

CHAPTER 2

PALMYRA'S USES ENQUIRY

(*Case Study* 159)

21 Exact Enunciation

Some years ago, the American mail brought us a query from the Library of the University of Mannitoba. One of its clientele wanted to know about a Tamil poem enumerating 801 uses of the palm tree. He would like to have a copy of the poem if it was a short one. He would also like to have a reference to an English translation of it. He would like to buy a copy of it. The American library had exhausted all its resources. It did not succeed. Therefore, the Mannitoba Library naturally thought about some library in the Tamil country as the most hopeful collaborator in the pursuit of this problem. It therefore wrote to the Madras University Library. Here the enunciation of the problem was exact. It gave us no difficulty.

22 Path of Pursuit

221 Inside Catalogues of Libraries

Our catalogue was first examined, then the catalogues of the other local libraries, and lastly the fairly exhaustive catalogue of the Tamil books and manuscripts of the British Museum. None of these threw any light on the problem.

222 Among Manuscripts

As the next step, we addressed the Manuscripts Library at Tanjore Palace. That too gave a negative reply. Then we approached some Tamil scholars, and in particular Mahamahopadhaya Dakshinatya Kalanidhi Dr V Swaminatha Iyer, the septagenarian doyen of Tamil scholarship. He had brought into print for the first time nearly a hundred classics and other pieces in Tamil. He still had many unpublished manuscripts; and he knew them all. But he too could not give us any help.

223 Inside Second-Hand Book Shops

Then personal visits were made by members of the staff to second-hand book-shops and to pedlars of ballad songs to try the off-chance of picking up an old copy of the poem. But here too no success.

224 Inside Printed Books

The botanical and agricultural books dealing with palms were searched. But no clue could be found.

2241 WATT'S DICTIONARY

Almost in despair we tried our luck in Watt's *Dictionary of economic products of India*. Page 495 of volume 1 contained a small light. It illuminated a certain angle immediately in front of it:

"Every part of this plant is made use of in some way or other. A tamil poem enumerates some 800 uses to which the various parts are put. The *Tropical agriculturist* (June 1884) publishes a list of the more important of these uses."

2242 TROPICAL AGRICULTURIST

Then we looked up the *Tropical agriculturist*. We found in page 913 of volume 3 the following encouraging piece of information:

"From the *Tala vilasam*, a Tamil poem describing 'in brief an account of one (?) out of the 800 items of things connected with the palmyra tree, which is emphatically the Kalpa tree of the Earth' given in the appendix to a *Description of the palmyra palm of Ceylon* by William Ferguson, printed at the *Observer* Press in 1850, we extract the following. . . . Mr. William Ferguson's account of the palmyra palm has been so long out of print that we intend publishing a new edition of it. . . . We regret that we are not in a position to spare a copy."

225 Outside the Library Into Villages

The foreign inquirer had mentioned Kumbakonam as the home of the author of the poem. We, therefore, took to the desperate last recourse of writing to the Tahsildar (Revenue official) of Kumbakonam taluk. He zealously unwound his red-tape and transmitted the inquiry through his revenue inspectors to the headmen of hundreds of villages in his taluk. But to our disappointment the return was 'nil' from everywhere.

23 Persistance in Hope

We were at our wit's end. Still we were too reluctant to give a negative reply to our foreign correspondent. For, our ideal in long-range reference service is, in the words of Hanuman the arch-priest of service:

"Hope is the root of all service. Search again, I will, wherever I have not yet searched. Hope is the greatest happiness. It is hope that always directs us in all our endeavours. It is that which brings all the efforts of beings to fruition. Therefore, I shall continue my hopeful attempts." [V6]:

अनिर्वेदः श्रियो मूलमनिर्वेदः परं सुखम् ।
भूयस्तत्र विचेष्यामि न यत्र विचयः कृतः ॥
अनिर्वेदो हि सततं सवार्थेषु प्रवर्तकः ॥
करोति सफलं जन्तोः कर्म यत्तत्करोति सः ।
तस्मादनिर्वेदकरं यत्नं चेष्ठेऽहमुत्तमम् ॥

In hope therefore we were biding our time. We were keeping the problem open. The life of the file was kept on. The problem was kept ever alive in the minds of all our reference librarians. At long last hope did materialise. Delight did come.

24 Ultimate Location

Ethelbert Blatter's *Palms of British India and Ceylon* arrived at the 'recent additions shelf'. The title was tempting. But the epithets added to the author's name sent a wave of cold shiver through us. For, the author was put down as a professor of Botany and that too in Bombay, far from the Tamil country. The first reference librarian, perusing it, put it aside with a sigh of disappointment. For, most of the pages, dipped into by him, confirmed the book to be a dry-as-dust systematic one. Still another reference librarian took it up with higher hopes. He too dropped it in disappointment. And yet another said "I have a lucky hand" and opened the book. His hand was lucky indeed. For the page opened by him — page 203 — contained in its middle the word *Talavilasam.* But the page-heading was made up of the forbidding Latin term 'Borassinae.' This was probably the reason for the others missing it.

241 Triumph of Success

At the announcement of *Talavilasam*, all the other reference librarians rushed for the book. Their colleague was holding it out triumphantly in his hand. The first words of Blatter were very consoling.

"I searched a long time for that poem, of which nothing but the title seemed to be known, and when I found it at last I was astonished that I had not discovered it sooner."

A few lines further down we read,

"The poem was written by 'Arunachalam, a poet of Terrukkudantei, the same with Combaconam in the province of Tanjore."

But our delight reached its climax when we read in the next page,

"We trust that our readers will not object to our reproducing the poem *in extenso*."

Object! Surely it was a mockery to us. We would have objected if he had not reproduced the poem *in extenso*! We were thankful that he gave us at least an English translation. It extended to nine pages.

25 Happy Popular Saying

Our minds began to sing in unison the words of Sita [V7] and Bharata [V8] exclaiming the old saw:

कल्याणी बत गाथेयं लौकिकी प्रतिभाति मे।
एति जीवन्तमानन्दो नरं वर्षशतादपि॥

"Happy seems to me the popular saying 'If only one would keep on to life, delight is assured even though it may take a hundred years in coming'."

Immediately steamed forth our epistle carrying the glad tidings to the sister library in the New World.

CHAPTER 3

PRE-COLUMBIAN HINDU COLONISATION OF AMERICA

(*Case Study* 160)

31 Enunciation Wide of the Mark

Exactly thirty years ago an octogenarian wrote from an up-country town for books on pre-Columbian America. He was Salem Vijayaraghavachariar. He was a famous man. He had once occupied the then highest position in the gift of the Indian nation—Presidentship of the Indian National Congress. His request was obviously simple.

32 Supply of Bibliography

The next mail delivered into his hands a type-script of several titles including some articles in some periodicals. The library's letter concluded with the words:

"The anthropological books dealing with the native races of America contain many suggestions about the inhabitants of the country in the pre-Columbian days."

33 Announcement of Two Books

Some months later, the prospectus of two publications of the American Geographical Society was received in the library. It had the display heading *The discovery of America in the years* 1000 *and* 1492. This information was promptly relayed to the octogenarian.

34 Exact Enunciation

He replied:

"Thank you for your kind letter of yesterday's date. I have been anxious to secure one or more books on America before its discovery by Columbus. As I believe you are aware, long ago I read somewhere that Hindus went to America through North Eastern Asia and founded or established its civilization there and that there was plenty of evidence in Mexico and Peru to prove the similarity if not the identity of Indian and American civilizations. If you can tell me what are the books on the subjects I shall be glad. The price or prices of such cannot be much. I am prepared to pay up to Rs. 100 if you advise me."

It took three months for his problem to be thus definitely enunciated as "Hindu civilisation in pre-Columbian America." The resources of our own library and of the others in our country were too meagre to throw any considerable light on this problem.

35 Foreign Aid Sought

Therefore, we approached the Library of Congress for help. We asked in particular,

"Can you kindly let me have a list of books suggesting at the same time two or three items which appear to be the best or the latest among them in your opinion."

36 Fifty Sheets of Bibliography

Within three months the secretary of the Congressional Librarian forwarded to us a :

1 Memorandum on the subject prepared by the chief bibliographer of the Library of Congress;
2 Clipping from a contemporary issue of the *Washington post* which announced certain latest discoveries of the ruins of the Mayan Empire; and
3 Fairly exhaustive type-written *List of references to writings on pre-Columbian art in America* and *Mayas, antiquities and culture: a bibliographical list.*

These consisted nearly of fifty sheets of matter compiled some five years earlier for some other purpose. The secretary's letter concluded with the characteristic sentence:

"The Library of Congress is precluded, because of its official position, from expressing an opinion as to the 'best' on any subject."

37 Delight of Personal Contact

In the meantime, we had ourselves located some relevant articles in *Inter-America.* Their list and the fifty sheets of the Library of Congress were sent to the octogenarian enquirer. He was evidently moved by this service. And he wrote a private and personal letter:

"Dear Mr. Ranganathan

My warm and grateful thanks to you for the great trouble you have taken in behalf of my request. I expect to go to Madras shortly, when I shall call and see you. Then in personal consultation with you the first batch of books might be selected.

With kind regards,
I am,
Yours sincerely,
Vijayaraghavachari

Sometime later, he called at the library. Age and fame sat lightly on him. This chastened all of us. We all felt elevated by his sincerity, child-like simplicity, and scholarly pursuit. His visit was a great honour. We were delighted.

38 Further Distribution of the Fruits

A year later His Holiness Jagadguru Sri Sankaracharya of Kamakotipitham camped in Madras after an interval of several decades. In some of his public discourses, he referred to the penetration of Hindu civilization into various other lands including America in the distant past. This brought to the library a stream of enquirers. The fruits of our labour, undertaken at the instance of the octogenarian, were freely distributed to all these inquirers.

Thus an exhaustive bibliography prepared for reference service at a library in Washington served in reinforcing reference service in Madras continuously for about a year.

CHAPTER 4

PAMBAN BRIDGE ENQUIRY

(*Case Study* 161)

41 Exact Enunciation

A local college was leading an exursion of students to the Pamban Straits, separating the mainland of India from the Rameswaram Island at its south eastern end. A batch of enterprising young men called at the library and wanted to have exhaustive information about the Pamban bridge connecting the mainland with the Island. Here the problem was definitely enunciated at the outset.

42 Routeing

The range for search had to be progressively narrowed down. The absence of any book exclusively on the Pamban bridge was first ascertained. It was known to be a recent construction. How recent was the question.

43 Upper Limit to Period of Search

Volume 19 page 377 of the *Imperial gazetteer of India* (1908) contained the sentence:

"Proposals are now under consideration to bridge the channel and to carry the railway across it to Rameswaram."

This fixed the upper limit to the period for literature-search. Another sentence in the preceding page of the *Gazetteer* gave a clue as to the periodical likely to give further information. It read:

"The first proposal to deepen this channel for traffic was made by Colonel Manmuel Martimers who brought the matter to the notice of Mr. Lushington then collector of southern provinces and afterwards Governor of Madras. . . . His (Major Sim's) reports will be found at length in the *Journal* of the Royal Geographical Society Vol. IV" (1837).

This made us examine the back volumes of this periodical. But the cumulative index covered only up to 1912. It did not mention Pamban bridge.

44 Lower Limit to Period of Search

In order to fix a lower limit before searching the individual volumes of the periodical, some books on Indian geography, commercial geography, and bridge-engineering were looked into. Dudley Stamp's *Indian empire*; v 2; p 97 contained the remark,

"But now there is a railway to Pamban on the Chain of Islands towards Ceylon."

This book was published in 1926. Therefore, this year was taken as the lower limit. Students were asked to search for information in the *Journal* of the Royal Geographical Society for the years 1912-1926. But they gave a nil report. The reason for this will be seen later.

45 Further Narrowing of Period of Search

In the meantime other attempts were made to narrow the time limit still further. S Playner's *Southern India, its history, people, commerce and industrial resources* gave, on page 573, 24 February 1914 as the date of opening of the Pamban route to Colombo. The students were then asked to examine the *Journal* of the Royal Geographical Society for 1914. But again they reported nil. Pamban did not appear in the index. But a more careful scrutiny of the index disclosed to the reference librarian the entry "India: railway connection between India and Ceylon, 693." This page fell in the *Monthly record section* for February; and the information given was very meagre. However, the record began with the sentence:

"The Indian papers report that the connection effected on the 24th February last between the Indian and Ceylon railway systems is already working successfully."

46 Location

Accordingly, the *Hindu* and the *Mail* for 24 and 25 February 1914 were examined. The *Mail* of 24 gave three columns of information with a map, in addition to an editorial article. The issue of 25 gave three more columns of information. The *Hindu* of 25 devoted its leader to the *Indo-Ceylon link*. It also gave a full page to a description of the bridge, the opening function, the governor's speech etc. This gave just the information wanted by the students.

47 Assimilation

While on this problem we looked up the *Minutes of proceedings* of the Institution of Civil Engineers. Pages 377-387 of volume 199 gave a full description of the construction of the Pamban viaduct and of the two-leaved rotating-light bridge. All these references were given cross reference entries in the catalogue of the library to facilitate future use.

CHAPTER 5

DEVIL WORSHIP OF TULUVA ENQUIRY

(*Case Study* 162)

51 Enunciation Wide of the Mark

Here is an example illustrating the difficulties in the enunciation of the problem by the enquirer even better than the case of the octogenarian described in chapter 3 of this Part. The enquirer was a much travelled gentleman with a university doctorate in Fine Arts. He was also known as an enthusiastic student and an exponent of Indian music and dance. He was a European. He struggled with the catalogue cards in the battery of cabinets for a while. He was just leaving the library with a look of disappointment. Mr C Sundaram, the Chief Reference Librarian, was just then coming back from lunch. He met the enquirer at the entrance. His facial expression and his hesitant gait were enough to induce Sundaram to introduce himself and to ask him if he would like to have help on any particular topic.

52 Book on Dance

"Have you any book on dance?"

"Yes."

"But you don't seem to have it. However let me have a look at your catalogue of books on dance once again with you."

The enquirer and Sundaram came to the catalogue room. The appropriate tray was pulled out. The cards were being turned. The enquirer involuntarily made his question a little more definite.

53 Books on Indian Dance

"I want books on Indian dance. But I find only the texts or translations of the ancient Sanskrit classics on the subject."

"Do you want a modern exposition of Indian dance?"

"Yes."

"We have a few. Do you want any book in particular?"

"Yes. What I want is not exactly dance but only an aspect of it."

"I see. Can you say what exactly you want?"

"Folk dance."

"The books on folk dance have been written mostly by anthropologists. The focus of interest in such books is cultural evolution rather than the technique of dance. You won't find such books on the shelves containing Fine Arts."

54 Book on Indian Folk Dance

Then they both stepped into the stack-room; and they entered the gangway containing anthropology. In a short while Hambly's *Tribal dancing* was picked up. It gave a world-survey of folk dance. But, only pages 64-68 dealt with India.

"I want more sumptuous information."

"I am sure we can collect a good deal more from other books in this class."

Now the learned doctor appeared to go into a reverie with half closed eyes contemplating on the stupendous task of examining every book. Almost unconsciously he blurted out, something closer to his search.

55 Burnell's Book on Indian Folk Dance

"I have heard that A C Burnell had a book on it."

"On folk dance in India?"

"Yes. But your catalogue does not show it."

"I have not heard of such a title by Burnell. Anyhow let me make an attempt."

Then, the chief bibliographical sources were examined. Neither the *Dictionary of national biography* nor the *Dictionary of Indian biography* mentioned such a book in the bibliographical note under Burnell.

"Do you happen to recollect anything more about the contents of the book. That may help me to pursue the matter further?"

"Well. It is obvious you don't have it. Don't worry yourself. I have already taken too much of your time."

"Please don't feel so embarrassed. My time is entirely for this kind of work. In fact I must thank you for giving me this engagement."

"Oh! It is very kind of you; but it is not fair that I should. . . . "

"Never mind. We don't seem to have exact information about the title or the contents of the book. Let us spend some more time on it before abandoning it as hopeless. Please see if you recollect anything more about it."

551 Burnell's Book on Kannada Folk Dance

"I think I have heard it said that he had dealt with the subject elaborately. I believe it is on folk dance as practised in his days in the West Coast among the Kannada speaking people if I remember right."

This brought to the mind of Sundaram the gazetteers of Mysore and South Canara. The *District manual of South Canara* (1894) had marginal headings. They ran their eyes down the margins. The first hopeful term to turn up was 'demonology'; and the next page mentioned 'devil dancing.'

It was already exciting experience for the learned doctor. As they skipped through the paragraphs their eyes simultaneously fell on the passage:

"Good accounts of a devil dance are given by Mr. Walhouse in the *Journal* of the Anthropological Institute Vol V and detailed description by the late Dr Burnell was published by Major Temple in the *Indian antiquary* for January and February 1894." With great avidity Vol 23 of the periodical was pulled out. But the contents page irritatingly read:

"The late A C Burnell CIE—*See* Major R C Temple."

But as a consoling factor, however, Temple's name appeared on the verso. There were quite a number of items under this name.

552 Burnell's Paper on Tuluva Devil Worship

"The Devil worship of the Tuluvas from the papers of the late A C Burnell, CIE, 1, 29, 85, 183" was the very first entry.

The learned doctor was really in ecstasy. These references yielded 71 quarto pages. The eyes of the doctor gleamed. Sundaram exclaimed to him with even greater ecstasy.

"Hallo, doctor! (They had already become sufficiently intimate) We are really lucky to-day!"

"Yes, 71 quarto pages! Imagine, I was about to go away muffling the remark: "This is a rotten library. All mere fuss!" If you had not pitted against me at the door. . . ."

"Doctor, you are such an easy guest. Satisfied so easily and so soon!"

"You are really uncanny! Have you hit upon another find?"

"Yes, doctor. *To be continued*!"

"God knows where!"

"Surely a doctor should not be impatient. I shall find out for you in a trice."

56 Idiosyncrasy of the Index

The *Author's index* 1872-1921 was summoned to our table. 'Burnell' however was disappointing. The only volume cited was the one already examined by us.

"I am sorry for you, librarian!"

"He laughs best who laughs last. Please turn to 'Temple'."

And he did. But the poor doctor had to plough through five double column pages of entries. He grew desperate.

"What the devil do they mean by this arrangement! Did I say 'arrangement'? No, no! I should have said 'derangement' or, better, 'chaos'."

"Doctor! It is perfect cosmos there. If your mind thinks chaos, I am afraid you have to look for it there."

"Librarian! Be more reasonable. Look here. 'Growse'; then 'Burton'; then 'Knowle'; then 'Grierson' I suppose this is librarian's cosmos!"

"My dear doctor, it *is* cosmos! Only it is of its own kind. The entries are arranged volume by volume and within each volume according to page number. But in the case of continuation articles all the continuations are shown together at the reference to the earliest volume, whatever be the later volumes in which the articles may be continued. You remember that the first instalment of the article appeared on page 1 of V 23. Now turn the pages until you reach the reference to Vol 23!"

57 Location in Full

The learned doctor read out with delight:

"The Devil worship of the Tuluvas, (a) XXIII, 1, 29, 85, 183; XXIV, 113, 141, 211, 242, 267; XXV, 61, 216, 237, 272, 295, 328; XXVI, 47, 60".

Thus the learned doctor's imagined *Dance* by Burnell had to be battered by slow degrees into the *Devil worship* by Temple and that too of the small localised community of Tuluvas, and what was asserted to be a book turned out to be matter big enough to form a book but scattered in seventeen different places in the volumes of a periodical!

And all the Five Laws of Library Science were duly propitiated.

CHAPTER 5

SHADOW PLAYS ENQUIRY

(*Case Study* 163)

61 Wrong Requisition Slip

A research worker of experience sent a requisition slip for the book "R Pischel: Altindische Schattenpiel, 1906." The reference librarian could not recollect having handled any such title. Hence the catalogue was looked up and it confirmed his impression. The research worker was known to be usually thorough and reliable in furnishing details for the books sought by him—heading, title, year of publication, name of the periodical if an article etc. The book was therefore presumed to exist. The library did not possess a copy. And so, the messenger had to go back empty handed.

62 Search for Bibliographical Data For the Book

The reference librarian took steps to procure a copy of the book for the library. For, an important member of the research staff had felt the need for it. He started collecting the necessary bibliographical details about the book for transmission to the Book Order Section. The British Museum catalogue and the catalogue of the India Office Library did not mention the book.

63 Doubt about the Very Existence of such a Book

This raised a doubt whether it was a book at all. Much light could have been gathered if the research worker had come in person. Perhaps the place from which he picked up the reference would have given some hints. But that help was not available. Hence the *Dictionary of Indian biography* was looked up. Keith's *History of Sanskrit literature* and *History of Sanskrit drama* were next examined. The former was of no help; but the latter had a section on 'Shadow plays' and 'Puppet plays'. The particular title being sought however was not mentioned. We looked for Winternitz's *Geschichte der indischen Literature*, well known for its bibliographical thoroughness. But it was unfortunately out on loan at the moment. As another alternative we looked up Schuylar's *Bibliography of the Sanskrit drama*. But it mentioned only Pischel's *Home of the puppet play*—

both the German original and the English translation. However, we did not regard this as a conclusive negative as its year of publication was the same (1906) as the one furnished in the loan slip of the research worker.

64 Location

At this stage Sten Konow's *Indische Drama* was thought of. To our relief section 55 which was headed "Schattenspiele" mentioned Pischel as the first authority. The footnote mentioned "Schatt." What could it mean? The Abkurzungen, p. 136, gave the answer:

"Schatt R Pischel, Das altindische Schattenpiele. Sitzungsberichte der Koniglich preussischen Akademie der Wissennchaften, 1906, S. 482 f"

And all along, the bands of the Sitzungsberichte had been mutely mocking at us. It was like dying of thirst on the brink of a river in full floods.

65 Sharing the Joy

Immediately the research worker was "dragged bodily" into the library, to make him share with us the pleasure brought by this find. He was also shown other articles on the subject by Hillebrandt and Luders. They were all lying secreted in the same periodical. Of course, he was immensely delighted.

66 Fulfilment of the Laws of Library Science

If the reference staff had not been actuated by the urge to secure a copy of the title in question for the library, the research worker would have surely gone unserved and the Second and the Third Laws of Library Science would have had legitimate ground for the indictment of the library to its eternal shame. And so we all congratulated the young man in the reference staff on the prompting given by him to pursue the problem at least on the book selection side and thus redeem the reputation of the library by finding a reader for this article (Third Law) and the material for the research worker (Second Law), without wastage of one minute of his time (Fourth Law).

CHAPTER 7

KRA CANAL ENQUIRY

(*Case Study* 164)

71 Collaboration of the Enquirer

Twenty-three years ago, a young graduate stepped into the library. Mentioning an alleged agreement between Siam and Japan, he asked for information on Kra Canal. We were absolutely ignorant of Kra. But the graduate collaborated with us in pursuing the problem. With the help of the atlas, Kra was found to be the name of the isthmus in the Malay Peninsula, at the head of the China Sea and near the southern tip of Lower Burma. According to the enquirer, the distance from the Eastern Coast of this neck to the nearest point on the river Pakcham, running across this isthmus to the Bay of Bengal on the west, was only a short one. The Kra Canal Scheme was just to connect this river with the China Sea.

72 Books on Siam

The encyclopaedia was searched; but it gave no light. Then the following books on the geography and history of Siam were skipped through:

1 McCarthy (James): *Surveying and exploring in Siam*;

2 Graham (W A): *Siam: A handbook of practical commercial and political information*; and

3 Graham (W A): *Siam*; 2 v.

None of these mentioned the Kra Canal.

73 Books on Japanese Foreign Policy

Japan was interested in the problem. This information was furnished by the enquirer. Therefore, the following only books in the library dealing with the foreign policy of Japan were examined. But they too gave a negative result:

1 Allan (G C): *Modern Japan and its problems*;

2 Young (A M): *Japan in recent times*;

3 Nitobe (I): *Japan: Some phases of her problems and development*;

4 Etherton (P J) and Tiltman (H H): *Japan: Mystery of the Pacific*; and

5 Peffer (N): *Japan and the Pacific.*

74 Books on Singapore Naval Base

The enquirer was collaborating with us all along. He dropped down a remark about the opening of the Kra Canal possibly nullify-ing the Singapore naval base. This led us to examine the books dealing with the Federated Malaya States and the books directly or indirectly dealing with British imperial interests involved in the Singapore naval base. The following books were looked into but no light came from any of them.

1 Winstedt (R O): *Malaya: the straits settlements and the federated and unfederated Malaya States*;

2 *Handbook to British Malaya*;

3 Wright (A): *Malay peninsula*;

4 Wheeler (L R): *Modern Malay*;

5 Sweetenham (F): *British Malaya*;

6 Herbertson (A J) and Howarth (O J R): *Oxford survey of the British empire*; V 6: *General survey*;

7 Stokes (R): *New imperial ideals*;

8 Stoye (J): *British empire: its structure and its problems*;

9 Demangeon (A): *British empire: a study in colonial geo-graphy*; and

10 Hall (W P): *Empire to commonwealth: thirty years of British imperial history.*

75 Books on Far Eastern Problems

Then we switched on to books on Far Eastern problems, the following books were examined. But they too were of no avail.

1 Soyeshima (M): *Oriental interpretations of the far eastern problem*;

2 Vinacke (H M): *A history of the east in modern times*;

3 Morse (H B) and MacNair (H F): *Far eastern international relations*; and

4 Mogi (S) and Redman (H V): *The problem of the far east.*

Then we delved into the following sets and books. But still no benefit came.

1 *Survey of International affairs*—Consolidated index to 1920-1930 and later volumes;

2 *Problems of the pacific* being the proceedings of the conferences of the Institute of Pacific Relations: Conference, 1, 3, 4 and 5;

3 Bodley (R V C): *The drama of the Pacific*;

4 Hoffman (W G): *Pacific relations*; and

5 Pickens (R S): *Storm clouds over Asia.*

76 False Hope

But we were loathe to send away such a participative enquirer unserved. When in that pensive and reluctant mood, it struck one of us that the *Geographical journal* had been left unexamined. The cumulative index gave to our delight one entry answering the very question of the enquirer. But our hopes were all shattered once again, on turning to that reference—page 421 of volume 6 (1895) as directed by the index. For, it gave only seven lines on the subject. These lines simply said "tremendous harbour works and very expensive dredging would have to be resorted to." Giving this article to the inquirer was virtually no better than giving him nothing.

77 Location

Everybody was just entering into despair. Suddenly, the periodical *Pacific affairs* emerged into conscious memory. Several eyes began to scan the pages of its volumes. In a few minutes, the one with the lucky hand shouted "eureka, eureka!" Immediately all rushed to him, with the enquirer leading. He was triumphantly waving v 9. Page 406 was headed "The KRA CANAL: A SUEZ FOR JAPAN?" All the succeeding rectos up to page 415 continued to carry this title as page-heading. The foot of every page was studded with bibliographical references—a delightful treat! These footnotes put us on to the correct volumes of the *Parliamentary debates*. From them, the inquirer was able to extract authentic official information. There were two references to the London *Times*. Our collection was examined. But unfortunately it disclosed a lacuna just in the period sought. We later managed to fill up this gap by persuading one of the subscribers to this daily to make a gift of his file to the library.

78 Delight

The feeling of delight and satisfaction radiating from the face of the enquirer and filling our heart is best described in the words of King Dasaratha addressed to the sage Visvamitra on his sudden appearance in the Royal Court.

"Welcome to thee, the great revered one. I consider your coming as the coming in of nectar. It is as welcome as the coming of rain during draught, as the getting of a son by the wedded wife of one long left childless, and as the recovery of the fortune totally lost. I find in this as much joy as in a great festivity." [V1]

यथामृतस्य संप्राप्तिर्यथा वर्षमनूदके ।
यथा सदशृदारेषु पुत्रजन्माप्रजस्य च ।।
प्रनष्टस्य यथा लाभो यथा हर्षो महोदये ।
तथैवागमनं मन्ये स्वागतं ते महामुने ।

CHAPTER 8

DEFERRED EGO-LESS JOY

81 Service without Attachment

Reference service—particularly long-range—blesseth him that takes and him that gives. The benefit for the reference librarian is unique. It habituates him to involuntary service, without any thought or expectation of any return to himself. It trains him from hour to hour and from day to day to act without flirting with the fruits of action. To him, the words of the Lord gradually cease to be mere words. They become a wholesome reality. The Lord says,

> Your right is only to do service.
> Flirt not ever with fruits.
> Let not the fruit of action be the incentive.
> Let there not be for you attachment to inaction. (B3)
>
> कर्मणि एव अधिकारः ते ।
> मा फलेषु कदाचन ।।
> मा कर्मफलहेतुः भूः ।
> मा ते संगः अस्तु अकर्मणि ।।

Ultimately, a reference librarian has a good chance to get himself established in this standard of the *Bhagavad-Gita*. Ultimately, he will get himself attuned even to hear words of gratefulness without their touching the little ego in him. He will be able to hear words of praise, as if he were not the person praised. Sri Ramakrishna had this quality in him inherently in abundance. A reference librarian can acquire it by the virtue of his very daily life. This quality is of a supreme order. It enables one to live life in pure delight. It enables one to transcend the inhibiting, corrupting, realities of ordinary life. In the case of an ordinary man, without spontaneous spiritual blossoming, its benefit can be realised only late in life. It will be deferred benefit. A young reference librarian will have to take the testimony of the older ones in this matter. With faith in that testimony, he should persistently practice reference service without attachment.

82 A Reader in His Last Moments

(*Case Study* 165)

It was 1938. A young man walked into my room in the library. He looked sad and perturbed. I took him to be a student.

"Can I help you?"

"My father sent me to you, sir,. . .with a request."

"Sit down; and tell me what it is."

"He is dangerously ill. He is almost in his last moments. He wishes to do something to the library. . . ." The young man broke down in sobs.

"Pick up courage, young man. What is the name of your father? What was he? Do we know each other?"

"Yes sir", the young man faltered, "He is not a graduate. But he was fond of books. You were good enough, it seems, to admit him as a member of your library as a special case."

"I do it for every serious reader. For, this is the only lending library in our city."

"Moreover, sir, it seems you have been helping all these years in selecting books for his study. He says that he enjoyed all of them. He says he derived immense benefit from them. He wishes to do something for the library."

"Is he rich?"

"No, sir. We are poor. His salary was only one hundred rupees."

"Then, why should he spend any money on this library. It is quite well off. It is maintained by public funds. It gets a good statutory grant from the Government."

I was much moved by this wish of his. I immediately went to see that member of the library. The moment I saw him, I recalled his coming to the library regularly for nearly twelve years. He developed interest in books on literature, religion, and philosophy. He was always beaming and cheerful. I saw him then in his last struggle.

"Why did you come yourself to this humble cottage, sir? I did not ask my son to bring you here."

"Never mind. Your son did not ask me to come. I wished to see you."

"Sir, I owe the happiness of this life of mine to your library. It is true, I was poor in the ordinary sense. But your library made me rich in every other way." He was struggling for breath. He lisped, "Here is something. Please buy books for the library."

It was a sum of one hundred rupees, in ordinary reckoning. But its true value!

83 Salem Fruit Gardener
(*Case Study* 166)

It was an afternoon in 1943. I was in the midst of being purified by the fire of World War II. It was showing the futility of being attached to do anything. It was bringing home the harm of attachment. I was being led to see the harm flowing from my attachment to the university library. The words of the *Bhagavad-Gita* began to tame me saying, "It was good for you to have thrown yourself unsparingly into its development. But it was bad for you to have developed an attachment for it." These words of the *Gita* were still without a full meaning to me. Therefore, the fire of purification got intensified in other ways. One of the ways took the form of a ruthless tyranny of the new man entering a place in the top management. It was further intensified by the reprehensible conduct of a creature of his installed in the library. It looked as if the ugly spirit of resentment, revenge, and misery would swallow up everything in me. A bitter struggle was induced by these apparently unfriendly forces. The words of the *Gita* struggled to make me continue to do the work intensively but without attachment to the library or sensitiveness to the hatred from which the tyranny sprang. At that moment, a well-dressed cheerful middle-aged man walked into my room. His radiation was soothing. I took him to be a reader.

"Can I help you?"

"No, sir. I really came to thank you."

"For what?"

"Perhaps, you don't recognise me."

"Honestly I don't. I am sorry. Can you help me?"

"Of course, you can't. You meet so many every day. And, it is now fifteen years since I visited your library last. I had just then graduated. I was poor. I had nobody to help me into any position. I took work under a cloth merchant on twenty rupees. He was a ruthless man. One morning, he turned me out. I was the very embodiment of misery. My only harbour was this library. I used to it in the easternmost seat in the last row. In many of your rounds of the reading room, you used to speak to me with kindness. You used to suggest several books to read. One day, you introduced me to a set of books on fruit growing. I devoured them. . . .

I am now a fruit-grower. I have extensive gardens near Salem. Through your help and blessing, I am now enjoying affluence in every respect. The ruthless conduct of that cloth merchant turned out to be a good in disguise. I really came to express my gratefulness to you for your having put me on the way."

"Gratefulness is due unto God. A librarian is only a means or a channel used by Him. Are you grateful to the postman handing over the money or to the sender of the money order?"

This experience did the conversion. Light flashed. The words of the *Gita* became real. No more sense of misery. No more hatred of the ruthless man without or of his creature within. Attachment dropped out. Work was thenceforth done even more thoroughly than ever before. All was light. All was joy. Greater and wider opportunities to serve flowed in. Yes. Flirt not with fruits. No, not even when they fall on the lap.

84 Florida Fruit Gardener

(*Case Study* 167)

It was June 1950. The Library School in Albany, New York, had invited me to deliver the valedictory address. A day after return to New York City, there was a letter from Albany.

The writer of the letter had just then reached Albany. He was a native of that place. But, he had been living for long in Florida. He happened to see a picture of me in a local paper. It also gave a report of my work in Albany. He recalled the name. He had been longing to meet me for several years. He immediately ran up to the Library School. But, I had left. The Head of the School gave my probable New York address. Could he come down to New York? Could he be given a few minutes?

I wrote back that it would be unnecessarily expensive to come all the way down to New York. He might get his work done by correspondence. I did not know anything about him. Nor could I guess his probable business with me. I was a stranger to him and to his country. Could he be a publisher?

That evening, I was working in my room in the library of the Columbia University. I was all alone in that huge building. For the library had been closed that afternoon, on account of the university convocation. They had really locked me in. There was a telephone call for me.

"I am the person from Albany. I wrote to you yesterday."

"I posted my reply about an hour ago. It will reach you to-morrow."

"I am now here in New York, sir. The Head of the Albany School had told me that you would soon be leaving to other universities. I did not want to take any risk. I therefore came over here without waiting for a reply. May I now come to see you? I want only a few minutes."

"I am sorry. It will not be possible. I am in a room in the library. The building is closed on account of the convocation. You can't enter it."

"I shall manage all that, sir. Will you kindly agree to receive me?"

In a few minutes, he was shown into my room by the janitor. He was beaming with a sense of achievement. What was it all about?

"How did you know that I am here? How did you get my telephone number?"

"I am a business man, sir. Necessity is the mother of invention, as they say. It was a question of now or never for me. The Head of the Albany School gave me your New York address; and I worked from it."

"You seem to be very resourceful. Tell me what I can do for you?

"Nothing in particular, sir. I had been longing for years to see you: I owe to you all that I am to-day."

"Me! How can it be? I do not know you at all."

"You may not know me, sir. But I can not forget the help I received from you."

"What did I do? I do not remember ever having done anything to you. I am afraid you are making some mistake."

"No sir. I am not making any mistake. Allow me to explain. Twenty four years ago, I was a young man looking for some work. It struck me that I could find an opportunity in Florida. I wished to grow mangoes. I could not get much help from the local libraries on the subject. But, the librarian got through you some books on Indian mango. That gave me a start. I am now having a flourishing business. I always remember you. I am glad of this opportunity to see you. I have in my garden descendants of your malgoa variety. They are delicious."

I reached my room in the hostel that evening. The receptionist handed over a basket. There was also a note. It read, "Kindly accept this. Do not refuse. I would not dare to mention about this when I was with you. I was afraid that you would decline to take it.

I felt like that in your presence. This is but a token of my appreciation of the help you did to an unknown man."

Yes. Service as reference librarian lays down a firm path to the living of the words of the *Gita*. Years later, he may have a chance to see the benefit of the service having done good to others. He may not even remember his having given service. He will have the delight of his hearing about it without any attachment. To be disciplined to this state is not easy. Reference service makes it possible.

BIBLIOGRAPHY

Note:

1 This bibliography is restricted only to the documents on library science and a few other books, referred to or quoted from, in the positive exposition of the subject of this book.

2. The reference books and the documents used, in the pursuit of the illustrative problems and case studies, are listed in Index 2 at the end of this book.

3 Column 1 of this bibliography gives the serial number of the documents included in it. Each serial number consists of a letter of the Roman alphabet followed by Indo-Arabic numerals. This serial number is given also at the point in the text where the document listed in the bibliography against the serial number is referred to or quoted from. In the text, the serial number is enclosed within square brackets.

4 Column 2 of this bibliography gives the number of the section in the text, where the reference to the document is made. If it is referred to in two or more sections of the text, column 2 gives the numbers of all such sections.

5 This bibliography gives also cross reference from the

1 Name of the host document in which the document referred to occurs, in case it is not an independant document;

2 Name of the sponsoring body of a host document, whenever it has a sponsoring body; and

3 Name of each of the collaborators of a document, which has collaborators, whether it be an editor, or joint author, or translator.

6 In the case of a cross reference entry, column 2 is left blank. But the serial number of the main entry in the bibliography is added at the end in circular brackets in the style "(P3)".

A1 ADELPHI (P3).

A2 C48 ALDRICH (Ella V). Two thousand freshmen and the library. (Bulletin, American Library Association. 33; 1939; 675-676).

A3 ALL ASIA EDUCATIONAL CONFERENCE (R66).

A4 ALL INDIA LIBRARY CONFERENCE. (P4).

A5 AMERICAN LIBRARY ASSOCIATION. Bulletin. (A2).

A6 H555 —, CATALOGUING AND CLASSIFICATION (Division of —). Catalog rules: Author and title entries, ed 2 ed by Clara Beetle. 1949.

A7 —, EDUCATIONAL (— Committee). (S1).

A8 ANNALS OF library science. (R7; R19; R20; R42).

A9 ASSOCIATION OF SPECIAL LIBRARIES AND INFORMATION BUREAUX (R68).

A10 E42 AUROBINDO. Mother. 1928; 58-64.

B1 J466 BACON (Francis). New atlantis. (Works ed by James Spedding. 1887; 3; 164).

B2 C351 BESTERMAN (Theodore). Beginnings of systematic bibliography. 1936; 29.

B3 K81 BHAGAVAD-GITA. Chap 2; verse 47.

B4 J34 —. Chap 5; verses 8-9 (from Message of the Gita by Anilbaran Ray. 1939; 85).

B5 D14 BLAKE (William). Jerusalem. Stanza 10; lines 10-13.

B6 H61 BLISS (Henry Evelyn). Organisation of knowledge in libraries and subject approach to books, ed 2. 1939; 307-308.

B7 B22 BOETHIUS. Consolatione philosophie tr by Geoffrey Chaucer. Book 1; prose 5. (from Complete works by Geoffrey Chaucer ed by Walter W Skeat. 1906; 138).

B8 B46 BROWN (James Duff), *Ed.* Open access libraries, their planning, equipment and organisation. 1915; chap 5.

B9 BULLETIN, American Library Association. (A2).

B10 BULLETIN, Indian Standards Institution. (R54).

C1 CHAUCER (Geoffrey). (B7).

C2 C357 CUTTER (Charles Ammi). Rules for a dictionary catalogue, ed 4. 1904; 12.

D1 DEUTSCHER MATHEMATIKER VEREINIGUNG. (K3).

D2 D221 DUTTA (Satyendranath). Methar (=Cleanser=Scavenger) tr by Rabindranath Tagore. (Visva Bharati quarterly. 3; 1925; 148). (Harijan. 1 of 1; 11 Feb 19). (Tendulker (D G). Mahatma: Life of Mohandas Karamchand Gandhi. 1930-34; 3; 236).

G1 GIRIJA KUMAR. (R66).

G2 J1371 GORDON (Niel E). Literature service for chemists. (Science. 90; 1939. 330).

H1 HARIJAN. (D2).

I1 INTERNATIONAL STUDY CONFERENCE ON CLASSIFICATION AND INFORMATION RETRIEVAL. (R6).

I2 ISI bulletin. (R54).

J1 JAHRESBERICHTE, Deutscher mathematiker Vereinigung. (K3).

J2 F60 JAST (L Stanley). Libraries and the living. 1932; 154.

K1 F223 H541 KAULA (Prithvi Nath). Alphabetisation. (Library herald. 1; 1959; 186-190).

K2 B32 KOCH (Theodore Wesley). On university libraries. 1924; 27.

K3 D751 KRONECKER (Leopald). (In Jahresberichte, Deutschen Mathematiker Vereinigung. 2; 1892; 19). (Quoted in Memorabilia mathematica by R E Moritz. 1914; 269).

L1 LIBRARY HERALD. (K1; P7).

L2 LIBRARY QUARTERLY. (L5).

L3 LIBRI. (R38).

L4 LONDON MERCURY. (W1).

L5 C345 LUND (John J) and TAUBE (Martimer). Non-expansive classification system . . . period class.fication. (Library quarterly. 7; 1937; 373-394).

M1 B45 McCOLVIN (Lionel R). Library extension work and publicity. 1927.

M2 MADRAS LIBRARY ASSOCIATION. (R18; S5).

M3 D85 MATERLINCK (Maurice). Life of the bee, tr by Alfred Sutro. Chap 3; sec 54.

M4 B231 MAKKARI. History of the modern dynasties of Spain.

M5 C351 MAUNSELL (Andrew). Catalogue of English printed books. 1595.

M6 H623 MELLON (Melvin Guy). Chemical publications: their nature and use. 1928; 110, 119.

M7 MEMOIRS, Madras Library Association. (R18; S5).

M8 MODERN LIBRARIAN. (R32; R50; R52; R67).

M9 MORITZ. (Robert Edward). Memorabilia mathematica. (K3).

P1 B45 PETERSON (Mildred Othmer). Library publicity methods. (Papers offered to the All Asia Educational Conference; Benares; 1930; Library Service Section).

P2 PHADNIS (S P). (P7).

P3 B53 PLOWMAN (Max). Living element. (Adeplhi. 16; 2; 1939 Nov; 44-46).

P4 D302 PROCEEDINGS, All India Library Conference. 2; Patna; 1935; 20

P5 PROCEEDINGS, International Study Conference on Classification and Information Retrieval. (R6).

P6 PUBLIC ADMINISTRATION. (W2).

P7 H552 PURANIK (K D) and PHADNIS (S P). Chaos in arrangement of Indian names. (Library herald). 1; 1959; 78-85.

R1 RAMAYANA. (V1 to V8).

R2 A66 RANGANATHAN (Shiyali Ramamrita). Bibliography of reference books and bibliography. 1941.

R3 H01 —. —; sec 5111-5115.

R4 B43 —. Classification and communication. 1951.

R5 C34 —. —; sec 321

R6 B43 —. Classification as a discipline. (Proceedings, International Study Conference on Classification and Information Retrieval. Dorking; 1957; 2-12).

R7 J54 —. Classification of environmented entity. (Annals of library science. 5; 1958; 113-121).

R8 C3511 H55 H557 —. Classified catalogue code with additional rules for dictionary catalogue code, ed 4. 1958; sec 022.

R9 C352 —. —; sec 028.

R10 H555 —. —; sec 18.

R11 H556 —. —; sec 185.

R12 C354 RANGANATHAN (Shiyali Ramamrita). part 3.

R13 B44 D351 —. —; chap 52.

R14 C355 —. —; chap 53.

R15 D351 —. —; chap 71 and 77.

R16 C34 —. Colon classification, ed 6. 1960; part 1 sec 027.

R17 J54 —. —; sec 0586.

R18 B241 —. Culture through books. (Memoirs, Madras Library Association. 1: 1940; 12-14).

R19 J125 —. Documentation in many lands: 1 Terminology and function. (Annals of library science. 2; 1955; 1-12).

R20 A56 B44 —. Documentation in many lands: 2 Evolution (Annals of library science. 2; 1935; 117-122).

R21 A71 —. Education for leisure, ed 4. 1961; chap J.

R22 J55 —, Elements of library classification, ed 3. 1961.

R23 B41 —. Five laws of library science, ed 2. 1957; sec 15, 341, 51, 54, 614, 616, 743, 747, 748.

R24 A61 B11 —. —; sec 177-18.

R25 A61 B122 —. —; sec 47-478.

R26 A61 B13 —. —; sec 54-544.

R27 A61 B141 —. —; sec 66-665.

R28 A61 —. —; sec 662

R29 C23 —. —; sec 743, 747, 748.

R30 B151 —. —; sec 851-855.

R31 C352 —. Heading and canons: Comparative study of five catalogue codes. 1955; sec 43-44.

R32 D302 —. Idiosyncrasies of periodical publications as viewed by the reference staff. (Modern librarian. 6; 1936; 67-76).

R33 B42 —. Library administration, ed 2. Chap 26.

R34 B36 —. —. Sec 2713.

R35 J135 —. —. Sec 2813.

R36 B46 —. —. Sec 2833:5

R37 A521 F68 J61 —. —. Sec 33.

R38 J55 —. Library classification and its added uses. (Libri. 2; 1952; 33-34).

R39 D31 D702 —. Library classification: Fundamentals and procedure. 1943; sec 435.

R40 J426 —. Library tour 1948: Europe and America: Impressions and reflections; 1950. sec 531-53136.

R41 C52 —. Organisation of libraries, ed 3. 1960.

R42 J55 —. Postulational approach to classification. (Annals of library science. 5; 1958; 33-51).

R43 C344 —. Prolegomena to library classification, ed 1. 1937; 132.
R44 C344 —. —, ed 2 1957; sec 171.
R45 C3451 —. —; sec 172.
R46 J125 —. —; sec 235.
R47 J125 —. —; sec 362-368.
R48 D32 —. —; chap 65.
R49 B43 —. —; chap 88.
R50 H37 —. Regression in book production, the problem of loose-leaf books. (Modern librarian. 11; 1941; 23-26).
R51 H557 —. Rendering of South Asian names: A report to Unesco. 1953. (unpublished).
R52 B38 —. Salesmanship in libraries—its advent. (Modern librarian. 4; 1934; 71).
R53 C52 —. School and college libraries. 1942.
R54 H557 —. Standard practice for specifying author's name (personal author). (ISI bulletin. 6; 1954; 120-125).
R55 B34 —. Theory of library catalogue. 1938; 25-26.
R56 H558 —. —; 60-61.
R57 C3511 —. —; 70-72.
R58 D31 —. —; 109-112.
R59 D32 —. —; 112.
R60 B44 —. —; part 3.
R61 C352 —. —; chap 32
R62 D353 —. —; chap 33.
R63 F223 H541 —. —; chap 64.
R64 B7 —. —; 369-370.
R65 —, *Ed.* Papers offered to the Library Service Section of the First All Asia educational Conference (P1).
R66 J462 —and Girija Kumar, *Ed.* Social science research and libraries, 1960; sec 8; resolution 4.
R67 H555 —and SIVARAMAN (K M). Rendering of Hindu names in headings: Function vs Position. (Modern librarian. 10; 1940; 61-75.
R68 J211 REPORT OF proceedings, Association of Special Libraries and Information Bureaux, Conference, 15; 1928; 37.
R69 ROY (Anilbaran). Message of the Gita. (B4).

S1 C283 SCHOOL LIBRARY year-book. 1; 1927; part 2.
S2 SCIENCE. (G2).
S3 SIVARAMAN (K M). (R67).
S4 SPEDDING (James). (B1).
S5 J122 SUNDARAM (C). Reference service in Indology. (Memoirs, Madras Library Association. 1; 1940; 37-38).
S6 SUTRO (Alfred). (M3).

T1 TAGORE (Rabindranath). (D2).
T2 TENDULKER (D G). (D2).

T3 J232 THOMPSON (Francis). Mistress of vision. Stanza 21.
T4 E1 TAITTIRIYA-UPANISHAD. Siksha-adhyaya; sec 3-4.
T5 C356 TOWNSHEND (Frank). Becoming. 1939; 101.
T6 B54 —. Earth 1935; 83.

U1 UNESCO. (R49).

V1 K78 VALMIKI. Ramayana. Bala-khanda; sarga 18; verses 47-59.
V2 E31 —. —. —; sarga 52; verses 21-22.
V3 D422 —. —. —; sarga 63; verses 16-27
V4 E33 —. —. Ayodhya-khanda; 91
V5 F51 —. —. Aranya-khanda; sarga 9; verse 24.
V6 K23 —. —. Sundara-khanda; sarga 12; verses 10-12.
V7 K25 —. —. —; sarga 34; verse 6.
V8 K25 —. —. Yuddha-khanda; sarga 129; verse 2.
V9 A77 VATSYAYANA. Kama-sutra. Adhikarana 2; chap 2; verse 32.
V10 VISVA-BHARATI quarterly. (D2)

W1 D732 WEST (Geoffrey). Integrated society. (London mercury. 39; 1939; 83).
W2 B37 WHITEHEAD (Harold). Salesmanship in the public service: Scope and technique. (Public administration. 11; 1933; 268).
W3 B323 WYER (James I). Reference work. 1930; 3.

INDEX 1

Note:

1 This index is restricted to the ideas inherent in the development of the subject of the book.

2 The documents referred to or quoted from in the positive exposition of the subject of the book are listed in the bibliography preceding this index.

3 Index 2 covers all the other documents used as illustrative materials or quoted in the case studies.

4 The index numbers are the numbers of the section, part, or chapter as the case may be.

5 The following contractions are used:

irt = in relation to; and
rirt = referred in relation to.

INDEX 2

Note:

1 This index is restricted to the

11 Documents described as reference books frequently used as source books in reference service;

12 Documents of other kinds used in the pursuit of the problems in the case studies; and

13 Documents ued to illustrate the need for reference help.

2 The documents referred to or quoted from in the positive exposition of the subject of the book are listed in the bibliography preceding the Index 1.

3 The ideas inherent in the development of the subject of the book are listed in Index 1.

4 The index numbers are the numbers of the sections or chapters as the case may be.

5 The following contractions are used:

irt = in relation to;
qirt = quoted in relation to; and
rirt = referred in relation to.

INDEX